the tablehopper's guide
to dining and drinking in
san francisco
find the right spot for
every occasion

MARCIA GAGLIARDI

TEN SPEED PRESS
Berkeley

Library of Congress Cataloging-in-Publication Data

Gagliardi, Marcia.
  The tablehopper's guide to dining and drinking in San Francisco : find
the right spot for every occasion / Marcia Gagliardi. — 1st ed.
      p. cm.
  Summary: "An insider's guide to the San Francisco culinary scene,
organized by dining occasion, from one of the city's hippest and
most-connected food writers"—Provided by publisher.
  Includes index.
  1. Restaurants—California—San Francisco—Guidebooks. 2. Dinners and
dining—California—San Francisco—Guidebooks. 3. Bars (Drinking
establishments—California—San Francisco—Guidebooks. 4. San
Francisco (Calif.)—Guidebooks. I. Title.
  TX907.3.C22S3635 2010
  647.95794'61—dc22
                        2009046952

ISBN 978-1-58008-128-3

Printed in the United States of America

Design by Ed Anderson
Typesetting by Colleen Cain
Cover design by Ed Anderson and Betsy Stromberg

10 9 8 7 6 5 4 3 2 1

First Edition

To my loving parents, my precious sister,
and my remarkable grandmother.

contents

Acknowledgments

Thank you to all of the talented people in the restaurant and bar industry of San Francisco and beyond. My job would cease to exist without your vision, skills, knowledge, hard work, passion, late hours, and commitment to creating quality food, drinks, and establishments that make people feel good, happy, and cared for. My waistline can attest to all the hospitality and generosity you have shown me over the years (thank you, really).

Speaking of ceasing to exist, this book would not be here if it weren't for my extraordinary literary agent, Carole Bidnick, who took a chance on a talkative woman who sat next to her at a book luncheon (that would be me), and who taught me what *bashert* is. I also want to express my gratitude to Roberta Klugman, my culinary fairy godmother, who invited me to the luncheon to begin with. It has been a sincere pleasure working with Melissa Moore and the entire Ten Speed Press team—I am so fortunate to work with such talented folks, yes indeed!

My heart swells with gratitude for my parents, Carmen and Kathy, whose strong love, support, and guidance have brought me such happiness in this life. And thank you for all the years of letting me pick a "nice restaurant" for my birthday dinners; I was able to start researching for this book at a very early age. I raise my glass to my grandmother Judy ("Mom"), who taught me about the joys of indulgence and is the reason I love Champagne as much as I do. And to my sweet sister Erica Rose, one of my very favorite people to eat with—yup, we really are cut from the same cloth, and in burritos and eggs we trust. Love and *bacioni* to all of my relatives, past and present.

A big cheers to all my dining partners, dear friends, and culinary compatriots who have helped me immensely with this book, and my business. Thank you for all the times you patiently let me take pictures of food before we eat it.

A wholehearted *grazie* to my enthusiastic readers, who know tablehopper is an e-column and not a blog, and who keep me motivated and in the loop. A backhanded thanks to all the magazine editors who never responded to my pitches; you inadvertently inspired me to start my own column. And a hearty thanks to all the publicists and kind colleagues who keep me informed— sometimes too informed, heh.

Fond remembrances of my Aunt Mary Hays, who always gave me such wondrous books as a child, and of class with Dr. Fisher, my English teacher my freshman year of high school, who I credit for turning me on to American literature.

Much love to my precious panther, Linus Mendenhall, whom I wish were here to see this book happen (and to style me for my book jacket photo and author appearances, hellllo!). Then again, you've been on my shoulder the entire time.

My excitement about having food in front of me has never waned.

Why, hello there. Thanks for picking up this book. You must be hungry, or perhaps looking for somewhere to celebrate your anniversary dinner or host your rager of a birthday party. Well, let's hop to it.

But first, some backstory. Since I'm the daughter of an amazing cook (my mother) and a former pizzeria and deli owner (yes, my father is Italian, and I've got an "i" at the end of my last name to prove it), it would not be an understatement to say my entire life has revolved around food. And even better, good food. Homemade food. Food made with love. A random smattering of childhood memories includes watering our family's garden full of tomatoes and fava beans, picking olallieberries, cracking crab at grandma's, coming home from school to a house that smelled of homemade bread (I know, my mother is off the charts in cumulative Mom points), and rolling tiny meatballs for our Christmas lasagna. It's really no surprise that I figured out how to make a living out of eating.

I've been adventuring throughout San Francisco like a culinary swashbuckler for the past fifteen years, and writing about food since 2002. I eat everything, from street food to sweetbreads to stinky *fromage*, and adore retro diners and four-star restaurants with equal passion. I launched my cheeky weekly tablehopper e-column in 2006 (you can subscribe for free at **www.tablehopper.com**), and it has since become a trusted insider source for learning what's new, coming soon, and, of course, delicious in the San Francisco restaurant and bar scene (and beyond). It's chock-full of news and gossip, covering what's hot and what's opening or closing, along with restaurant reviews of both new and established places, mentions of culinary and wine events, weekend getaway ideas, and a very popular section covering star sightings in bars and restaurants. After taking a trip I include write-ups of the restaurants and bars I visited in those cities, from Sydney to New York to New Orleans. I also cover places closer to home, like the Wine Country, for those looking for weekend getaway ideas.

I have been an unofficial concierge for years, recommending restaurants to friends and family since I was a teenager. Once I launched tablehopper, my readers started to ask me for restaurant recommendations, so I launched my "tip please" service, acting as a restaurant matchmaker and answering more than 1,500 dining inquiries. Those recommendations became the inspiration for this book, since I soon realized that both locals and travelers don't pick their restaurants by category (French, Financial District, $$$), but by occasion: dinner with the girls, first date, lunch with the parents. Diners plan their meals around their lives. Most guidebooks are organized by neighborhood, by cuisine, or even by their rating (and I use them all), but I thought there needed to be a guide organized by how we really eat: by occasion. And based on all the recommendations I've made, I think there are some diners who would agree with me.

Before we dive in, here's a little something you should know about me. No, it's not that I secretly enjoy eating Lean Pockets with ranch dressing (and, for the record, I don't eat Hot Pockets either). But you may find this tidbit of information useful while reading my recommendations: I'm thirty-eight, which means I can appreciate places that have some style and verve, but my suggestions for date places might veer toward being too hip or noisy for some folks in their sixties (which is why I have special chapters on quiet restaurants, or dining with the 'rents, or "serious" meals, like business dining). Only you know where you fall on the age spectrum: are you a night owl in your fifties, or perhaps a very serious twenty-eight? Just a little something to keep in mind. Then again, you're not likely to find me in a restaurant packed with college kids doing tequila body shots. In fact, it's not likely at all.

I have tried to include a variety of places for everyone, with all kinds of tastes and budgets, but many fall within the moderate to spendy price range. What can I say? I blame San Francisco for having so many fabulous restaurants (even though I love me some cheap eats, too).

Here's the price breakdown on listings:

$	Thrifty: average main course under $9
$$	Moderate: average main course $9–$17
$$$	Spendy: average main course $18–$29
$$$$	Very Spendy: average main course or tasting menu $30+

NOTE: Restaurants that serve small plates can be a little tricky, so in those cases the price category refers to what you'd spend on, say, a couple of plates.

This is not a guidebook of every single restaurant in San Francisco (which has about three thousand and counting, by the way). It's more about my choices for what places are appropriate for which occasions. These are places where I like to go and that I think are worth the money—where I've had good dining experiences, and I hope you do too. So did some big-name places get left out? Yes. Your neighborhood favorite? It's quite possible. And some of them may be very good—but just not right for this book—or a place I don't know very well, or inconsistent. And besides, I have a word-count limit to abide by (trust, this could have been a three-volume set).

For each occasion you'll find at least a few minireviews, plus a listing of "OTHER IDEAS" about where to go. Many of the places listed in "OTHER IDEAS" have reviews elsewhere in the book, so be sure to look at any cross-referenced page numbers for their write-up and additional details. You will also see a "TIP" or "NOTE" section following certain reviews, with special hints, such as which table to request or other insider tidbits.

One challenge in writing this book was that we're in the middle of a nasty recession (summer 2009). It's a tricky situation, because it's hard to determine if some places will make it. Time will tell. As a result, I went with more tried-and-true favorites and fewer "fresh outta the gate" or "funky" places, since these restaurants are subject to change (or end) very quickly. Which also means you should call a place before heading over for lunch—who knows, they might not serve lunch anymore, even though this book says they do.

I also opted to not mention a lot of executive chefs or bartenders by name since they tend to move around. (So chefs, don't get snippy with me if I left your name out, sorry.) But in the case of a chef-owner, I sometimes included a name.

There are so many unique and under-the-radar concepts currently happening in San Francisco, from pop-up restaurants to mobile food carts, so I recommend subscribing to tablehopper (at **www.tablehopper.com**) if you want to keep up on all the very latest.

I have also included a roundup of destination-worthy locations in the East Bay, the Peninsula, the South Bay, and the Wine Country. And if you're just passing through and want to eat your way through the city, be sure to take a look at the one-, two-, and three-day culinary itineraries, which were designed both for those who have planned ahead and for those who showed up at the last minute. (Locals will want to peek at these itineraries as well—there's a lot to chew on!)

Note that many of the places listed in this book have also been written up on tablehopper.com, so if you want even more details (or sass), take a look in the archives under "Fresh Meat" and "The Regular."

My father's hilarious Vietnam buddy Bob Jaskolka spontaneously came up with a variety of funny titles for this book when I was trying to nail one down. One of them was *You Only Live Once, But You Can Eat a Lot!* (I agree), and another winner was *Fork Your Way Around the Bay*. I couldn't have said it better myself.

Let's eat.
~Marcia

We checked, we called, we proofread, and we researched, but things like restaurant hours and special dishes and late-night dining at bars are changeable things. Very changeable. So please accept our apologies for any errors or differences in detail—at press time, this is where things stood. Our best advice: call first (especially if it's your wifey's birthday, ahem). Cheers!

FOR THE LADIES

Girls' Night Out

Girls, they wanna, wanna have fun! Fun scene? Yes. Cocktails and wine by the glass? Natch. Food that's easy to share, even with your picky friend in tow? Sure! Places worthy of your sassy style, kitten heels, and fabulous handbag? Checkity check check! Whether it's just you and your BFF or a flock of five, here's where to go hit the town.

Beretta $$ *1199 Valencia St. at 23rd St., 415-695-1199, berettasf.com*
There's a bunch of reasons this place has taken off like a *casa* on fire: impeccable craft cocktails, late hours, heart-of-the-Mission location, and well-priced Italian food you don't have to think about too much while you're hanging out with your gal pals (think antipasti like the fave eggplant *caponatina* with burrata, and thin-crust pizzas). The vittles aren't *perfetto,* but it's one of those places where the raucous vibe, cuties at the communal table, and swish cocktails tip the scale. Speaking of the cocktails, since they take a while to make, let alone order, request your next drink as soon as you get your first one in front of you, no joke. The all-day weekend brunch/lunch is a bonus.

TIP: If your group is big enough (six or more), you can reserve a table and avoid the walk-in madness—but try to get an upstairs table, since the downstairs has less of a scene. If your group is smaller than six people, you can call ahead to get your name on the list while you circle for parking.

Dosa $$–$$$ *1700 Fillmore St. at Post St., 415-441-3672, dosasf.com*
The second (and newer) location of this South Indian stunner covers all the bases: chic and colorful interior, upbeat vibe, urban crowd, well-composed wine list, inspired cocktails (cardamom and Kaffir lime on the loose), and a unique menu of spiced goodies that's a pleasure to explore and share—especially if there's a vegetarian or vegan in the posse. Try the *vadas* (South Indian crab cakes), Kerala fish *moilee* (a spicy, creamy, and savory preparation), and the crepe-like dosas (they come with a variety of fillings—the spinach and fennel version is particularly tasty). The tasting menu is also a good way to go. Bonus: The build-out was very eco-friendly (just like the ingredients in the food).

TIP: The Sundance Kabuki Cinemas (1881 Post St. at Fillmore St., 415-929-4650) is right across the street in case you want dinner before catching a chick flick—or you can have a nightcap at Dosa afterward.

NOTE: The original Dosa (995 Valencia St. at 21st St., 415-642-3672) is cozier and more rustic, with wood tables, persimmon walls, dim lighting, and a candlelit bar. This location attracts an upbeat crowd ranging from tattooed vegans to young professionals, so anyone will fit in here. There's no full bar, but they'll help you pick out a good wine, like a killer Riesling.

Terzo $$$ *3011 Steiner St. at Union St.,*
415-441-3200, terzosf.com

We know how much the ladies like to drink vino (hic!), and this spot in Cow Hollow is primed to fill your glass with something liquid (and the Euro-heavy list means your vino will most likely have an accent). The daily-changing menu of seasonal Cal-Med-Ital cuisine can verge on the spendy, but eat, sister—we don't want you falling off your stool when you're done with your first glass of *rosato*. (At least tuck into the swoon-worthy hummus with warm made-to-order pita.) Besides, a couple of small plates is all a girl needs when she's trying to avoid muffin-topping in her low-rider jeans. That said, just in case you're a bad girl, the crispy onions are delicious. The look is postmodern rustic hip, just like your sexy boots. Oh, and there's a posse-perfect back corner table with room for seven, as well as a private room with space for sixteen.

nopa

TIP: Terzo has a petite front patio (twenty seats in all), and did you know you can reserve a table there ahead of time? Heh, now you do.

The alfresco restaurants on Belden Place and Claude Lane (two pedestrian alleys near Union Square) could be a fun place for a night of touring with a culinary Eurorail pass (of sorts). For example, you could go to Café Claude (p. 31), Gitane (p. 24), and Plouf (40 Belden Pl., 415-986-6491) for drinks and bites (flirting with accented hottie waiters at each destination).

OTHER IDEAS: A16 (p. 58), Bar Crudo (p. 121), Bar Tartine (p. 33), Betelnut (p. 82), Bocadillos (p. 102), Contigo (p. 49), Delfina (p. 137), Destino (p. 24), District (216 Townsend St., 415-896-2120), Farina (p. 127), Florio (p. 57), Gitane (p. 24), Heaven's Dog (p. 74), J Lounge (p. 15), Laïola (p. 30), Mamacita (p. 16), nopa (p. 17), Oola (p. 55), Ottimista Enoteca-Café (1838 Union St., 415-674-8400), Range (p. 59), RN74 (p. 128), SPQR (p. 51), Umami (p. 57)

Bachelorette Blowout (No Hairdryer Needed)

There are two types of bachelorette parties: those with the veil, and those without (you know which group you fall into). If you're in the former, AsiaSF (a.k.a. Asian tranny HQ; 201 9th St., 415-255-2742) is known for being bachelorette party central, but here are some less "Girls Gone Wild" options to consider.

Bar Bambino $$–$$$ *2931 16th St. at S. Van Ness Ave., 415-701-8466, barbambino.com*

Over in the Mission is this Italian charmer, complete with a slick design, friendly staff, and a handy all-day lunch. The communal table in the front is where you wanna be with your estrogen crew. Start getting lit on well-chosen wines by the glass (and bottle, to make up for the lack of booze here) along with Italian eats like bruschetta, stuffed olives, salumi, pasta, and heartier dishes like brisket and meatballs. But, just like with men, sometimes you'll pick a winner and other times you won't: a few dishes falter or are underseasoned. How handy that you have all of 16th Street and its many bars to terrorize when you're done. There's also a back patio if you want to dine alfresco.

rnm $$–$$$ *598 Haight St. at Steiner St., 415-551-7900, rnmrestaurant.com*

Pass through the chain mail curtain of this Lower Haight restaurant and hopefully Robert will be hosting that night (he wrote the book on charm). You can reserve the mezzanine for some private-party ambience (it fits twenty-five people seated). Justine Miner's American food with French twists is easy to share, like the mussels, mushroom pizza (easy on the truffle oil!), and famed mini burgers (good salads as well). Full bar with cocktails too, woot! It's also a good date-night place. A $28 three-course prix-fixe menu is available Tuesday through Saturday 5:30 p.m.–7 p.m.

TIP: If you want to stay in the Haight, you can start the night with some vino at Uva Enoteca (p. 28), then head to Nickie's (466 Haight St., 415-255-0300) for more cocktails after dinner.

Velvet Cantina $–$$ *3349 23rd St. at Bartlett St., 415-648-4142, velvetcantina.com*

Ay ay ay, this place is like a Reagle Beagle in Tijuana with its groovy décor. And there's *más:* pitchers of margies, *la musica* is bumping, the bartenders are *caliente,* and you can munch on affordable fiesta food: chile con queso, nachos, enchiladas, and more. Plus, the Mission is just outside the front door. Have fun out there, tigress.

OTHER IDEAS: Balboa Cafe (p. 21), Beretta (p. 4), BIN 38 (3232 Scott St., 415-567-3838), butterfly (DJs Thurs.–Sat., p. 138), Cha Cha Cha (1801 Haight St., 415-386-5758; 2327 Mission St., 415-648-0504), Chez Papa Resto (4 Mint Plaza, 415-546-4134), Dosa (Fillmore; p. 4), Foreign Cinema (p. 32), Isa (p. 83), Kan Zaman (1793 Haight St., 415-751-9656), La Folie Lounge (do a buyout; p. 197); La Mar (p. 134),

Mamacita (p. 16), Medjool (2522 Mission St., 415-550-9055), Orson (p. 15), Osha Thai (the best party location is at 4 Embarcadero Center, 415-788-6742), Ristorante Ideale (p. 50), Slanted Door (private room; p. 98), Straits Restaurant (Westfield Centre, 845 Market St., 4th Floor, 415-668-1783), Umami (p. 57)

Finally, here are a few suggestions for bar stops during your night out: karaoke at the Mint (1942 Market St., 415-626-4726); salsa dancing at Cigar Bar & Grill (850 Montgomery St., 415-398-0850), cocktails and flirting in lower Nob Hill at Cantina (p. 211), the Tunnel Top (p. 195), Rye (p. 203), and Swig (561 Geary St., 415-931-7292); and stumbling around the Lower Polk at Vertigo Bar (p. 195), R Bar (1176 Sutter St., 415-567-7441), Koko Cocktails (p. 206), and Blur (p. 206). If you're in the Mission, the entire neighborhood is your oyster.

Bridal or Baby Shower (Brunch or Lunch)

No veils here—just ladies coming together over good food, handwritten congratulations cards, and maybe a saucy negligee or sippy cup in the mix.

Absinthe Brasserie & Bar $$$ *398 Hayes St. at Gough St., 415-551-1590, absinthe.com*

Sure, you know about the Ginger Rogers (gin, mint leaves, ginger syrup, lime juice, and ginger ale) they serve here, and the French onion soup, and maybe you know about their $5 shots of rye at the bar, but did you know Absinthe has a primo private dining room? Reserve it for brunch or lunch, but whatever you do, that table better have some cones of frites on it. You can even arrange to have cocktail service for your party (uh, yes please). The croque madame and burger also please. And you can all do some tipsy shopping afterward in Hayes Valley (Gimme Shoes is only fifty feet away).

Foreign Cinema $$–$$$ *2534 Mission St. at 21st St., 415-648-7600, foreigncinema.com*

This place is almost a no-brainer for a weekend get-together. Let's do the math: spacious outdoor tables on the patio (good for groups), a chic interior, stellar Bloody Marys, an array of fresh oysters (except none for the expectant mother, sorry), fruit "Pop Tarts," and spot-on egg dishes that could make a vegan think twice about their lifestyle. Oh yeah, and Billecart-Salmon Champagne on the wine list, pop!

TIP: Saturday is the only day Foreign Cinema serves their delicious burger. Be sure to get it with bacon (you were going to do that anyway, weren't you?).

Samovar Tea Lounge $–$$ *498 Sanchez St. at 18th St., 415-626-4700; 297 Page St. at Laguna St., 415-861-0303; Yerba Buena Gardens, Upper Terrace, 730 Howard St. at 3rd St., 415-227-9400, samovarlife.com*

Feeling a little Zen? Get the ladies together and enjoy the soothing style at Samovar. Bountiful tea service (go English, Russian, Chinese, or Japanese) can be ordered with fresh and light dishes ranging from quiches and salads to *jook* (a comforting Chinese porridge) and sandwiches (including good curry egg salad). It's also very vegetarian-friendly. Such exotic teas—take your pick. The newest Hayes Valley (excuse me, "Zen Valley") location has a table for fifteen you can reserve in advance, while the sunny Castro location has a comfortable sunken table for eight to ten.

OTHER IDEAS: 2223 Restaurant (p. 91), Americano (Hotel Vitale, 8 Mission St., 415-278-3777), Bar Jules (p. 31), Bar Tartine (p. 33), The Butler & The Chef (p. 131), Crown & Crumpet (p. 12), Dosa (p. 4), La Mar (lunch, p. 134), Lobby Lounge at the Ritz-Carlton (600 Stockton St., 415-773-6198), Lovejoy's Tea Room (p. 13), Magic Flute Garden Ristorante (p. 132), Olea (p. 85), The Rotunda (p. 10), Slanted Door (p. 98), Sociale (p. 37), Vitrine (St. Regis, 125 3rd St., 415-284-4049), Zuni Café (p. 52)

Take Your Girlfriend/Wifey/Mistress Out for Her Birthday

This is not the night to screw up. Make your reservation waaaay in advance. Otherwise, if it's a busy Saturday night you'll end up doing drive-through and get zero nookie for a month.

INEXPENSIVE $–$$

TIP: Check out "Cheap Date" (page 40) for more ideas.

Manora's Thai Cuisine $ *1600 Folsom St. at 12th St., 415-861-6224, manorathai.com*

It's her birthday, so you don't want to feel like a cheapskate, which means you'll need a little more atmo than an ethnic joint with fluorescent lighting. You also can't quite go to dinner at 5:30 p.m. and say, "Babe, just order the prix-fixe menu, cool?" because she will cut you. Presenting Manora, a cozy Thai place in SoMa that still has some cute style in spite of the cheapity-cheap prices; you get cloth napkins, fresh flowers, pretty good Thai dishes, carved wood panels and artwork, and kind service. The full bar is a bonus, too. If you go on the later side, things are definitely quieter (read: more romantic). Don't miss the mango sticky rice for dessert.

OTHER IDEAS: Burma Superstar (p. 66), Charanga (p. 96), Dragonfly Restaurant (420 Judah St., 415-661-7755), Hotei (1290 9th Ave., 415-753-6045), Indian Oven (233 Fillmore St., 415-626-1628), Khan Toke (p. 96), Pagolac (655 Larkin St., 415-776-3234), Park Chow (1240 9th Ave., 415-665-9912), Piqueo's (830 Cortland Ave., 415-282-8812), Ploy II (1770 Haight St., 415-387-9224), Thep Phanom Thai Restaurant (400 Waller St., 415-431-2526), Zadin (p. 114)

MODERATE $$–$$$

Firefly $$–$$$ *4288 24th St. at Douglass St., 415-821-7652, fireflyrestaurant.com*
Someone would have to have a heart of stone not to be charmed by this Noe Valley neighborhood nook. And fifteen-plus years of making people happy counts for a lot. The seasonal menu includes the stalwart shrimp and sea scallop pot stickers and inspired desserts. It's also a good spot for vegetarians, and the $35 prix-fixe menu (Sun.–Thurs., take your pick of anything on the menu) is downright kind. The artsy and candlelit atmosphere is intimate and cozy, and there's also a bar where you can perch if you two like counter dining instead.

OTHER IDEAS: Aziza (p. 79), Bar Bambino (p. 6), Bar Jules (p. 31), Blue Plate (p. 19), Café Claude (p. 31), Contigo (p. 49), Da Flora (p. 25), Foreign Cinema (p. 32), Koo (408 Irving St., 415-731-7077), La Ciccia (p. 138), Le Charm French Bistro (315 5th St., 415-546-6128), Loló (p. 32), Piccino (p. 52), Sociale (p. 37), Terzo (p. 5), Universal Cafe (p. 26), Woodward's Garden (1700 Mission St., 415-621-7122), Zaré at Fly Trap (p. 112)

SPENDY $$$–$$$$

Chez Spencer $$$–$$$$ *82 14th St. at Folsom St., 415-864-2191, chezspencer.net*
This upscale French-California bistro is the secret weapon of many a savvy romantic. Sure, you'll wonder if you're going to get shanked on the street outside, but once you slip through the gate, you're transported to a place that's downright *magnifique*— and on a balmy night, the patio is magical. The vibe is industrial-meets-rustic (just smell that wood-burning oven), the tablecloths are crisp and white, the flowers are fresh, the lighting is oh-so-dreamy, and just wait until you taste the smoked duck breast salad. Even the bathroom is pretty. Could this place be any sexier? *Bisous!*

TIP: Chef Laurent Katgely offers a tasting menu for those who want to go that route, and there's live piano Friday and Saturday evenings.

OTHER IDEAS: Acquerello (p. 89), Bar Tartine (p. 33), Big 4 (p. 89), Boulevard (p. 80), Cafe Jacqueline (p. 37), Coi (p. 135), Dining Room at the Ritz-Carlton (p. 38), Fifth Floor (p. 101), Frascati (1901 Hyde St., 415-928-1406), Gary Danko (p. 37), Gitane (p. 24), Jardinière (p. 13), Kiss Seafood (p. 33), Kokkari (request table 2; p. 103), La Folie (p. 38), Moss Room (p. 68), Quince (p. 137), sebo (p. 53), Spruce (p. 100), Zuni Café (p. 52)

Ladies Who Lunch

"Ooooh, love the bag." "Your hair looks great." "He did not say that! What a pig." "Another bottle, please." All that and more. Girl, let's taaaaaaalk!

Café Claude $$ *7 Claude Ln., between Grant Ave. and Kearny St., off Bush St., 415-392-3505, cafeclaude.com*

What's one of the most important components of a ladies' lunch? Yup, hot waiters. French-accented *garçons* will serve you your pâté plate and *salade niçoise,* but if you're a girl after my heart, you'll order the steak tartare prepared tableside. This place has a charming authentic bistro atmosphere, and the alley location means you can dine outside on a warm day. Plus, its proximity to Union Square makes it a power (shopping) lunch spot. Equally tempting: a bottle of the crémant. Cheers, darling.

TIP: The roast chicken with lemon and olives, a lunch-only special, is delicious with a side of frites.

Rose's Café $$ *2298 Union St. at Steiner St., 415-775-2200, rosescafesf.com*

Whaddya know, another cute café surrounded by good shopping (but watch out, because Union Street will take all your money in a heartbeat). The sidewalk tables are the coveted spots, especially if you brought your little Precious along; the restaurant even has doggie biscuits for pets. The Italian-inspired dishes are seasonal and market-fresh, and there are plenty of salads, sandwiches, some light fish dishes, and irresistible pizzas (be sure to order one with an egg on top). All the baked goods are made in house, so for now, just say carbs be damned.

The Rotunda at Neiman Marcus Restaurant $$$ *150 Stockton St. at Geary St., 415-362-4777, neimanmarcus.com*

Uh, of course. It's like the place invented the genre. In addition to sweeping views of Union Square, you get ladies traipsing by in the latest fashions while you're communing with your complimentary popover (go ahead and slather that strawberry butter on—pretend it's your night cream). There are enough salads to make you feel like you might just fit into that size-six Escada after all, but then again, it's better to eat here *after* shopping so you can order the lobster club or Cobb salad without batting an eye. Faaaaahbulous idea.

OTHER IDEAS: A16 (p. 58), Absinthe (p. 7), Bar Jules (Wed.–Sat.; p. 31), The Butler & The Chef (p. 131), Café de la Presse (352 Grant Ave., 415-249-0900), Campton Place Bar and Bistro (p. 11), Chez Papa Bistrot (1401 18th St., 415-824-8210), Chouquet's (p. 124), Citizen Cake (p. 86), Garibaldi's (347 Presidio Ave., 415-563-8841), Mission Beach Café (p. 125), Perbacco (p. 102), Piccino (p. 52), Seasons (757 Market St., 5th Floor, 415-633-3737), Slanted Door (p. 98), Sociale (p. 37), Spruce (p. 100), Universal Cafe (Wed.–Sat.; p. 26), Vitrine (St. Regis, 125 3rd St., 415-284-4049), Waterbar (p. 105), Yank Sing (p. 97), Zuni Café (p. 52)

Ladies Who Lunch Like Dudes

Sure, it's nice to have a salad, but some ladies know how to shake it in more ways than one—like a two-martini lunch (or do you like it stirred?). Uh-huh, it's time to get your steak on and talk about closing deals . . . like the shoes you just saw on sale at Bloomies.

Campton Place Bar and Bistro $$$ *340 Stockton St. at Campton Pl., 415-955-5555, camptonplacesf.com*

It's an intimate and sophisticated hotel bar, and the perfect setting for a cloth-napkin burger and a cocktail. Or a glass of bubbles and fries, one of the more godly combinations on this earth. For the record, it's also a good downtown spot to mix business with pleasure. And for the nights you're solo, you can sit at the bar and the cheeky bartenders will keep you entertained.

TIP: Conveniently open continuously all afternoon, you can eat here after a shopping spree, or late into the evening (until 10:30 p.m.); the bar is open until midnight.

Lark Creek Steak $$–$$$ *Westfield San Francisco Centre, 845 Market St., 4th Floor, 415-593-4100, larkcreek.com*

Oh sure, it's in a mall, but this ain't no food court. Here you'll find a comfortable and well-appointed room—request one of the booths, or sit at the counter overlooking the grill and flirt with the kitchen staff. For lunch, take your pick from a bunch of different meaty burgers (the mushroom steak burger with Swiss cheese and roasted button mushrooms has made me love mushroom burgers), and they come with a pile of crisp steak fries (really good ones). The New York strip is one hell of a steak. And if you must do a salad, go for the little gem wedge salad with bacon, chopped egg, and buttermilk-blue cheese dressing—purr.

TIP: You cannot eat here without ordering the buttermilk biscuits with tomato jam and the andouille sausage-maple-pecan butter. I won't tell if you won't, deal?

Schmidt's Deli $–$$ *2400 Folsom St. at 20th St., 415-401-0200, schmidts-sf.com*
This is not part of the downtown lunch scene at all. It's actually in the Mission, but worth the trek if you have the time. This corner spot has a spartan yet comfortable café aesthetic, with communal tables made of walnut and a long bar where you can swill German beer and wine, 'cause, hey, it's 5 p.m. somewhere. Lunchtime is all about simple fare like wursts with house-made sauerkraut, veal schnitzel sandwiches with a fried egg, and potato salad. Cash only.

OTHER IDEAS: Balboa Cafe (p. 21), Big 4 (Thurs.–Fri, p. 89), Gio's (531 Commercial St., 415-362-0800), Hayes Street Grill (p. 62), Le Central (p. 100), Maxfield's (The Palace Hotel, 2 New Montgomery St., 415-512-1111), Sam's Grill (p. 100), Tadich Grill (p. 101), Wexler's (p. 104)

Two for Tea

Best friend wants to talk about the foolio who just dumped her? Been stressy and need to unwind over a cuppa? Maybe you have mom in tow and want to show her a civilized time. Here are a few places to chillax, catch up, and eat little sandwiches with the crusts removed.

Crown & Crumpet $$ *Ghirardelli Square, 900 North Point St. at Larkin St., 415-771-4252, crownandcrumpet.com*
Some locals hear "Ghirardelli Square" and raise an eyebrow, but a visit here is definitely worth braving the tourists, because it puts the *party* in *tea par-TAY*. No stuffy tearoom vibe here: it has a playful modern look that's been described as more Vivienne Westwood than granny (read: "doily-free zone"). Get ready for some fully dialed Technicolor: hot pink prevails. This place is total kryptonite to straight guys. There's also outdoor seating with a view, but then you miss out on the *charmant* décor. Indulge in crumpets and rather fantastic tea sandwiches.

TIP: There's a communal table in the corner that's perfect for a larger group (if you're in a book club, here's your next location). Plus, it has a great view of the bay.

Katia's Russian Tea Room $$ *600 5th Ave. at Balboa St., 415-668-9292, katias.com*
For a spin on the usual English tea service, pay a visit to the homey Katia's in the Inner Richmond. There's no flash or pretension here; it's almost like being in someone's modest but tidy house. And it's personal—the spunky, smart, and welcoming Katia may even come out to take your order and pull up a chair to chat with you. It's a choose-your-own-adventure of savory and sweet selections; I am quite taken with the eggplant caviar, a savory spread that is delicious on rye bread, and the sautéed *pel'meni,* like meat-filled Russian tortellini with lightly browned edges and a buttery curry sauce. You can finish up with teacakes, tarts, and blintzes. Your samovar will

contain Russian-style brewed tea or herbal tea, and the entire service with four savory and three sweet selections is just $25 per person, including tax and gratuity. And no dishes for you to do at the end—this ain't no gulag.

TIP: During the holidays this place makes total clutch-the-pearls sweet potato or pecan pies with an incredible buttery crust. Bring one as a hostess gift and I guarantee you'll score major culinary points.

Lovejoy's Tea Room $$ *1351 Church St. at Clipper St., 415-648-5895, lovejoystearoom.com*

This Noe Valley mainstay is a bastion of old-school civility and girlie charm. The room looks like the parlor of your quirky British Aunt Victoria who has a penchant for antiques—it's stuffed with mismatched china, a variety of seating areas, and, you guessed it, doilies. Groups of ladies (yes, some are in hats) cozy up over all kinds of tea service, but there are also some heartier options, like the shepherd's pie and sausage rolls. Bring on the double Devon cream, and be prepared to make a decision on the seventeen kinds of tea sandwiches. Reservations are recommended—and you can also take home some of the scones you are bound to fall in lust with. Be a darling and pass the lemon curd? Thank you, love.

TIP: Wondering where to bring your precious little niece? Here's your spot.

OTHER IDEAS: The Garden Court (Palace Hotel, 2 New Montgomery St., 415-546-5089), Imperial Tea Court (1 Ferry Bldg., 415-544-9830), Lobby Lounge at the Ritz-Carlton (Sat.–Sun. only; p. 38), Mo Bar (Mandarin Oriental, 222 Sansome St., 415-276-9888), Samovar Tea Lounge (p. 8)

Fancy Mom/Stepmom Dinner

Even if you're not that polished or poised, the mere fact you're choosing to bring your mommy dearest or stepmother (let's hope she's not a wicked one) to one of the places below shows some class. Now, sit up straight, dear. (See "Less-Fancy Moms" at the end of this section if your mom is, uh, less fancy.)

Jardinière $$$$ *300 Grove St. at Franklin St., 415-861-5555, jardiniere.com*

This Hayes Valley bastion of elegance has been in business for more than twelve years, hosting many a politico, operagoer, and anniversary. Arrive early for your reservation and enjoy a well-concocted cocktail at the spiffy horseshoe bar, or in the J Lounge if Mother doesn't sit at bars. Request a table upstairs, preferably one by the railing so that you can look down on the bar below (no jumping). Two things to strongly consider on Traci Des Jardins's seasonal French-Cal menu: the duck, and the cheese course (the cheese cave is a thing of beauty). Care to pony up for the elegant tasting menu? You're in excellent hands with the wine list here, so get something special to put in the glass Champagne bucket to help numb you for any ensuing discussions about what you're going to do with your life.

TIP: This may be one of the spendier places in the city, but the rotating Monday prix-fixe menu for $45 is a steal.

OTHER IDEAS: Absinthe (p. 7), Ame (p. 88), Big 4 (p. 89), BIX (p. 20), Boulevard (p. 80), Dining Room at the Ritz-Carlton (p. 38), Fleur de Lys (777 Sutter St., 415-673-7779), Gary Danko (p. 37), Kokkari (p. 103), La Folie (p. 38), Michael Mina (p. 53), Perbacco (p. 102), Piperade (p. 87), Quince (p. 137), Silks (222 Sansome St., 415-986-2020), Spruce (p. 100), Waterbar (p. 105)

LESS-FANCY MOMS: Aziza (p. 79), Bar Tartine (p. 33), Café Claude (p. 31), Citizen Cake (p. 86), Contigo (p. 49), Delfina (p. 137), Slanted Door (p. 98), Sociale (p. 37), Universal Cafe (p. 26), Woodward's Garden (1700 Mission St., 415-621-7122), Zaré at Fly Trap (p. 112)

Lesbian Hangouts

Gay men may have overtaken the Castro, but here are a few lesbian-friendly establishments where the odds are good you'll find more than two (i.e., more than just you and your girlfriend). And since San Francisco has a number of cute lesbian chefs, you'll often find their friends and followers at their restaurants. For bars, see "Lesbionic" on p. 208, and for date night, look at "Romantic Gay Dinner" on p. 25.

CAV Wine Bar & Kitchen $$ *1666 Market St. at Gough St., 415-437-1770, cavwinebar.com*

You into wine? Or maybe your date is (what a lovely trait). The front area of this centrally located wine bar and restaurant is a good pit stop for a glass of vino and cheese (or sweet potato fries!) with friends, and there are plenty of singles (both ladeez and gay gents) in the mix. Meanwhile, if you're there with a posse and you're getting hungry after that bottle of Chenin Blanc, you can move into the back dining room area and eat well; I'm a fan of the Cal-Med-French fare here. The minimalist look is modern and sleek, with candles on the bar and tables that warm things up.

TIP: The house-made charcuterie plate is bountiful, loaded up with terrines, headcheese, and more—one of the better deals in the city as far as cured-meat plates go.

J Lounge at Jardinière $$–$$$ *300 Grove St. at Franklin St., 415-861-5555, jardiniere.com*

You might as well call this the "L" lounge based on the number of ladies who love ladies you'll find here. The downstairs lounge is sexy and comfortable, with whoa-nelly cocktails and bar bites (just try not to finish the bowl of fried olives, I dare you). The only bummer is this place can be utter madness before the symphony or opera, so if you're hoping for a quieter atmosphere, it's best to call ahead and check.

Orson $$$ *508 4th St. at Bryant St., 415-777-1508, orsonsf.com*

Chef-owner Elizabeth Falkner is a fan of urbanity, art, innovation, and living sexy—and her most recent restaurant tucked away in SoMa is a testament to her vision. The place is très chic and provides a stunning set for the weekly ladies' night on Thursdays. Big hits on the seasonal and inventive brasserie-inspired menu include the duck fat fries with brown butter béarnaise, a deluxe hamburger, the mussels, and wood-fired pizzas like one with pastrami, kraut, and Russian dressing (yes, just like a Reuben). The horseshoe-shaped marble bar is one of the prettier bars in the city, and the lounge is an alluring place for some bubbles and a tête-à-tête.

OTHER IDEAS: 2223 Restaurant (p. 91), Absinthe (p. 7), Da Flora (p. 25), Gialina (p. 62), Pisco (p. 196), Weird Fish (p. 111), Woodward's Garden (1700 Mission St., 415-621-7122), Zuni Café (p. 52)

FOR THE FELLAS

Guys on the Town

Some guys like to just go out for a burrito and get some drinks. Others want the whole package: good food, cold cocktails, and a hot scene. Here are a few places to find that winning combo. The night is young—take no prisoners. Wolverines!

The Alembic $$ *1725 Haight St. at Cole St., 415-666-0822, alembicbar.com*

Even though this Upper Haight spot is more of a bar than a restaurant, there's plenty of stellar man food on the chalkboard to calm the beast in your belly, like beef tongue sliders, pork belly, and baby back ribs. Oh yeah, and jerky. Rawr. The wall of bourbons and ryes is enough to cause a twinkle in any chap's eyes (even the chocolate pudding has bourbon in it), and listening to the bartender beat the hell out of a bag of ice for a proper mint julep is positively invigorating. The style has a bit of a rustic East Coast feel to it, and the music is always choice. Cool cocktail-loving chicks come by, too. Careful, you might not ever leave.

Mamacita $$–$$$ *2317 Chestnut St. at Scott St., 415-346-8494, mamacitasf.com*

"Upscale" Mexican that makes good dude food, like *queso fundido* (yup, a bowl of baked cheese with beans and more), a flavorful guac, a slew of tacos, and *gorditas* (a pocket of corn masa stuffed with beef and cheese—keep eating those and you'll be "a little fat one" too). On the lighter side, the ahi tuna tacos in jicama wraps are pretty tasty (make all the tuna taco jokes you want). There's quite a din from folks getting lit on mojitos, sangria, and pitchers of margies (they must have known to ask the bartenders to go light on the ice), while beer drinkers appreciate the nice touch of a Tecate can dipped in salt. Always a scene, and plenty of honeys to flirt with (there are even more after you've had a couple drinks—it's like magic, dude).

nopa $$–$$$ *560 Divisadero St. at Hayes St., 415-864-8643, nopasf.com*

Since you probably didn't call ahead for a reservation (guys don't tend to make them),
luckily there's a big communal table where you can hover for a spot and be social
with strangers at the same time. The long concrete bar is prime seating, but you
have to have lady luck on your side to score a couple of seats. Consistently loud, fun,
and packed, in spite of its not-in-the-Mission address. The flatbread, pork chop, and
grass-fed burger all score high marks (and are made with ultra-seasonal ingredients).
It's basically Zuni Café for the younger generation. The curated list of cocktails, beers,
and wine shows they really know what the hell they're doing here. Like, getting you
buzzed, for starters.

TIP: The kitchen has an irresistible closing time of 1 a.m.

OTHER IDEAS: 15 Romolo (p. 209), Americano (happy hour; p. 107), Anchor & Hope
(p. 94), Balboa Cafe (p. 21), Bar Crudo (great beers; p. 121), Beretta (p. 4), BIN 38
(3232 Scott St., 415-567-3838), Eastside West (3154 Fillmore St., 415-885-4000),
farmerbrown (p. 64), The Front Porch (p. 65), La Trappe (p. 205), Medjool
(2522 Mission St., 415-550-9055), Monk's Kettle (p. 23), Oola (p. 55), Salt House
(545 Mission St., 415-543-8900), Suppenküche (p. 72), The Tipsy Pig (p. 94), Town Hall
(p. 103), Tres Agaves (130 Townsend St., 415-227-0500), Tsunami Sushi (this one:
1306 Fulton St., 415-567-7664), Umami (p. 57), Velvet Cantina (p. 6)

Bachelor Party Patrol

*What you do after dinner is entirely up to you (I've seen you guys
stumbling out of Gold Club on a Saturday night, hundreds of dollars
lighter), so you should start the night with some proper bedrock. Like a
cocktail from Ty at the Big 4 (p. 209). And then it's time to go lay a meat
foundation (I'm talking about a steak, you scallywag).*

If you want to smoke cigars after dinner, look into The Cigar Bar & Grill (850
Montgomery St., 415-398-0850), Palio d'Asti (they have a patio for cigar service; p. 107),
or Paragon (701 2nd St., 415-537-9020), or try getting into the Guanxi Lounge at
Shanghai 1930 (133 Steuart St., 415-896-5600)—just call ahead and see if it's booked.

Espetus $$$ *1686 Market St. at Gough St., 415-552-8792, espetus.com*

Come hungry to the meat parade. Turn the dial on your table to green (which means
"bring it on"), and gaucho servers descend upon your table to shave slices of meat
off skewers onto your plate. Is this heaven? Welcome to the world of Brazilian
churrascaria. Now, one small bit of strategy: don't fill up on the cheaper meats they
first bring out (chicken leg, sausage), because you're gonna want to hold out for

the top sirloin and filet mignon. The prawns are also pretty juicy, and don't knock the pineapple until you've tried it. There's a monster salad bar so you can take an occasional break from the meat-tastic evening (vegetarians can hang out with it all night). There's also a full bar.

Harris' $$$–$$$$ *2100 Van Ness Ave. at Pacific Ave., 415-673-1888,*
harrisrestaurant.com

How could this place possibly improve? It can't. Big-ass booths, a spacious dining room with tycoon décor that makes you feel like you're in the movie *Giant,* a house Manhattan that comes with a little extra (in a carafe on ice—genius!), and oh dear god, the steaks. The rib eye rules, but so does the dry-aged Harris Steak—a bone-in New York. (The prime rib is no slouch, either.) There's also a side lounge with low-slung roller chairs and live music if you want to retire for a nightcap. Oh wait, scratch that. You're just getting started. Anyway, this place is a bit formal, so it's better for a "gentleman's bachelor party."

Oyaji $$–$$$ *3123 Clement St. at 32nd Ave., 415-379-3604, oyajirestaurant.com*

Want to save your money for the dancers later? Understood. Besides, it's time to see the city's most notorious dirty man (and boozehound), chef-owner Hideki Makiyama. This rowdy *izakaya* is all about drinking to eat and eating to drink. Dishes are built to share, so dig in to the Oyaji beef (a saucy version of Japanese fajitas), pork belly with mustard, at least ten different grilled skewers *(kushiyaki),* and yellowtail collar. Take a cab out here, since you're gonna be ordering bottles of shochu and beer while toasting Hideki (he will drink you under the table, so don't even try). Make. A. Reso.

Izakaya A publike drinking establishment in Japan where you go with your friends after work to drink and eat. On the menu: small plates of beer- and sake-friendly food, like *yakitori* (grilled chicken), *kushiyaki* (grilled items on skewers), and fried dishes like croquettes.

OTHER IDEAS: 5A5 (p. 104), Betelnut (p. 82), Baby Blues BBQ (p. 23), Balboa Cafe (p. 21), BIX (p. 20), The Cigar Bar & Grill (850 Montgomery St., 415-398-0850), House of Prime Rib (p. 158), Mamacita (p. 16), Nihon Whisky Lounge (1779 Folsom St., 415-552-4400), Ozumo (p. 105), Poleng Lounge (p. 72), Sotto Mare (get the private room; p. 42), The Tipsy Pig (p. 94), Town Hall (p. 103), Toyose (p. 151), Tres Agaves (130 Townsend St., 415-227-0500), Umami (p. 57), Velvet Cantina (p. 6)

No small plates tonight. Here's where to take your fella out for dinner on his special day.

Does your man just want a burger? If that's the case, you can go a little more spiff! For excellent cloth-napkin burgers, see p. 143.

INEXPENSIVE $–$$

B Star Bar $–$$ *127 Clement St. at 2nd Ave., 415-933-9900, bstarbar.com*
It's no news flash that the lines at Burma Superstar (p. 66) are serious business, but this sister restaurant down the street scores bigger points because they take reservations. You can still partake in the famed tea leaf salad and *samusa* soup (a hearty lentil-based soup), and the pan-Asian menu includes dishes like pulled pork sliders, basil-chili tofu, miso cod, and a number of curry and noodle dishes. Vegetarians will find plenty to eat, and there are a variety of tasty desserts to put a candle in. The look is nice—kind of Pier One bistro goes to the flea market in Philly— and there's a heated back patio with cozy ambience.

OTHER IDEAS: Baby Blues BBQ (p. 23), Chow (215 Church St., 415-552-2469), El Zocalo (p. 155), farmerbrown (p. 64), The Front Porch (p. 65), Gamine (p. 70), Little Star Pizza (p. 115), Limón Rotisserie (p. 49), Los Jarritos (p. 145), Magnolia (p. 30), Monk's Kettle (p. 23), Nopalito (p. 130), Park Chow (1240 9th Ave., 415-665-9912), Pizza Nostra (p. 134), Pizzeria Delfina (p. 66), Puerto Alegre (546 Valencia St., 415-255-8201), Q (225 Clement St., 415-752-2298), Schmidt's Deli (p. 12), Starbelly (3583 16th St., 415-252-7500), Street (2141 Polk St., 415-775-1055), Thep Phanom Thai Restaurant (400 Waller St., 415-431-2526), Tony's Pizza Napoletana (p. 96)

MODERATE $$–$$$

Blue Plate $$–$$$ *3218 Mission St. at Valencia St., 415-282-6777, blueplatesf.com*
The name should clue you in to what this New American place is known for: its meatloaf and mac and cheese. Personally, I veer toward chef Cory Obenour's pork chop, plus there's good focaccia, too. This is also the site of one of the city's best garden patios (it's heated, and dang, it's first come, first served), so at least reserve an indoor table overlooking the garden. Eclectic and comfy with just a touch of hipster, it's got mismatched silverware, tight tables, and groovy art. Not into wine? Your man can happily order up a can of Oly for $1. Save room for dessert—you'll want to finish with some pie. Pie!

Spork $$–$$$ *1058 Valencia St. at 22nd St., 415-643-5000, sporksf.com*
This cool Mission spot with cozy booths, soft lighting, and a quirky repurposed-meets-retro style was once a KFC (chef-owner Bruce Binn says that enough chickens died here, so you'll never see it on the menu). The clever Cal–New American menu features unique flavors and executions, with good house-made pastas, mussels with pork, and complimentary pull-apart rolls with whipped honey butter that will make you pine for them later. The In-side-Out burger is a man-pleaser (with two patties, word). The restaurant's proximity to Mission bars makes this a good launch pad for the night.

TIP: This place has one of the better (secret) outdoor patios in the Mission, and they play vinyl records out back. Check it out for brunch, when you should be sure to order the Mission Eggs, a heavenly pile of broken eggs over carnitas.

You dating a steak man? The following places have tasty steak frites: Absinthe (p. 7), Chez Papa Bistrot (1401 18th St., 415-824-8210), Chouquet's (p. 124), Florio (p. 57), Fringale (570 4th St., 415-543-0573), Le P'tit Laurent (699 Chenery St., 415-334-3235), and South Park Cafe (p. 155).

OTHER IDEAS: A16 (p. 58), Anchor & Hope (p. 94), Anchor Oyster Bar (p. 48), Aziza (p. 79), Balboa Cafe (p. 21), Bar Crudo (p. 121), Fish & Farm (339 Taylor St., 415-474-3474), flour + water (p. 61), Foreign Cinema (p. 32), Incanto (p. 92), Koo (408 Irving St., 415-731-7077), La Ciccia (p. 138), Lark Creek Steak (p. 11), Maykadeh Persian Restaurant (p. 71), Namu (p. 65), Nihon Whisky Lounge (1779 Folsom St., 415-552-4400), Oola (p. 55), Perbacco (p. 102), Range (p. 59), The Richmond (615 Balboa St., 415-379-8988), Ristorante Ideale (p. 50), Serpentine (p. 59), Slow Club (p. 30), SPQR (p. 51), Wexler's (p. 104), Zaré at Fly Trap (p. 112)

SPENDY $$$–$$$$

BIX $$$–$$$$ *56 Gold St. between Jackson St. and Pacific Ave., off Montgomery St., 415-433-6300, bixrestaurant.com*
When you want a celebration to feel all swank and swish, here's the spot. Such a San Francisco classic. Head down the alley into an oasis with snappy white-jacketed servers, the music of cocktail shakers all night (wait until you see the bar), and a classic Deco-esque supperclub atmosphere that all conspire to transport you into full-tilt special-occasion mode. Yeah, baby. Stars on Bruce Hill's New American menu are the potato pillows, the city's best steak tartare (hand-cut and prepared tableside—just wait for the spritz of Cognac), house-made mozzarella, and the bavette steak. For dessert, dive into the bananas Foster. Oh yes, and what I consider to be the best cloth-napkin burger in the city (there's also a super-deluxe version with truffled pecorino on rye).

OTHER IDEAS: 1300 on Fillmore (p. 128), Boulevard (p. 80), Coi (p. 135), EPIC Roasthouse (p. 91), Gary Danko (p. 37), Harris' (p. 18), House of Prime Rib (p. 158),

Kokkari (p. 103), La Folie (p. 38), La Mar (p. 134), Michael Mina (p. 53), Piperade (p. 87), RN74 (p. 128), sebo (p. 53), Spruce (p. 100), Town Hall (p. 103)

21

for the fellas

Guys' Lunch (Dude Food)

Dude, you hungry? Yeah, me too. Let's go eat.

Balboa Cafe $$–$$$ *3199 Fillmore St. at Greenwich St., 415-921-3944, balboacafe.com*
This classic restaurant is dude central at lunch, with business getting discussed, sports highlights getting rehashed, and burgers getting scarfed (this place goes through fifty thousand burgers a year, no joke). Bun or baguette? Your pick, but the baguette is a fave. House-made fries, it's on. High points for the chopped salad, too. With white tablecloths, timeless SF atmosphere, and a full bar, it's a shoo-in. (And it's a total cougar den in the evening, if you happen to like ladies of a certain age, rawr.)

Giordano Bros.

Morty's Delicatessen $ *280 Golden Gate Ave. at Hyde St., 415-567-3354, mortysdeli.com*
No frills, nothing fancy, just big piles of perfectly sliced meat between two pieces of bread. Well, the sandwiches aren't that simple, really; they happen to make a delicious Reuben, the kind that will keep you coming back and asking for another hit (it's quite literally the John Belushi of sandwiches). Nice folks, nice tunes, and, as the sign says, "a nice sandwich." Definitely worth a trip to the armpit of the Tenderloin, and it also stocks PBR, in case you're thirsty.

Phat Philly $ *3388 24th St. at Valencia St., 415-550-7428, phat-philly.com*
They're not joking with the name: these sandwiches are indeed phat (and you'll be f-a-t yourself if you eat here more than once a month). The interior is diner-spartan, but your steak sandwich won't be. Start with a classic cheesesteak, since they do it so right (the Amoroso rolls are flown in from Philly); you can choose a seven-inch sandwich or order that puppy phat and get a twelve-incher. Take a trip to the pepper bar and do your steak up to your liking. The quality beef they use makes all the difference, and the house-made Newcastle Brown Ale cheddar sauce doesn't hurt either.

TIP: Delivery service is available within the Mission. Living large, indeed.

SEE "OTHER IDEAS," PAGE 214.

Just Wanna Watch Sports and Eat My Wings

The game is on, but you want some good chow to go with all those action replays, right? Unfortunately, no one in town does really outstanding bar food, but here are some spots where you can get decent grub and your game on at the same time. Take it easy with the belly bucking, okay dude?

Connecticut Yankee $ *100 Connecticut St. at 17th St., 415-552-4440, theyankee.com*

This Potrero Hill bar (a.k.a. the Yankee My Cranky) is a hangout for many a homesick New Englander (and they even dish out a little tough guy 'tude, just in case you miss it from back home, ya heah?). Baseball is the first love here. There's a big outdoor patio, and brunch, lunch, and dinner are served, so you'll get fed no matter what time your game is on. The Cobb salad, cleverly named sandwiches, and chowdah keep regulars and neighbors returning.

Kezar Pub & Restaurant $ *770 Stanyan St. at Waller St., 415-386-9292*

Whoa, how many TVs did they manage to fit in this place? Formula 1, March Madness, football (i.e., soccer, mate), World Cup, Wrestlemania . . . they play it all at this Upper Haight pub. A total man hut (plus women on the prowl) and local hang, it's known for their truly spicy Buffalo wings (some would say the best in the city) and nachos.

TIP: If you're meeting someone, be sure you have the right Kezar, since there are two. The Kezar Bar & Restaurant (900 Cole St., 415-681-7678) is more of a bar/restaurant, with just one TV (wah), but it's the sort of place you can bring your girl and still sneakily keep your eye on the game.

Giordano Bros.

Pete's Tavern $$ *128 King St. at 2nd St., 415-817-5040, petestavernsf.com*

Dude's name, check. Tavern, check. It's right across the street from the ballpark, so be prepared for an overwhelming number of bodies on game days (read: nice staff, but slow drinks). It's quite cavernous, with three floors, huge flat-screens, a big horseshoe bar, and pool tables. The vibe is casual, and ditto on the menu of no-frills pub fare, like nachos, zucchini sticks, mini-corn dogs, and garlic fries. There's also a house-smoked brisket sandwich, or gumbo with Louisiana hot links on Wednesdays if you want something meaty besides a burger or the sliders.

OTHER IDEAS: 21st Amendment Brewery (563 2nd St., 415-369-0900), Double Play (cheeseburger; 2401 16th St., 415-621-9859), Durty Nelly's (chicken pot pie, steak sandwich; 2328 Irving St., 415-664-2555), Eastside

West (3154 Fillmore St., 415-885-4000), Giordano Bros. (HQ for Pittsburgh Steelers games; 303 Columbus Ave., 415-397-2767), Harry's Bar (p. 119), Il Pirata (get the wings; 2007 16th St. 415-626-2626), Kennedy's (South Indian food; 1040 Columbus Ave., 415-441-8855), Knuckles (555 North Point St., 415-486-4346), Martin Mack's (1568 Haight St., 415-864-0124), Nickie's (466 Haight St., 415-255-0300), Nova Bar & Restaurant (steak salad; 555 2nd St., 415-543-2282), Paragon (701 2nd St., 415-537-9020), Perry's (monster portions, chicken and biscuits; 1944 Union St., 415-922-9022; 155 Steuart St., 415-495-6500), The Phoenix Bar & Irish Gathering House (p. 116), Pier 23 (outdoor screen, perf for sunny days; Pier 23, The Embarcadero at Broadway, 415-362-5125), The Taco Shop at Underdogs Sports Bar & Grill (p. 159), The Tipsy Pig (p. 94), Zeke's (600 3rd St., 415-392-5311)

Bromance (We're Not Gay, Just Friends)

There are no white tablecloths, candles, or mood music at these spots; they're just easygoing places where you can hang out, eat some dude food, laugh at each other's jokes, and silently think, "I love you, man."

Baby Blues BBQ $$ *3149 Mission St. at Precita Ave., 415-896-4250,*
babybluessf.com

Man, meat, and fire: it's a winning combination that can't be messed with. There are plenty of options to choose from, but you might as well go for the Big Blue (three meats, two fixin's)—just make sure the pork ribs and collard greens end up on your plate. Ask for the "XXX" sauce (you know you like it hot). The burger is also outta hand, and to finish get the banana pudding, complete with Nilla Wafers. The music is on loud, the crowd is mostly twenty- or thirtysomething, and it has a friendly staff. Plenty of bars in the neighborhood for a nightcap, too. Done.

Houston's $$–$$$ *1800 Montgomery St. at Francisco St., 415-392-9280,*
houstons.com

Big-ass baked potatoes, French dip sandwiches, bad-for-you spinach-and-artichoke dip (ask for some bread, which is tastier than the chips it comes with), good steaks, killer baby back ribs with coleslaw—the menu is a guy's playground. (Just have 'em put the Lipitor in the pepper grinder.) You want big portions? Wait until you see the sundae. I normally don't write up chain restaurants, but this urban steakhouse on the Embarcadero has a lot of things going for it, including an outdoor patio and full bar. Oh yeah, and there's free corkage if you happen to be a cork dork.

Monk's Kettle $–$$ *3141 16th St. at Valencia St., 415-865-9523,*
monkskettle.com

Nothing like a couple dudes bonding over some beers. Or, even better, geeking out over some beers poured in proper glassware. This Mission hotspot with a cool reclaimed style is not lacking in options for quality suds. It's small and busy (weekends can mean long lines—just grab a beer at neighboring Gestalt Haus while waiting), so there's lots of jockeying for a spot at the bar or one of the small booths. Stars on the menu are the warm pretzel (dip that puppy into the cheddar ale sauce) and the burger. All come with suggested beer pairings. Plenty of chicks come by, so buy them a glass of wine and may the best man win. The kitchen is open late (until 1 a.m.).

NOTE: Sidewalk seating is slated to come in early 2010.

OTHER IDEAS: The Alembic (p. 16), Balboa Cafe (p. 21), Beretta (p. 4), Blue Plate (challenge the waiter to shotgun a can of Oly with you; p. 4), Church Key (p. 205), farmerbrown (p. 64), Fly Bar (p. 196), The Front Porch (p. 65), Hard Knox Café (2526 3rd St., 415-648-3770), Izzy's Steaks & Chops (3345 Steiner St., 415-563-0487), Little Star Pizza (p. 115), Magnolia (p. 30), nopa (p. 17), Poleng Lounge (at the bar; p. 72), Street (p. 115), Suppenküche (p. 72), The Tipsy Pig (p. 94), Tommy's Mexican Restaurant (p. 60), Tres Agaves (130 Townsend St., 415-227-0500)

"Actually, We Are Gay" Dinner

So you have a hot new boyfriend and want to take him out and show him off. Looking for a place where you can play footsie without anyone cocking an eyebrow? (Do I get a point for getting the word "cock" in that sentence?) And how novel: none of these places are in the Castro. Come on, you can do it.

Destino $$–$$$ *1815 Market St. at Octavia St., 415-552-4451, destinosf.com*
Well, it's close to the Castro, in case you're afraid of suffering from separation anxiety. Don't worry, there are bartenders shaking up mighty delicious pisco sours and caipirinhas, because hey, I know how you boys like to drink. The ceviches will help you maintain your gym bunny body, or you can go full steam ahead and order the *arepas*, corn patties filled with oozing Fontina cheese. There are also tasty steak dishes in case you're feeling all Atkins. Don't miss the dulce de leche–filled *alfajores* at the end (did someone just say whore?). The look is colorful, comfortable, bohemian, and with a touch of drama, just how you like it. Oh yeah, and it's gay-owned (and the owner is a cutie).

TIP: There's a handy pay lot (a cheap one, kind of like your last trick) at Market and Buchanan. For those cabbing it, head next door to Pisco for more cocktails.

Gitane $$$ *6 Claude Lane between Bush St. and Sutter St., 415-788-6686, gitanerestaurant.com*
Can this Union Square boîte have any more style? *C'est impossible!* In a word, it's fiercely fabulous. Wait, that's two words. No matter. The downstairs bar is plush and lush, while the dining area on the mezzanine feels like you just walked in on

your friend Luc's after-hours dinner in his apartment in Paris, circa 1972. Or maybe Barcelona. Anyway, it's a soiree, Mary. The menu has some crowd pleasers, like the bacon bonbons, plus the tajines and pizzas. Or ribs, if you're feeling especially indulgent. And beignets for dessert. Someone is gonna get lucky tonight—go look in the mirror in the chic bathroom to see who.

TIP: Be sure to look up the address on your iPhone before going—it's a bit stealth.

OTHER IDEAS: 1550 Hyde Café & Wine Bar
(1550 Hyde St., 415-775-1550), Absinthe (p. 7), Bar Jules
(p. 31), Blue Plate (p. 19), COCO500 (p. 90), Conduit
(p. 67), Contigo (p. 49), Delfina (p. 137), Dosa (p. 4),
flour + water (p. 61), Loló (p. 32), Maverick (3316 17th St.,
415-863-3061), nopa (p. 17), Orson (p. 15), Plouf
(40 Belden Pl., 415-986-6491), Range (p. 59), rnm (p. 6),
sebo (p. 53), Slow Club (p. 30), Universal Cafe (p. 26),
Zuni Café (p. 52)

sebo

If you really have to stay in the 94114, there's Anchor
Oyster Bar (p. 48), Eureka Restaurant-Lounge (4063 18th St.,
415-431-6000), L'Ardoise (p. 36), Poesia (4072 18th St.,
415-252-9325), and Starbelly (3583 16th St., 415-252-7500).

Romantic Gay Dinner

*It's date night! Here are a few ideas for where to stage the perfect
dinner date. Of course these are places that look fab, just like
you in those jeans.*

Da Flora $$$ *701 Columbus Ave. at Filbert St., 415-981-4664, daflorasf.com*
Do you have a reservation? Good, because walk-ins tend to get on the owner's
prickly side. This quirky corner gem in North Beach is intimate and full of "good
date" ambience, with vermilion walls, candles, and antiques. Once you decipher the
handwritten Venetian menu, don't pass up the *baccalà mantecato* (like a brandade—
a whipped salt cod dish that is *delicioso*), the egg and asparagus, the decadent sweet
potato gnocchi with sherry cream and bacon (every first-timer *must* try this dish), and
the pork loin. In fact, it's quite the lovely carb-fest here, because you'll go crazy over
the house-made focaccia (some of the city's best), and for dessert, the lemon-almond
pistachio cake. Owner Flora is quite the oenophile (with Amarones galore on her list),
so let her choose for you—you're in excellent hands.

TIP: Pay cash and make Flora very, very happy. Which is something you want to do.

Universal Cafe $$–$$$ *2814 19th St. at Florida St., 415-821-4608,*
universalcafe.net

Just on the outskirts of the Mission is this vibrant local fave that's been going steady
for years. It has a chic industrial interior that's warmed up with fresh flowers and
candlelight—I mention these details because I know you will appreciate them, unlike
some straight guys (le sigh). Ah yes, where were we? Leslie Carr-Avalos's daily-
changing New American menu might list a perfect Hoffman Farm chicken *(bwok!),*
and the flatbread and double-fried frites with aioli are worth every calorie (really). It's
a good place for a bistro-style hanger steak, too. The seasonal desserts can really hit
the mark, and check the chalkboard for international wines by the glass. I'm a fan of
dining at the counter (although it can be a little loud, be forewarned).

TIP: Universal also has a hugely popular brunch; read more on p. 132.

OTHER IDEAS: Chez Spencer (p. 9), Firefly (p. 9), Foreign Cinema (p. 32), Gary
Danko (p. 37), Jardinière (p. 13), L'Ardoise (p. 36), Le P'tit Laurent (699 Chenery St.,
415-334-3235), Quince (p. 137), Serpentine (p. 59), Sociale (p. 37), South Park Cafe
(p. 155), Spruce (p. 100), Terzo (put your toe in Cow Hollow, it's okay, it won't hurt a
bit; p. 5), Woodward's Garden (1700 Mission St., 415-621-7122), Zaré at Fly Trap
(p. 112), Zuni Café (p. 52)

JUST THE TWO OF US

Ahhh, dating and (hopefully) mating. In an attempt to make this as painless as possible, below are suggestions for various settings during the many stages of courtship. Now, everyone has their own style: some like to start inexpensively and break out the big guns on date three, while others are all about closing the deal on date two, and dialing the romance to eleven. Just take your pick from dates one, two, or three, depending on how you move. And remember, whoever did the inviting pays—no going dutch on date one.

Let's Meet Up: Online Dating ;)

So you've checked out each other's profiles, made contact, and are finally ready to meet up. Or perhaps this is the blind date your friend wanted to set you up with (let's hope your buddy did you right). Here are a few inexpensive cafés and wine bars where the atmosphere isn't too romantic or sterile but there's some personality—spots where you can talk easily and stay for just twenty minutes (sorry it didn't work out) or for two hours. For places to meet over a cocktail, see "Blind Date or First Date" (p. 192).

Café du Soleil $ *200 Fillmore St. at Waller St., 415-934-8637*
It's like this corner place in the Lower Haight was custom-made for Internet dating first meetings, with an easy Frenchie café vibe and plenty of seating (including outdoor tables if it's a sunny day). You can grab a coffee, glass of wine, or beer or cider on tap, depending on what time of day you're meeting up (a beer is not cool in the morning, for the record). There are also munchies like salads, tartines, and easy snacky items, plus Bay Bread sweets in case you want to share a treat.

Crossroads Café $ *699 Delancey St. at Brannan St., 415-836-5624,*
delanceystreetfoundation.org
This SoMa gem has a spacious and peaceful outdoor patio that's ideal for a daytime meet-up. There's also a cafélike area inside with a sofa and small tables and chairs—it's comfortable but not super stylee, FYI. Plus there's a bookstore and magazine stand if you need to kill time. Tasty food, beer, and wine, including an ice cream bar.

Four Barrel Coffee

TIP: The bagels are flown in from H&H in New York, in case you want to come back for breakfast. Maybe even together, heh.

SFMOMA Rooftop Coffee Bar $
151 3rd St. at Howard St., 415-243-0455, sfmoma.org

Wanna know how to impress a first coffee date? Meet them at the sculpture garden on the roof of the SFMOMA, buy them a Blue Bottle drip coffee (or a macchiato, but that's how I roll), and share a slice of Thiebaud cake; the fact you even know how to pronounce it will score you double points. Or if that seems too posture-y, just go with the Mondrian cake. This place is the perfect intersection of class, culture, and the culinary. Pass go, collect $200.

NOTE: Access to the café requires museum admission. The coffee bar's hours are 11 a.m.–5 p.m. (open at 10 a.m. in the summer). Don't forget the SFMOMA is closed Wednesdays, which means the café is closed as well, but it is open late on Thursdays, so you can enjoy the garden until 8 p.m.

Uva Enoteca $–$$ *568 Haight St. at Steiner St., 415-829-2024, uvaenoteca.com*
This chic wine bar in the Lower Haight has a charming style, a comfortable bar, and quality wines that pair well with a plate of charcuterie or cheeses; in short, it feels like a total find in a somewhat sketch 'hood. If things go well, you can head on over to rnm (p. 6) for dinner or a cocktail and some sliders.

SEE "OTHER IDEAS," PAGE 214.

Now, if you're like me, you actually prefer the ease of dining at the bar with a new prospect. You get to sit close to each other, play footsie (if you're feelin' it), share food easily, and there's also the wonderful distraction of a bartender in case things are feeling a touch awkward. The trick is finding a place where you can walk in and score some bar seats. Sometimes hotel bars are a bit less busy than popular restaurant bars around the city, so they offer an intimate "getting to know you" setting, and you won't have to jockey for a space like you would at a place like nopa (p. 17). But, alas, they are also a bit spendier. For more suggestions, check out "Date and Dine at the Bar" (p. 50).

Local Kitchen & Wine Merchant $$–$$$ *330 1st St. at Folsom St., 415-777-4200, sf-local.com*

Ola Fendert's restaurant and wine bar is in a quieter part of SOMA, so sometimes it can be a bit on the mellower side. You have three counters to choose from: a wine bar in one corner where you can start with a glass of something special (there's a good wine list here), the marble counter overlooking the kitchen, or the communal table. The Cal-Ital fare is approachable, so even picky eaters will be at ease, but don't expect any culinary epiphanies. Plus it's shareable, with dishes like salads, truffle Parmesan fries, and pizza. The look is sleek and modern; some people might deem it chilly, while others will be right at home. It does have nice lighting, so both of you will look good (sorry, I can't help with your goiter). Gents, be sure to hold open the door for your date; it's massive and heavy, so you can look like a total stud.

TIP: Don't book your date on a Sunday, the all-you-can-eat-pizza night; save that for later in the dating game, snarf snarf. They also serve lunch during the week and weekend brunch.

OTHER IDEAS: Ame (sushi bar; p. 88), Anchor & Hope (p. 94), Bar Crudo (p. 121), Bar Jules (p. 31), Bar Tartine (p. 33), BIX (p. 20), Campton Place Bar and Bistro (p. 11), CAV Wine Bar & Kitchen (p. 14), COCO500 (request seats 11–12; p. 90), Farallon (sit at the oyster bar; p. 82), Firefly (p. 9), Garibaldi's (347 Presidio Ave., 415-563-8841), Heaven's Dog (p. 74), Hog Island Oyster Co. (p. 151), Kokkari (p. 103), Laïola (p. 30), Michael Mina (p. 53), Oola (p. 55), Ottimista Enoteca-Café (1838 Union St., 415-674-8400), Range (p. 59), The Ritz-Carlton Bar (600 Stockton St., 415-773-6198), rnm (p. 6), Seasons Bar (757 Market St., 5th Floor, 415-633-3737), South (p. 74), Spruce (p. 100), Universal Cafe (p. 26), Zinnia (500 Jackson St., 415-956-7300)

Date One

It's the first date (good luck, you player, you!), which means you don't want anything too romantic, too expensive, or too quiet, and you need ample access to alcoholic beverages (or at least good wine) to help quiet the nerves. Reserve a table in advance where possible. Let's rock.

Laïola $$–$$$ *2031 Chestnut St. at Fillmore St., 415-346-5641, laiola.com*
It can be a packed Marina scene on the weekends, so I'd recommend this Cal-Spanish hangout for a midweek date instead. The seasonal tapas-style menu means you'll have plenty to choose from and share, like bacon-wrapped dates, crisp chickpea *croquetas*, and grilled squid (and there are enough vegetable dishes in case either of you is a vegetarian). Sharing the chocolate dessert with olive oil and sea salt is like a prelude to that hopeful hot kiss you'll have later. It's a comfortable and handsome room, with a long copper bar overlooking the open kitchen, a variety of high and low tables, a few outdoor seats, and a warm glow from the pressed copper ceiling. Creative cocktail program as well—cheers to a good first date.

Magnolia Gastropub & Brewery $$ *1398 Haight St. at Masonic Ave., 415-864-7468, magnoliapub.com*
Is your date a little laid-back? This casual Haight Street mainstay will keep everyone's nerves in check—or is that the secondhand pot smoke from outside? It's always busy with a friendly crowd and has a vintage-meets-East Coast style. (It's the kind of place most straight guys would be comfortable with.) The gastropub fare is approachable (think burgers and killer sausages), and house-made with seasonal and local ingredients. The artisanal beers are house-brewed (things like this keep a fella relaxed), but there are wines on offer, too. Try to score a booth.

Slow Club $$–$$$ *2501 Mariposa St. at Hampshire St., 415-241-9390, slowclub.com*
I can personally vouch for this place as an in-the-pocket first date spot: the lighting is dim and sexy, but the room's industrial style keeps it from getting too romantic; the tight Cali menu changes daily, is easy to navigate, and delivers on deliciousness (there's a great flatbread, and you can come back for the burger when you're an item). The vibe is the right amount of upbeat (if a touch on the noisy side), and it's also secluded, so you can be a bit incognito.

TIP: Come early and loosen up with an excellent cocktail (or two) at the back bar before your reservation.

Since this is such an important date, here are my five other top picks for a first date: Blue Plate (p. 19), Contigo (p. 49), Dosa (Valencia; p. 5), Namu (p. 65), and Range (p. 59).

OTHER IDEAS: A16 (p. 58), Bar Bambino (p. 6), Bar Crudo (p. 121), Betelnut (p. 82), Bocadillos (p. 102), Burma Superstar (prepare to wait; p. 66), COCO500 (p. 90), Delfina (p. 137), Florio (p. 57), The Front Porch (p. 65), Gamine (p. 70), the house (p. 49), Koo (408 Irving St., 415-731-7077), Limón Rotisserie (p. 49), Los Jarritos (inexpensive; p. 145), Nihon Whisky Lounge (1779 Folsom St., 415-552-4400), nopa (p. 17), Plouf (40 Belden Pl., 415-986-6491), Ristorante Ideale (p. 50), rnm (p. 6), Ryoko's (p. 40), Serpentine (p. 59), South (p. 74), Spork (p. 20), SPQR (p. 51), Tsunami Sushi (1306 Fulton St., 415-567-7664), Weird Fish (wait for your table next door at The Corner; p. 111)

Date Two

So, things went well on date one, eh? Good work. Let's dial that romantic vibe up a little more. It's time for a proper tête-à-tête.

Bar Jules $$$ *609 Hayes St. at Laguna St., 415-621-5482, barjules.com*
This Hayes Valley honey is undeniably cute (like a kitten!), with French bistro rattan chairs, soft candlelight, brightly colored walls, and lovely floral and fresh produce displays (it's very Chez Panisse that way). The daily rotating menu is short, with just a few starters and entrées each night (so it's not good for picky eaters). (You can check out the menu ahead of time on the website in case you have diet or control issues.) It's all listed on chalkboards and has a homey and market-fresh sensibility. Full disclaimer: some dishes, like the soups and salads, really shine, but every once in a while something will just be "fine." Bummer on the no-reservations policy, but once you snag your precious little table (or place at the counter), you'll slide right into date mode. The volume in the room can be a bit lively, but it keeps the atmosphere from becoming awkwardly tooooo hearts and flowers (the eclectic music has the same effect). The Chocolate Nemesis for dessert is your secret weapon.

Café Claude $$–$$$ *7 Claude Lane between Grant Ave. and Kearny St., off Bush St., 415-392-3505, cafeclaude.com*
Nothing quite says romance like Paris, *non?* This *très charmant* and cozy café is ensconced off a quiet downtown alley, and the entire interior is actually from a café in Paris, shipped over lock, stock, and barrel. Start with an aperitif at the petite bar, then sit down for a dinner of bistro classics like charcuterie, steak tartare prepared tableside, or coq au vin. For dessert, get the *moelleux au chocolat* (soft chocolate cake topped with crème

nopa

anglaise). The warm lighting, wood floors, white tablecloths, and waiters with accents all ensure some kisses (French? Meow.) at the end of the meal.

TIP: Be aware that the live jazz Thursday through Saturday (7:30 p.m.–10:30 p.m.) might drown out any intimate conversation, depending on who is playing.

Foreign Cinema $$–$$$ *2534 Mission St. at 21st St., 415-648-7600, foreigncinema.com*

I never tire of dining here. Walk down the candlelit hallway off grungy Mission Street, and at the end you're suddenly greeted with a spacious outdoor patio with a film flickering on the back wall (meanwhile, the interior has vaulted ceilings and a fireplace). Start with a classic cocktail at the back bar, or the slam-dunk combo of oysters and bubbles. Then move to your table, where the approachable Cal-Med menu (including a wonderful pork chop—hey, it's the other white meat!) will satisfy without totally emptying your wallet.

TIP: Psssst, request corner table 4 or 16 if you're eating inside.

Loló $$ *3230 22nd St. at Bartlett St., 415-643-5656, lolosf.com*

A little nervous about transitioning to candlelight just yet? Okay, try this place on for size. Loló totally takes me to my happy place: it has one of the most unique (and colorful) interiors in the city (factoid: one of the owners designs furnishings in Guadalajara). The food is an unexpected mix of Mexican with Turkish and other international touches, including the incredible panko-crusted shrimp in jicama "tacos" (so good you'll want to order it twice). Great Mission scene and friendly energy.

TIP: After a successful dinner, you can hang out at a variety of bars, from the Latin American Club (p. 206) to the Make-Out Room (heh; p. 206), or there's always the bohemian Revolution Café (3248 22nd St., 415-642-0474), which is the city equivalent of center camp at Burning Man, but with dogs.

OTHER IDEAS: 1550 Hyde Café and Wine Bar (1550 Hyde St., 415-775-1550), Chapeau! (126 Clement St., 415-750-9787), Coi (lounge; p. 135), Destino (p. 24), Firefly (p. 9), Isa (p. 83), La Ciccia (p. 138), Le Charm French Bistro (315 5th St., 415-546-6128), Le P'tit Laurent (699 Chenery St., 415-334-3235), Le Zinc French Bistro (4063 24th St., 415-647-9400), Oola (p. 55), Orson (p. 15), Piccino (p. 52), Poesia (4072 18th St., 415-252-9325), Ristorante Ideale (p. 50), The Richmond (615 Balboa St., 415-379-8988), RN74 (p. 128), sebo (p. 53), South Park Cafe (p. 155), Terzo (p. 5), Universal Cafe (p. 26), Zaré at Fly Trap (p. 112)

Okay, you know what this means: cue Barry White at the end of the meal (if you can even make it to dessert). Let's get lovey (so don't eat too much, right?). Oooh, someone is gonna have a walk of shame tomorrow. And oh yeah, you might want to bring that credit card.

Bar Tartine $$–$$$ *561 Valencia St. at 17th St., 415-487-1600, bartartine.com*
Smack dab in the Mission, this enclave is romantic, but not romantic in a way that would give most guys the heebie-jeebies—just soft lighting that makes you look good. The urban-artsy interior has wood floors, an antler chandelier, cool paintings, fresh flowers, and a marble bar overlooking the bar and kitchen that's my usual place to park. Attentive and really dialed-in service. The rustic Cal-French menu is ingredient-driven, with the kitchen sourcing the best local and seasonal products out there. And since this is a sister to Tartine Bakery, the bread and desserts are delicious.

TIP: Bar Tartine is also a spiffy destination for weekend brunch (rise and shine with the boozy sorbet). Oh, and there's no sign, so look for the address.

Kiss Seafood $$$–$$$$ *1700 Laguna St. at Sutter St., 415-474-2866*
Uh-huh, the name should give you a clue. Be sure you've made a reservation in advance for this tiny jewel box of a restaurant—there are only two tables for two, and you want one of them. Kiss is known for its authentic and delightful Japanese *omakase* tasting menu, so let's hope your dining partner is into food, and surprises. The atmosphere is a bit minimalist/nondescript, but it's subdued and calming, ideal for intimate conversation. The food is delicate, thoughtful, and sublimely fresh. Wow, you're in love. (I'm talking about the food.) Be sure you write the address down, though, because there's no sign.

TIP: Send chef Nakagawa-san a bottle of his favorite, Asahi Black.

Omakase [say: ohm-AH-caw-say] My preferred way to order in a sushi restaurant: it basically means you trust the chef to whip up something for you on the fly. It literally translates to "it's up to you/I am in your hands" and is usually a chance for the chef to assemble the freshest, most impressive, unique, seasonal, and off-the-menu items for you. As you can imagine, it's usually a bit expensive. I only order *omakase* at restaurants I know well and trust.

OTHER IDEAS: Absinthe (p. 7), Acquerello (p. 89), Ame (p. 88), Aziza (p. 79), BIX (p. 20), Chez Spencer (p. 9), Coi (p. 135), Da Flora (p. 25), Frascati (ask for table 21 or 33; 1901 Hyde St., 415-928-1406), Gitane (p. 24), Jardinière (p. 13), Quince (p. 137), Sociale (p. 37), Spruce (p. 100), Zuni Café (p. 52)

"Morning After" Breakfast

You scallywag—good work on closing the deal the night before. Now you're hungry and ready to make eyes at each other over some eggs. Let's get you both fed. You'll see that I've separated the options for weekday and weekend breakfast; but if a place serves weekdays, you could also go there on the weekend. (See "Playing Hooky," p. 110, for more ideas.)

OPEN WEEKDAYS FOR BREAKFAST

Brenda's French Soul Food $ *652 Polk St. at Eddy St., 415-345-8100, frenchsoulfood.com*
Chef-owner Brenda Buenviaje understands breakfast like only a New Orleans native can. (Lunch, too.) This tiny little slip of a spot is personal, friendly, and funky, and everything is made with love. It's pure pleasure (just like the night before, right?). Favorites include hands-down the best biscuits in the city; the crawfish-stuffed beignets (I heart them); hearty omelettes like one made with andouille and cheddar plus *sauce piquant;* and house-made granola for the healthy set. It can get packed, but it's so worth the wait. Wake up and smell the chicory coffee.

Pork Store Café $ *1451 Haight St. at Ashbury St., 415-864-6981*
Sometimes you just want perfect bacon, eggs, and hash browns. Here's your spot—total diner style (tight quarters), and a godsend after a boozy night (though not a good choice if you have a fancy-pants on your hands).

TIP: The second Pork Store location, in the Mission (3122 16th St. at Valencia St., 415-626-5523), has outdoor seating and a full bar.

St. Francis Fountain $ *2801 24th St. at York St., 415-826-4200, stfrancisfountain.com*
Rise and shine, it's time for hipster brunch. This diner gets crazy busy on the weekends—consider yourself warned—but is ideal for weekday breakfasts. The tiny booths will assuredly have you squeezed in close together, just how you like it. Get your engine running with a Guinness Float (you are so hardcore that way), or perhaps just go with the strong coffee. The lengthy menu has a bunch of breakfast classics, from omelettes to scrambles to waffles to fluffy pancakes, plus all kinds of vegetarian, vegan, and lactose-intolerant options. Buy your sweetie some vintage Magnum P.I. trading cards on the way out.

Zazie $–$$ *941 Cole St. at Carl St., 415-564-5332, zaziesf.com*
This sunny place is all about dining in the backyard garden patio. The breakfast and
brunch menus are loaded with seductive morning munchies like challah French toast,
the "miracle" lemon ricotta pancakes, and some of the city's better eggs Benedict
dishes (take your pick from seven variations). Make eyes at each other over the big
latte bowls and toast your good taste in lovers with a mimosa.

OTHER IDEAS: Arlequin Café (p. 122), Art's Cafe (p. 141), Boogaloos (3296 22nd St.,
415-824-4088), The Butler & The Chef (p. 131), Café Divine (1600 Stockton St.,
415-986-3414), Café Flore (2298 Market St., 415-621-8579), Chloe's Café (p. 132), Chow
(215 Church St., 415-552-2469), The Curbside Café (2417 California St., 415-929-9030),
Dottie's True Blue Café (p. 110), Eddie's Café (800 Divisadero St., 415-563-9780), John's
Ocean Beach Café (2898 Sloat Blvd., 415-665-8292), Just For You Café (732 22nd St.,
415-647-3033), Kate's Kitchen (471 Haight St., 415-626-3984), Los Jarritos (p. 145),
Mama's (1701 Stockton St., 415-362-6421), Mission Beach Café (p. 125), Samovar Tea
Lounge (p. 8), Tartine Bakery (p. 131), Weird Fish (p. 111)

Dim sum could also be super-fun if you're getting up late: go hit City View
(662 Commercial St., 415-398-2838), Dol Ho (808 Pacific Ave., 415-392-2828), Imperial
Tea Court (1 Ferry Bldg., 415-544-9830), S&T Hong Kong Seafood Restaurant (p. 147),
Ton Kiang (5821 Geary Blvd., 415-752-4440), or Yank Sing (p. 97).

OPEN FOR WEEKEND BRUNCH

Pomelo $$ *1793 Church St. at 30th St., 415-285-2257, pomelosf.com*
Get here when they open at 10 a.m. and you can take your pick of the outdoor tables.
But it better be a warm day, because there's one small catch: it's not on the sunny side
of the street. Or snag a table inside, and sit in an intimate room packed with couples
(see, you're one of them now). The international vittles at this Noe neighborhood
spot are not your usual brunch suspects. A trio of flavorful *arepas* (stuffed corn
patties) takes you to South America, while the rich smoked trout and red potato hash
is an homage to Seattle. No matter what you order, the chipotle corn bread with
maple butter is a delicious side trip—you can take turns licking each other's fingers.
(Actually, save that PDA for home, okay?)

TIP: Pomelo has a second location (92 Judah St. at 6th St., 415-731-6175), but it
doesn't serve brunch.

OTHER IDEAS: Absinthe (p. 7), Balboa Cafe (p. 21), Bar Jules (p. 31), Bar Tartine
(p. 33), Canteen (p. 67), Chouquet's (p. 124), Dosa (p. 4), Foreign Cinema (p. 32),

Gamine (p. 70), Home (2100 Market St., 415-503-0333), Le Zinc French Bistro (4063 24th St., 415-647-9400), Magnolia (p. 30), Maverick (3316 17th St., 415-863-3061), Olea (p. 85), Park Chow (1240 9th Ave., 415-665-9912), The Phoenix Bar & Irish Gathering House (p. 116), Piccino (p. 52), Serpentine (p. 59), Slow Club (p. 30), Universal Cafe (p. 26)

"Morning After" Brunch with a Vegan You don't want to make your vegan brunch partner cranky at a place that serves only egg dishes, so head to Boogaloos (3296 22nd St., 415-824-4088), Greens (Sundays only; p. 112), Olea (p. 85), The Plant Café Organic (p. 144), Pomelo (p. 35), St. Francis Fountain (p. 34), Toast (1748 Church St., 415-282-4328; 3991 24th St., 415-642-6328), and Weird Fish (p. 111).

Romantic Date

So it's date night, and you've been seeing each other for a while (glad to see someone's making it work). You bring the hearts, and most of these places will supply the flowers (on the tables, that is). Refer to "Date Two," p. 31, and "Date Three," p. 33, for more ideas.

Are you thinking about popping the question? Really? You sure you want to do that in a restaurant? It's such a personal occasion that I really don't know what to recommend. Your fiancée may be happier at The Ramp than The Rotunda; I have no idea. Good luck. (And don't hide the ring in the food, seriously.)

MODERATE $$–$$$

L'Ardoise $$ *151 Noe St. at Henry St., 415-437-2600, ardoisesf.com*
Ready for date night? *Allez*. Thierry Clement's corner bistro in the Duboce Triangle is an intimate one, with soft light, red tones, and a vibe that's romantic without being oppressive. Add in equal numbers of straight and gay couples and zippy (and cute) servers, too, with accents as thick as a slice of filet mignon. Faves include the tiger prawn *raviole*, the *pommes landaises* (these spuds involve duck fat and bacon—buckle up), and steak frites, *naturellement*. There can sometimes be small missteps with the food, but the place has heart, so you let it slide.

Sociale $$–$$$ *3665 Sacramento St. at Spruce St., 415-921-3200, caffesociale.com*
Walk down the flower-laden alley to the enclosed courtyard and you'll start getting
a loud and clear reading on the romance meter. Since the inviting patio has heat
lamps and umbrellas, you'll stay toasty and dry, even on the drizzliest of nights.
Inside is cozy, a bit Pac Heights in décor, but pleasing. Classic dishes on the Cal-Ital
menu include the famed fried olives and a juicy brick chicken; if it's springtime, hope
for the asparagus lasagna (total *amore*). For dessert, the panna cotta. They are very
passionate about wine here, so you'll have fun with fellow swirlers (if you're into that
kind of thing). *Cin cin.*

OTHER IDEAS: 1550 Hyde Café and Wine Bar (1550 Hyde St., 415-775-1550), Aziza
(p. 79), Café Claude (p. 31), Contigo (p. 49), Firefly (p. 9), Florio (p. 57), Foreign Cinema
(p. 32), Isa (p. 83), Le Zinc French Bistro (4063 24th St., 415-647-9400), Plouf (40 Belden
Pl., 415-986-6491), Range (p. 59), Serpentine (p. 59), South Park Cafe (p. 155), Universal
Cafe (p. 26)

EXPENSIVE $$$–$$$$

Cafe Jacqueline $$$–$$$$ *1454 Grant Ave. at Union St., 415-981-5565*
There are all kinds of classic items for two, like chateaubriand and scorpion bowls.
And here's a new one to add to the roster: soufflé. For more than thirty years,
Jacqueline Margulis has hand-beaten countless eggs for the soufflés here. One by
one, and for couple by couple. So don't expect things to move quickly—leisurely is the
name of the game (even though there are only twelve tables). And you'll be inhaling
the scent of butter, sugar, and chocolate the entire time. Oh, and they're *huge*.
Quintessential Frenchie restaurant atmo, with white tablecloths, fresh flowers, soft
music—the works (including occasionally abrupt treatment from the waitstaff). The
chocolate may tempt, but the lemon or strawberry soufflé for dessert is the way to go.

TIP: Take a trip to the restroom in order to walk by the kitchen and get a peek of
Jacqueline hard at work. Bonus: Maykadeh Persian Restaurant (p. 71) around the
corner has valet parking for $15.

Gary Danko $$$$ *800 North Point St. at Hyde St., 415-749-2060, garydanko.com*
Say what you like, but man, Danko sure knows how to do foie. This restaurant also
really knows how to do service, with some of the best in town. And flambé dessert.
There's a monster wine list (1,500 bottles and counting), as well as a knowledgeable
staff who will make your pairings sing. Plus the gorg glazed oysters, delicious duck,
a drool-inspiring cheese cart—and you gotta love the breakfast cake they send you
home with. Is the refined Cal-French cuisine here groundbreaking? Not necessarily,
but it's definitely luxurious and impeccably prepared. The room is one of the city's
sexiest, with dramatic lighting, artsy flair, inspired floral displays . . . and wait until
you experience the Zen/spa bathroom (complete with shoe polisher). The dining room
is a lovely set for whatever scene you're about to play out.

TIP: You can book two months in advance. Still can't score a reso? There's an eleven-seat bar where you can park yourself (first come, first served) starting at 5 p.m. The cheese cart will even wheel on up (but no flambé). It's also a good idea to check for last-minute cancellations on the day (or day before) you're trying to get in.

OTHER IDEAS: Absinthe (p. 7), Bar Tartine (p. 33), Big 4 (p. 89), BIX (p. 20), Chez Spencer (p. 9), Da Flora (p. 25), Dining Room at the Ritz-Carlton (p. 38), Fleur de Lys (777 Sutter St., 415-673-7779), Frascati (ask for table 21 or 33; 1901 Hyde St., 415-928-1406), Gitane (p. 24), Jardinière (p. 13), Kiss Seafood (p. 33), La Folie (p. 38), Quince (p. 137), Spruce (p. 100), Zuni Café (p. 52)

Super-Important Date (Anniversary, Honeymoon, Big Birthdays)

Did ya just tie the knot? Or perhaps that was twenty years ago (cheers!). Either way, here are places that are custom-made for special celebrations (which also means they're going to be a little spendy). Be sure to call way in advance for reservations.

Dining Room at the Ritz-Carlton San Francisco $$$$

600 Stockton St. at California St., 415-773-6198, ritzcarltondiningroom.com
Good thing the room is gorgeous and that seat is comfy because you're going to be here for a while. Enjoy the salt-and-pepper tasting menu or the nine-course tasting menu ($100 less than the French Laundry's); each menu comes with a cavalcade of

amuse-bouches, mid-courses, and more. If you go with the nine-courser, you and your honey will most likely be served different dishes, so you get double the tastes. Chef Ron Siegel is one of the city's most shining talents—full of creativity, with a Franco-Japanese aesthetic, plus modern and playful flair (just wait until you have the quail egg with smoke and caviar). Breathtaking wine list, full of Champagnes. Both a cheese cart and candy cart will pop flavor wheelies for you, and the service is so gracious it makes you wish it was the norm everywhere else. Here's to the good life, all the better when shared with you, darling.

La Folie $$$$ *2316 Polk St. at Green St., 415-776-5577, lafolie.com*

Chef and owner Roland Passot is one of the hardest-working chefs on our local scene—and if you dine here, the odds are very good that he will be in the kitchen himself (nope, he's definitely not one of those

Jardinière

"phone it in" chefs). His wife is here a lot, too—a true restaurateur couple. And his brother! Since this esteemed restaurant is celebration central, the attentive servers know exactly what is needed to make it a memorable night (the only seams you'll see are on your stockings, you hussy). The foie gras and frog's legs are legendary here, but a vegetarian tasting menu is also available. Don't wear your tight dress or pants, because all the decadences on the tasting menu will challenge your waistline containment. The décor isn't stuffy or overwrought—just classy and, in fact, relaxing. Or is that the expensive wine you're drinking that's getting you all loosey-goosey?

TIP: Request table 11 or 30, the oh-so-desirable corner tables, for maximum romance.

OTHER IDEAS: Acquerello (p. 89), BIX (p. 20), Boulevard (p. 80), Cafe Jacqueline (p. 37), Chez Spencer (p. 9), Coi (p. 135), Fifth Floor (p. 101), Fleur de Lys (777 Sutter St., 415-673-7779), Gary Danko (p. 37), Jardinière (p. 13), Kiss Seafood (p. 33), Masa's (p. 136), Quince (p. 137), Spruce (p. 100)

Late Date

That 10 p.m. kitchen cutoff can be challenging for couples who like to go out for a drink after work—suddenly it's 9:30 p.m. and you're tipsy and hungry. Here's where to get a late-night dinner that is worthy of your date night. (If you're game for something a little more casual, check out "Late-Night Chow," p. 118.)

The Brazen Head $$–$$$ *3166 Buchanan St. at Greenwich St., 415-921-7600, brazenheadsf.com*

This Marina hideaway should be every dater's secret weapon. There's no sign outside, so immediately you look like you're a total insider (unless it's your first time and you can't find the dang place). And, unbelievably, the kitchen serves until 1 a.m. nightly (the bar until 2 a.m.). Hallelujah. The atmosphere is pub-meets-gentleman's club, with low lights, lots of wood, and little nooks and private tables. Sidle on up to the bar, order some stiff classic cocktails (you don't want your buzz to wear off, do you?), and take your pick from standards like French onion soup, beef carpaccio, escargot, chicken Marsala in a mushroom cream sauce, or a New York strip pepper steak. And, of course, there's a burger. (Just stay away from the roasted garlic unless you've been dating a while.) There's an eclectic crowd and a laid-back atmosphere with a touch of clandestine deliciousness.

TIP: Hear the sound of that cash register? Yup, it's old school here: cash or ATM card only, buddy.

Ryoko's Japanese Restaurant and Bar $$$ *619 Taylor St. at Cosmo Pl., 415-775-1028*

You ready to descend into the sushi dungeon? (I promise, it's not a massage parlor.) It's more of a sushi speakeasy, with a bit of cabaret bar vibe thrown in—totally kooky. This place is dark, with DJs spinnin' it loud, low chairs with roller wheels, weird back rooms, a piano, and, uh, carpet. The friendly folks workin' the sushi bar are always fun to watch, heads bopping to the music. And wait, is that a full bar? Why, yes it is—just keep your order simple. Sure, there are better sushi joints around town, but none of them are this much fun at 1 a.m. on a Wednesday night. Just keep drinking. And get some fried chicken *karaage* (almost like Japanese Chicken McNuggets) to soak up some of the bottle you've been hitting all night.

TIP: No matter what people may say, the volcano roll with peanut butter and jalapeño is a bad idea. Don't do it. When have volcanoes ever led to anything good?

OTHER IDEAS: The Alembic (p. 16), Bar Crudo (p. 121), Beretta (p. 4), Bossa Nova (139 8th St., 415-558-8004), flour + water (p. 61), Heaven's Dog (p. 74), Magnolia (p. 30), Monk's Kettle (p. 23), Nihon Whisky Lounge (1779 Folsom St., 415-552-4400), nopa (p. 17), Oola (p. 55), RN74 (p. 128), Scala's Bistro (p. 92), Tsunami Sushi (1306 Fulton St., 415-567-7664), Zuni Café (p. 52)

The Alembic

Cheap Date

No one likes to be called a cheap date, but we all sure seem to like experiencing them (especially when we're the one paying). Here are some spots where it's okay to order the prix-fixe menu, in fact, it's why you're there to begin with. (Be sure to look at the "Inexpensive" section under "Take Your Girlfriend/Wifey/Mistress Out for Her Birthday," on p. 8 and "Casual Midweek Date Spots," on p. 48, for more ideas.)

Bodega Bistro $–$$ *607 Larkin St. at Eddy St., 415-921-1218, bodegabistrosf.com*

This Franco-Vietnamese gem in Little Saigon makes for a super date—it's food that's meant to be shared, and the price is right. The green papaya salad is a can't-miss flavor extravaganza (complete with Asian "beef jerky" bits), and the fried crab and mushroom rolls, shaking beef, roasted squab (don't mind the head and feet), and deep-fried squid are all super. Outstanding beef pho, too. Be sure to get the *bahn xeo* (imagine a Vietnamese quesadilla) on the Hanoi street food section of the menu. The décor is quirky, with magenta walls and bent bamboo chairs in effect, but upon taking a few bites of food, that's what you'll mostly be focusing on. Friendly service, too. Some random trivia for you: the name is not referring to a Mission corner store, but actually breaks down like this: bo-de-ga (Vietnamese for beef-lamb-chicken).

TIP: Get there on the early side if you want the squab since it often sells out, or the super-affordable oysters. Swing by Olive (p. 194) just up the street before or after dinner for a cocktail. Great location for large group dinners.

Lahore Karahi $ *612 O'Farrell St. at Leavenworth St., 415-567-8603, lahorekarahisanfrancisco.com*

Hopefully the two of you have been dating a while, because you're gonna walk out of here smelling like a campfire. This divey little Tandooriloin restaurant is a strong contender to the throne of best Pakistani-Indian in the neighborhood. Chef Guddu is Mister Personality and totally knows how to rock the *karahi* (wok). Menu stars include the chicken korma with hunks of tender chicken in a deeply flavorful curry, tandoori fish, and the *karahi* chicken with onion, tomatoes, and bell pepper. Sounds kind of "meh," but in fact it's totally meow. When the server takes your order, tell him how you really want it, and not how you think it will be served. Spicy is freaking spicy. Get a side of the basmati rice, which features Guddu's special spice mix.

TIP: The joint is BYOB, so you might want to place your order and then go on a beer run, since things can move a little slowly here. Oddly, the closest liquor stores don't have beer, so hit the one that's practically kitty-corner to the restaurant.

SEE "OTHER IDEAS," PAGE 215.

Offbeat Date Spots

Feel like being a little adventurous? Up for dealing with quirky owners and their restaurants? Here are a few ways to shimmy and shake things up.

Eiji $$–$$$ *317 Sanchez St. at 16th St., 415-558-8149*

This place cracks me up. The Japanese owner can be very nice, but be aware there are some rules, like a $10 minimum per person (no "just miso for me" diners), and if you've made a reservation, there are no last-minute changeups or additions—it totally sets the owner off (instant mad dog). And, god forbid, don't be late. Once you settle in, it's a tiny and peaceful place . . . well, unless someone is getting schooled for trying to add one more person to his or her party. Standout items include the custardlike *oboro* (house-made tofu), a salmon-skin salad with cured daikon peel, and strawberry mochi for dessert. The sushi is fresh, affordable, and solid—good *saba* (mackerel)—and be sure to check the specials board. I also like the *sunomono* (vinaigrette) selections, like the *tako* (octopus), and once I had one with bitter melon. On a foggy night, the *misonabe,* a miso-seafood casserole of sorts, totally hits the spot—super homey.

Ino $$$ *Miyako Bldg., 22 Peace Plaza, off Post St., 415-922-3121*

I think many of us must secretly like masochistic dining experiences. How else to explain the popularity of places with super-crotchety owners? So, are you ready to play *maguro* master and sushi servant? Then come to Ino, where the husband-and-wife duo have been holding down this tiny and tidy room for something like thirty years. Definitely request a seat at the sushi bar (you made a reservation, right?). Here are some rules to abide by: wait until Ino-san gives you the signal to order some sushi. Don't freak out when your *gari* (ginger) and sushi are plunked directly in front of you on the wood counter without a plate. (The wood is clean. Don't ask for a dish. Be cool.) Don't overpour soy sauce in your bowl—start with just a little. Do *not* ask for wasabi. This is probably the biggest thing that sticks in Ino-san's craw. He has a heavy hand and will place a plentiful swipe of wasabi in your nigiri, don't you worry your pretty little head about it. Here's what I like to order: the cucumber *sunomono,* the best *shoyu ikura* (salmon roe) in the city (I ask for it with a quail egg), the incredible *ankimo* (monkfish liver; I just wish it were sustainable—don't tell Michael Pollan), grilled *saba* (mackerel), and Oregon sardine. Enoki mushroom or clam miso at the end is also delicious. Stick with classic items (no funky rolls or spicy tuna) and just behave. This is not a place you want to get bounced from, because it's so good you'll want to be able to come back again.

Sotto Mare $$–$$$ *552 Green St. at Grant St., 415-398-3181, sottomaresf.com*

So many classic North Beach joints are long gone, but this place feels like it's been here forever. Local character Gigi Fiorucci has created an old-school fish joint that's personal, casual, and definitely quirky (a Swan Oyster Depot of North Beach?). The feisty staff will bring you oysters on the half shell (only $1.50 each); a delightful *baccalà* (Gigi's mother's recipe, *viva la mamma*!), made to be spread on the bread from Italian French Baking Company (it's just around the corner); and classics like sand dabs, cioppino, and linguine with clams. The crowd is a mix of regulars and lucky tourists who stumble upon it. There's also a mini-fish market in the front.

TIP: If you want the ultimate in "bonus room party spaces," you gotta see the downstairs room that's rentable for private parties (up to fifty). It's like Uncle Vito's man cave, begging for a poker game over a bottle of homemade grappa.

Spices II $–$$ *291 6th Ave. at Clement St., 415-752-8885*

So, you like it hot? You ready for a spice spanking? Okay then, because the heat level of some of the Szechuan/Taiwanese dishes here are infernally hot. Two words for you to heed: spicy twicey. The menu features more than one hundred sweat-inducing items, but here are the absolutely irresistible hotties: the numbing and incomparable beef tendon (do it, do it), the cumin lamb, the filling and meaty twice-cooked bacon, and the respite of the cooling cucumber. The décor is kooky, with pop videos and music playing, and a hodgepodge of all kinds of guests, plus an all-female staff of hottie Taiwanese waitresses. This place is a favorite of chefs, partly due to the late hours (until 11:45 p.m.).

TIP: There's also the smaller and less kooky Spices! a few blocks away (294 8th Ave. at Clement St., 415-752-8884), which is open until 11 p.m. You can try to stomach their claim to (dubious) fame, the stinky tofu, but the smell of it alone is reason enough for me to go to Spices II instead.

OTHER IDEAS: Hama-Ko Sushi (108 Carl St., 415-753-6808), Happy Shabu Shabu (1401 Fillmore St., 415-673-0416), It's Tops Coffee Shop (p. 119), Jai Yun (p. 126), Kappou Gomi (authentic Japanese; 5524 Geary Blvd., 415-221-5353), Marnee Thai (1243 9th Ave., 415-731-9999; 2225 Irving St., 415-665-9500), Minako (2154 Mission St., 415-864-1888), Shabu-Sen (fun with meat!; 1726 Buchanan St., 415-440-0466), Suppenküche (p. 72), Walzwerk (381 S. Van Ness Ave., 415-551-7181)

The One-Two: Drinks and Dinner (a.k.a. Slap and Tickle)

Sure, you can just go straight to dinner, but why not start somewhere for conversation and a drink first (or afterward)? Here are a few one-two combos within decent walking distance of each other in a bunch of neighborhoods—just be sure to double-check your choices on a map so the lady isn't schlepping more than two blocks in her heels, okay?

CASTRO

DRINKS: Blackbird (2124 Market St., 415-503-0630), Café Flore (2298 Market St., 415-621-8579)
DINNER: Anchor Oyster Bar (p. 48), L'Ardoise (p. 36), La Méditerranée (many Castro first dates happen here; 288 Noe St., 415-431-7210), Poesia (4072 18th St., 415-252-9325), Starbelly (3583 16th St., 415-252-7500)

COLE VALLEY

DRINKS: EOS (901 Cole St., 415-566-3063), Finnegan's Wake (937 Cole St., 415-731-6119), Kezar Bar & Restaurant (900 Cole St., 415-681-7678)
DINNER: Grandeho's Kamekyo (943 Cole St., 415-759-8428), Zazie (p. 35)

COW HOLLOW

DRINKS: Betelnut (p. 82), Eastside West (3154 Fillmore St., 415-885-4000), Jovino (2184 Union St., 415-563-1853), Ottimista Enoteca-Café (1838 Union St., 415-674-8400)
DINNER: Balboa Cafe (p. 21), Betelnut (p. 82), Gamine (p. 70), Pane e Vino (1715 Union St., 415-441-2111), Rose's Café (p. 10), Terzo (p. 5), Umami (p. 57)

DOGPATCH

DRINKS: Yield Wine Bar (2490 3rd St., 415-401-8984)
DINNER: Piccino (p. 52), Serpentine (p. 59)

DOWNTOWN/MINT PLAZA/UNION SQUARE

(see also Financial District and Lower Nob Hill)
DRINKS: Anú (43 6th St., 415-543-3505), Campton Place Bar and Bistro (p. 11), Cantina (p. 211), Chez Papa Resto (4 Mint Plaza, 415-546-4134), Grand Cafe (501 Geary St., 415-292-0101), Grandviews (if you're into some serious views and the 1970s; 345 Stockton St., 415-398-1234), Masa's (p. 136), Pied Piper Bar at Maxfield's (p. 210), Rye (p. 203), Swig (561 Geary St., 415-931-7292), Tunnel Top (p. 195)
DINNER: 54 Mint (p. 61), Chez Papa Resto (4 Mint Plaza, 415-546-4134), Lark Creek Steak (p. 11), Le Central (p. 100), Scala's Bistro (late bite; p. 92)

FILLMORE (LOWER)

DRINKS: 1300 on Fillmore (p. 128), Rasselas (1534 Fillmore St., 415-567-5010)
DINNER: 1300 on Fillmore (p. 128), Happy Shabu Shabu (1401 Fillmore St., 415-673-0416), Rasselas (1534 Fillmore St., 415-567-5010), Yoshi's (1330 Fillmore St., 415-655-5600)

FILLMORE (UPPER)/JAPANTOWN

DRINKS: Dosa (Fillmore; p. 4), Florio (p. 57), Wine Jar (1870 Fillmore St., 415-931-2924)
DINNER: Cassis (2101 Sutter St., 415-440-4500), Dosa (Fillmore; p. 4), Florio (p. 57), Ino (p. 42), Kappa (1700 Post St., 415-673-6004), Kiss Seafood (p. 33), Maki (1825 Post St., 2nd Floor, 415-921-5215), SPQR (p. 51), Woodhouse Fish Company (1914 Fillmore St., 415-437-2722)

DRINKS: Café Claude (p. 31), Gitane (p. 24), The Irish Bank Bar & Restaurant (10 Mark Lane, 415-788-7152), midi (185 Sutter St., 415-835-6400), Palio d'Asti (p. 107), Rickhouse (p. 211)
DINNER: Café Claude (p. 31), Gitane (p. 24), Great Eastern (649 Jackson St., 415-986-2500), Jai Yun (p. 126), Perbacco (p. 102), R & G Lounge (631 Kearny St., 415-982-7877), Wexler's (p. 104)

HAIGHT (LOWER)

DRINKS: Nickie's (466 Haight St., 415-255-0300), Uva Enoteca (p. 28)
DINNER: Indian Oven (233 Fillmore St., 415-626-1628), rnm (p. 6), Rotee (400 Haight St., 415-552-8309), Thep Phanom Thai Restaurant (400 Waller St., 415-431-2526)

HAIGHT (UPPER)

DRINKS: The Alembic (p. 16), Aub Zam Zam (1633 Haight St., 415-861-2545), Club Deluxe (p. 206), Hobson's Choice (1601 Haight St., 415-621-5859)
DINNER: The Alembic (p. 16), Citrus Club (1790 Haight St., 415-387-6366), Ploy II (1770 Haight St., 415-387-9224)

HAYES VALLEY

DRINKS: Absinthe (p. 7), CAV Wine Bar & Kitchen (p. 14), Hôtel Biron (p. 192), J Lounge (p. 15), Smuggler's Cove (650 Gough St., 415-869-1900)
DINNER: Absinthe (p. 7), Bar Jules (p. 31), CAV Wine Bar & Kitchen (p. 14), Jardinière (p. 13), sebo (p. 53), Zuni Café (p. 52)

"THE HUB"

This is that up-and-coming area flanked by the Mission, the Castro, and Hayes Valley. Note that visiting some of these spots will require a little bit of walking.

DRINKS: Conduit (p. 67), The Orbit Room (1900 Market St., 415-252-9525), Pauline's Pizza (wine bar; p. 72), Pisco (p. 196), Zeitgeist (p. 116)
DINNER: Conduit (p. 67), Destino (p. 24), Little Star Pizza (p. 115), Pauline's Pizza (p. 72), Sushi Zone (1815 Market St., 415-621-1114)

DRINKS: The Ambassador (673 Geary St., 415-563-8192), Bourbon & Branch (p. 56), Café Royale (800 Post St., 415-441-4099), Fish & Farm (339 Taylor St., 415-474-3474)
DINNER: Canteen (p. 67), farmerbrown (p. 64), Fish & Farm (339 Taylor St., 415-474-3474), Lahore Karahi (p. 41), Shalimar (532 Jones St., 415-928-0333), Sultan (340 O'Farrell St., 415-775-1709)

MARINA (A.K.A. "CAMPUS")

DRINKS: BIN 38 (3232 Scott St., 415-567-3838), California Wine Merchant (2113 Chestnut St., 415-567-0646), CIRCA (p. 77), Nectar Wine Lounge (p. 193), The Tipsy Pig (p. 94)
DINNER: A16 (p. 58), Bistro Aix (reopening in 2010; 3340 Steiner St., 415-202-0100), Isa (p. 83), Laïola (p. 30), Mamacita (p. 16), The Tipsy Pig (p. 94)

MISSION (16TH ST. AREA)

DRINKS: Bar Bambino (p. 6), Casanova Lounge (p. 200), The Corner (2199 Mission St., 415-875-9258), Dalva (3121 16th St., 415-252-7740), Elixir (p. 197),
DINNER: Bar Tartine (p. 33), Delfina (p. 137), Dosa (Valencia; p. 5), Farina (p. 127), Poc Chuc (2886 16th St., 415-558-1583), Ti Couz (3108 16th St., 415-252-7373), Weird Fish (p. 111)

MISSION (DEEPER)

DRINKS: Beretta (p. 4), Homestead (p. 196), Laszlo (2526 Mission St., 415-401-0810), Latin American Club (p. 206), Lone Palm (p. 193), Range (p. 59), Schmidt's Deli (p. 12), Shotwell's (3349 20th St., 415-648-4104)
DINNER: Foreign Cinema (p. 32), Limón Rotisserie (p. 49), Range (p. 59), Schmidt's Deli (p. 12), Spork (p. 20)

MISSION (OUTER)

DRINKS: Argus Lounge (3187 Mission St., 415-824-1447)
DINNER: Angkor Borei (3471 Mission St., 415-550-8417), Blue Plate (p. 19), The Front Porch (p. 65), Lotus Garden (3216 Mission St., 415-282-9088)

DRINKS: Bliss Bar (4026 24th St., 415-826-6200)
DINNER: Contigo (p. 49), Le Zinc French Bistro (4063 24th St., 415-647-9400)

NORTH BEACH/JACKSON SQUARE

DRINKS: 15 Romolo (p. 209), BIX (p. 20), Enrico's (p. 212), Quince (p. 137), Rosewood (go late; p. 196), Tony Nik's (1534 Stockton St., 415-693-0990), Tosca Cafe (p. 56), Vesuvio (p. 204)
DINNER: BIX (p. 20), Coi (p. 135), Da Flora (p. 25), the house (p. 49), Kokkari (p. 103), L'Osteria del Forno (519 Columbus Ave., 415-982-1124), Quince (p. 137), Ristorante Ideale (p. 50), Tony's Pizza Napoletana (p. 96)

POLK (LOWER)

DRINKS: Blur (p. 206), Olive (p. 194), R Bar (1176 Sutter St., 415-567-7441), Vertigo Bar (p. 195)
DINNER: Bodega Bistro (p. 40), Lers Ros (p. 75), Pagolac (655 Larkin St., 415-776-3234), Thai House Express (901 Larkin St., 415-441-2248)

POTRERO HILL

DRINKS: Blooms Saloon (great view; 1318 18th St., 415-552-6707), Lingba Lounge (1469 18th St., 415-355-0001)
DINNER: Aperto (1434 18th St., 415-252-1625), Chez Maman (p. 50), Chez Papa Bistrot (1401 18th St., 415-824-8210)

RICHMOND (INNER)

DRINKS: 540 Club (540 Clement St., 415-752-7276), Bitter End (441 Clement St., 415-221-9538), The Plough & Stars (116 Clement St., 415-751-1122)
DINNER: B Star Bar (p. 19), Burma Superstar (p. 66), Pagan (731 Clement St., 415-221-3888), Pot de Pho (p. 152), Spices! and Spices II (p. 42)

RUSSIAN HILL

DRINKS: Amélie (1754 Polk St., 415-292-6916), Bigfoot Lodge (1750 Polk St., 415-440-2355), La Folie Lounge (p. 197), Tonic (2360 Polk St., 415-771-5535)
DINNER: 1550 Hyde Café and Wine Bar (1550 Hyde St., 415-775-1550), Frascati (1901 Hyde St., 415-928-1406), Helmand Palace (2424 Van Ness Ave., 415-362-0641), La Folie (p. 38), luella (p. 84), Pesce (p. 51)

DRINKS: Epicenter Café (764 Harrison St., 415-543-5436), Oola (p. 55), Orson (p. 15)
DINNER: COCO500 (p. 90), LuLu (816 Folsom St., 415-495-5775), Oola (p. 55), Orson (p. 15), South Park Cafe (p. 155)

SUNSET (INNER)

DRINKS: Fireside (603 Irving St., 415-731-6433)
DINNER: Koo (408 Irving St., 415-731-7077), Park Chow (1240 9th Ave., 415-665-9912), Pomelo (p. 35)

WESTERN ADDITION/NOPA

DRINKS: Bar 821 (821 Divisadero St.), Candybar (p. 85), Madrone Art Bar (500 Divisadero St., 415-241-0202), Mini Bar (p. 207)
DINNER: Bar Crudo (p. 121), Little Star Pizza (p. 115), nopa (p. 17), Nopalito (p. 130), Tsunami Sushi (1306 Fulton St., 415-567-7664)

Casual Midweek Date Spots

You've been dating for a while (read: you have toothbrushes at each other's apartments), so the pressure is off. You're just looking for a location for a fun midweek date, and nothing too spendy. (For more ideas, see "Cheap Date" on p. 40.)

Anchor Oyster Bar and Seafood Market $$ *579 Castro St. at 19th St., 415-431-3990*

If seafood floats your date's boat, you can thank me later for pointing you to this little (and I mean little) gem. Anchor, which has been around since 1977, is an intimate spot for sharing classic and simple seafood like oysters, shrimp or crab cocktail (or Louie!), and steamed mussels while admiring your date's muscles. Share a bottle of white wine while perched at the marble bar or tucked in at one of the five zinc-topped tables. With a great East Coast fish house look and feel, it also has the nicest staff. It may be in the Castro but draws a mixed crowd. This tiny place can get crowded, so try to go early, and be sure to sign up on the white board if there's a wait.

TIP: You can also come back for lunch Mon.–Sat.

Contigo $$–$$$ *1320 Castro St. at 24th St., 415-285-0250, contigosf.com*
For starters, the name means "with you." I know, it's like you planned it that way,
you Casanova. Brett Emerson's Barcelona-by-way-of-Noe Valley neighborhood
spot is ridiculously *cariño,* with a cozy two-level dining room and all kinds of corner
tables, plus perfect lighting and a cute crowd. There's even an outdoor patio; on
warmer nights, the restaurant's full-length back windows open up to let in the
fresh air. The modern design scheme is heavy on the wood, so it feels warm and
almost Scandinavian in its simplicity. The extensive seasonally driven menu is meant
to be shared, full of small plates *(pica pica)* that will please all types of diners, from
vegetarians to pork belly sluts to seafood fanatics. The sardine and avocado toasts,
oxtail *croquetas,* and flatbreads are especially *bueno.* The affordable plates and well-
priced wine list ensure you can get dessert, which has to be the fried-to-order churros
you dip into a cup of thick hot chocolate (you almost want to get it to go so you can
lick it off each other at home, *ay, dios mio*!).

TIP: No reservations except for groups of six or larger—but the wait times aren't too
terrible, and there's an indoor counter where you can hang out over some vino and
almonds until your table is up.

the house $$$ *1230 Grant Ave. at Broadway, 415-986-8612, thehse.com*
This North Beach mainstay has proven that Asian fusion can be both dated and totally
delicious. Tables are close and the volume is high, so don't come if you're looking
to have a private conversation about your philandering boss or your drug-dealing
friend. What you should be looking for are the following dishes: barbecued oysters,
shrimp and chive dumplings, wasabi noodles with flatiron steak, chicken liver salad,
pork chop with pomegranate currant sauce, and the sea bass. Totally flav-o-flav. Good
wines, plus sake, too. Three words: Make. A. Reservation. And I hope you have some
good parking karma saved up.

Limón Rotisserie $$ *1001 South Van Ness Ave. at 21st St., 415-821-2134,*
limonrotisserie.com
This place is the picture of a casual midweek date place. The nondescript building is
a touch off the main Mission drag, but people still come out of the woodwork for
the juicy rotisserie chicken and Peruvian dishes here. I recommend getting a whole
chicken, a screaming deal for less than $20, especially since it comes with two sides
(the *yuca frita* rules). The interior is a little sparse, with ambience provided by a few
punches of color, candles on the tables, and the occasional fire flare-up in the kitchen.
Friendly service, and just a few blocks away from the Homestead (p. 196) for after-
dinner drinks.

Pizzetta 211 $$ *211 23rd Ave. at California St., 415-379-9880*
Out in the blustery Outer Richmond is this closet-size pizzeria, turning out some of the
city's better pies. There are barely any seats, so have your date put your name down
while you circle for a parking space. While waiting for your table, you can enjoy a
glass of wine sitting around the tree out front (they offer blankets too, awwwww!).
You'll each want to get your own thin-crust pizza (there are five rotating kinds to

choose from), and be sure one of them has an egg on it (the anchovy and pepperoni is also freaking incredible). Flourless chocolate cake with fresh whipped cream and a Blue Bottle coffee is a royal finish. Welcome to pizza nirvana.

TIP: They are closed Tuesdays and take *cash only*. Late afternoon is a great time to go Wednesdays through Saturdays. And this place is notorious for quirky service and running out of dough, so prepare for the unexpected.

Ristorante Ideale $$–$$$ *1315 Grant Ave. at Vallejo St., 415-391-4129, idealerestaurant.com*

I know, good Italian food in North Beach, really? Yes, really. It's a quality date spot: the location is cute and cozy, the staff is super chirpy, and the food is the surefire kind that makes you happy such as *mozzarella di bufala,* carpaccio, pastas like tender homemade ricotta gnocchi and *bucatini all'amatriciana,* classic thin-crust Roman pizzas, homemade bread, and whoa, there's a full bar. To be honest, I've never swooned over the entrées, so just stick with the carb-loaded dishes I mentioned. *Buon appetito!*

SEE "OTHER IDEAS," PAGE 215.

Date and Dine at the Bar

Dining at the bar isn't just for singles; it's my preferred seat for a date, actually (there's no pesky table between you). Sushi bars are also highly recommended for a sexy date locale—and besides, nigiri is built for two. See also "No Table Needed: Date One (or Two) at the Bar" p. 29.

Chez Maman $–$$ *1453 18th St. at Connecticut St., 415-824-7166, chezmamansf.com*

You better like dining at a counter, because that's what this casual French joint is all about. Just ten seats total overlook the hustling kitchen crew manning the grill, plus a few tables by the door and outside. That's it, *mon ami.* If you're not lucky enough to score two seats right away, head next door to Lingba Lounge for a cocktail, and a cute (and probably flirty) *garçon* will call you when your perch is ready. It's bistro fare, with a good croque madame on offer, but the hands-down winner is the burger. I like mine with Brie, while others swear by the Roquefort. The ciabatta-like bun is one of the best examples in its class, the side of grilled onions is genius, and the accompanying frites with fines herbes are worth every single calorie you'll have to work off later (indoor sports, anyone?). There are also savory crepes, panini, quesadillas, and classic bistro entrées, like a pork chop or mussels. Split a dessert crepe for your finale. *A bientôt!*

TIP: Weekend waits can be rough, but that's the only time you can get the French onion soup.

Pesce $$–$$$ *2227 Polk St. at Green St., 415-928-8025, pescesf.com*
For those who like a drink or two with your dinner, here's your spot. It's a small space that can get packed and a little loud, so it's ideal for a fun date, not a romantic one. Get things started with some oyster shooters, and then move through the Venetian-inspired menu of small plates called "cicchetti" (say chee-KET-ee), featuring bruschetta with *alici* (anchovies), crab linguine, plus some meaty dishes like milk-braised pork. To finish, order the *sgroppino,* a fantastic (and very Venetian) frothy blend of lemon sorbet, cream, vodka, and prosecco that's served in a Champagne flute.

SPQR $$–$$$ *1911 Fillmore St. at Bush St., 415-771-7779, spqrsf.com*
This popular Roman-inspired offshoot from the A16 crew has a lot of things going for it—especially if you're on a date. It's in close proximity to two movie theatres, and if you like to dine at the bar, there are actually two here (one overlooks the kitchen). Shelley Lindgren's wine list is a playground of Italian varietals; have fun. Friendly servers, and the always-busy space has a comfortable and clean look—it's a good "go to."

NOTE: There was a chef changeover in August 2009. But you can now make reservations here!

SEE "OTHER IDEAS," PAGE 216.

Sushi bars (some of these are quirky!): Ariake Japanese Restaurant (5041 Geary Blvd., 415-221-6210), Hama-Ko Sushi (108 Carl St., 415-753-6808), Ino (p. 42), Kappa (1700 Post St., 415-673-6004), Kiss Seafood (p. 33), Koo (408 Irving St., 415-731-7077), Kyo-ya (2 New Montgomery St., 415-546-5090), Ozumo (p. 105), sebo (p. 53), Takara (great cooked dishes, order sushi off the board; 22 Peace Plaza, Suite 202, 415-921-2000), Zushi Puzzle (1910 Lombard St., 415-931-9319)

Lunch Date (Another Kind of Nooner)

Sure, a dinner date is hot, but sometimes a lunch date is even hotter. Here are a few spots where you can admire each other's flushed cheeks by the light of day. And yes, you should most definitely have a glass of vino with your meal. How about some bubbles? Because, as my dear friend Roberta says, "A day without Champagne is just stupid." Cheers to that.

Piccino $$ *801 22nd St. at Tennessee St., 415-824-4224, piccinocafe.com*

Talk about cute overload. The petite corner café in Dogpatch is worth every mile needed to arrive to its where-the-hell-are-we location. The weather is always a little warmer here, so odds are good you'll want to snag one of the alfresco tables. Sheryl Rogat and Margherita Stewart's well-chosen Cal-Italian food is all made with such quality seasonal ingredients, it tastes like it was made with love. Salads are flavorful, sandwiches are spot-on, and there are some pizzas to choose from, all with a crisp crust and just the right amount of toppings. Linger over an expertly drawn Blue Bottle coffee (Piccino has their own blend) and a seasonal dessert. Let's just hope your date is worthy of all this perfection.

Zuni Café $$$ *1658 Market St. at Franklin St., 415-552-2522, zunicafe.com*

This beloved restaurant has been seducing diners for twenty-five years—no easy feat. While it's enchanting for dinner, I have to say I prefer Zuni for lunch, especially in the late afternoon. There are so many nooks and unique seating areas, the light is exquisite, and it's sexy and chic. Of course you have to start with some oysters (Casanova style, baby!), and then proceed to the signature Caesar, or anchovies and celery. Look, you simply must order the Tuscan chicken for two—it's like it's designed for dates. Sadly, it costs as much as a chateaubriand, so even if you opt for a more affordable pizza (don't get me wrong, those are delicious, too), you will still love your lunch. Caramel pots de crème for dessert, ooh la la!

TIP: The shoestring fries are transcendent with some Billecart-Salmon Brut Rosé. I'm just sayin'.

OTHER IDEAS: A16 (p. 58), Absinthe (have some caviar!; p. 7), Anchor Oyster Bar (p. 48), Bar Jules (p. 31), Boulettes Larder (p. 123), The Butler & The Chef (p. 131), Café Claude (p. 31), Café Tiramisu (28 Belden Pl., 415-421-7044), Canteen (Fri. only; p. 67), COCO500 (p. 90), Fringale (570 4th St., 415-543-0573), Hog Island Oyster Co. (p. 151),

Mission Beach Café (p. 125), Perbacco (p. 102), Piperade (p. 87), Pizzetta 211 (p. 49), Plouf (40 Belden Pl., 415-986-6491), Rose's Café (p. 10), Slanted Door (p. 98), Sociale (p. 37), Spruce (p. 100), Tadich Grill (p. 101), Ti Couz (3108 16th St., 415-252-7373), Universal Cafe (Wed.–Fri.; p. 26), Zazie (p. 35)

Sexy Dinner

There's date night, and then there's "I am assuredly going to do naughty things to you the second we get home from dinner" night. Here are a few sexy places where you two can feed each other bites, merely Act I in the hot night ahead of you.

Michael Mina (bar) $$–$$$$ *335 Powell St. at Geary St., 415-397-9222, michaelmina.net*

Nothing like some indigestion from an eight-course meal to put you in the mood, right? Right. Which is why dining at the bar at Michael Mina is one of the city's best-kept secrets, because you can actually pick and choose whatever sexy dishes you'd like off the tasting menu and make your own custom meal (have it your way!). Some of the simpler dishes, like a trio of Japanese fish or the house classic of the ahi tuna tartare, are as lovely to look at as they are to eat—and won't leave you feeling like you just consumed an immobilizing amount of fat grams. It's also a great bit of foreplay to the main event (I'm talking about a full-tilt dinner in the main dining room, which you can come back for another time). For dessert, I suggest you share the classic root beer float—it comes with ooey-gooey cookies that are as slutty as that girl you met in Spain when you were nineteen. The cocktails are spendy but expertly crafted and intriguing, and the beastmaster wine list is truly a page-turner.

TIP: Don't see any seats at the bar? Nab one of the low-slung cocktail tables first, and make sure your cocktail server knows you're eyeing the more intimate bar instead.

sebo $$$–$$$$ *517 Hayes St. at Octavia St., 415-864-2122, sebosf.com*

I don't know about you, but in my book sushi is one of the sexiest things to eat. So we might as well talk about my top place for sushi in San Francisco, right? Blink and you'd miss it (there's no sign, just some lettering on the window that's obscured with blinds). While everyone jockeys for the ringside seats at the small bar (it feels like you're dining at someone's home kitchen, which you kind of are), the wooden hexagonal tables are where you'll find a quieter setting—although the music can sometimes veer toward the edgier side. Meals here tend to run at a leisurely pace, so don't be in a rush to get to the symphony. Owners Michael Black and Danny Dunham are maniacally obsessed with sourcing pristinely fresh seafood, and it's best served simply (think nigiri, sashimi). I've had plenty of sushi epiphanies here—the kind that make me say "holy shiso!"—so take it easy on the soy sauce and wasabi. The fish is all sustainable and seasonal, so you won't find farmed salmon, or unagi (if you see *ankimo* on the menu, *get it*—they only buy it when they can verify the monkfish was caught sustainably). If you're into California rolls, this is not your place. *Omakase* (p. 33) is one way to go—say yes to wow. Beau Timken of True Sake up the street curates the sake list that reads like no other list in the city. (Psssst, you can actually buy sake from his store and bring it over without paying corkage.)

TIP: Sunday night is *izakaya* (p. 18) night, with no sushi and more of a focus on hot and home-style dishes. There's a bit of a relaxed party vibe, with many local chefs dining there on their night off, and parents bringing in their kids.

OTHER IDEAS: Aziza (p. 79), Bar Tartine (p. 33), BIX (p. 20), Chez Spencer (p. 9), Coi (lounge; p. 135), Foreign Cinema (p. 32), Gary Danko (p. 37), Gitane (p. 24), Harris' (lounge; p. 18), J Lounge (p. 15), Kokkari (p. 103), Oola (p. 55), Orson (p. 15), Quince (p. 137), Serpentine (p. 59), Slow Club (p. 30), Spruce (p. 100), Terzo (p. 5), Universal Cafe (p. 26), Zuni Café (p. 52)

Eat and Cheat

Nope, I'm not talking about dieting. Nor am I here to judge—I'm just here to give you recommendations. I offer no guarantees that you won't get caught dining with your lover, but here are a few places where the odds are certainly diminished. I also included some spots for drinks, you scandalous thing.

Luna Park $$ *694 Valencia St. at 18th St., 415-553-8584, lunaparksf.com*
This restaurant may be in a hopping part of town (the Valencia corridor), but it contains the ultimate cheater's tables: three private booths in the back (ask for 41, 42, or 43). The full bar means the two of you can relax over some cocktails and then be all flirty over goat cheese fondue. The eclectic menu is pretty straightforward, full of comfort food classics like chicken, pastas, short ribs, and the house special: mac, cheese, and broccoli (with the option of adding ham). There are also big salads (like a Cobb), and vegetarians and vegans have decent choices. Just keep in mind you're not totally here for the food—it's more about the booth, and booze.

Oola $$–$$$ *860 Folsom St. at 4th St., 415-995-2061, oola-sf.com*

For the *ne plus ultra* in cheater's tables, look no further than the private table upstairs at Oola. It's like having your own room. The restaurant has low lights; a sexy, clubby vibe; and a chic look—total date night material. Ola Fendert's American bistro menu includes glazed baby back ribs, decadent foie and chicken ravioli (just go for the small size, because they are super-rich, like a Rockefeller), and the French fries with Parmesan cheese and truffle (I loathe truffle oil in general, but these fries are an exception). Oh yeah, and get the milk chocolate ganache tart with fleur de sel. You can get all "rawr" over some oysters, and the late-night hours are handy. Well-made cocktails will get you saucier than you already are.

OTHER IDEAS: Alfred's Steakhouse (659 Merchant St., 415-781-7058), Big 4 (at the bar; p. 89), Bistro Clovis (1596 Market St., 415-864-0231), BIX (upstairs; p. 20), The Brazen Head (p. 39), Campton Place Bar and Bistro (p. 11), Cassis (bar; 2101 Sutter St., 415-440-4500), Chouchou (upstairs; 400 Dewey Blvd., 415-242-0960), Fish & Farm (339 Taylor St., 415-474-3474), Harris' (in the lounge; p. 18), Katana-ya (p. 151), Le Colonial (p. 84), Liverpool Lil's (2942 Lyon St., 415-921-6664), Maxfield's (The Palace Hotel, 2 New Montgomery St., 415-512-1111), Michael Mina (bar; p. 53), Moss Room (p. 68), The Phoenix Bar & Irish Gathering House (back booths; p. 116), Ryoko's (p. 40), Sam's Grill (private room/booths; p. 100), Vitrine (lunch; St. Regis, 125 3rd St., 415-284-4049)

Drinks: Bourbon & Branch (p. 56), Forbes Island (it's touristy, and an island—perfect; Pier 41, 415-951-4900), Hidden Vine (620 Post St., 415-674-3567), Hôtel Biron (p. 192), The Rite Spot Cafe (p. 207), Seasons Bar (757 Market St., 5th Floor, 415-633-3737), Top of the Mark (p. 212), Tosca Cafe (p. 56)

SHITUATIONS

Dump Him or Her: The Last Supper

For the record, I don't think it's appropriate to dump someone in a restaurant. It's actually the worst place to do it, because once the moment of dumping happens, there are usually tears, harsh words, and hasty exits. It's tacky. Here are a few bars to go to instead. And yes, there's booze handy.

Bourbon & Branch *501 Jones St. at O'Farrell St., 415-931-7292, bourbonandbranch.com*

The bummer about this speakeasy-inspired joint is your date might think the location is fabulously romantic, but then suddenly the needle will scratch across the record like the most painful train wreck any DJ ever committed. Reserve your table ahead of time on the website and get your password for the door—request a table in the back room in the far corner for the most privacy. The hand-crafted cocktails are bracing and refreshing, just what you need right now. The lights are incredibly low, you'll have your own private booth, and there's old-timey music so people can't hear every word of your "I'm sorry to do this to you" speech. Hey, if you're going to dump someone, you might as well do it with style.

TIP: The neighborhood is super-sketchy, so once the dumping happens, make sure whoever got dumped gets safely into a cab or to their car.

Tosca Cafe *242 Columbus Ave. at Broadway, 415-986-9651*

The scene: a dark moody bar with quieter tables and booths in the back, and tragic opera arias on the jukebox. The players: white-jacketed waiters shaking up strong cocktails so you can drink your courage. The bonus: the proximity to Broadway makes it easy to snag a cab when it's time to get the hell out of Dodge. And the one who gets left behind has good odds of meeting someone and hooking up when the dust settles. Nope, I don't think it can get better than this. Or worse.

OTHER IDEAS: 15 Romolo (during the week; p. 209), Big 4 (lounge; p. 89), Hôtel Biron (p. 192), Lone Palm (p. 193), The Rite Spot Cafe (p. 207), Seasons Bar (757 Market St., 5th Floor, 415-633-3737)

Awww hell, isn't it the worst? Dag. You need a place where you can get together with your friends and dish on the jerk or wench who just dumped your ass. On order: some comforting food, followed up with a really decadent dessert. We also need to get you liquored up, and maybe help you meet some new guys or dolls. Bartender!

Florio $$–$$$ *1915 Fillmore St. at Bush St., 415-775-4300, floriosf.com*
You need a good setting when you're hashing out the sordid breakup details with a friend, and some steak frites can only help. You've come to the right place: Florio's brasserie style is classy and homey, and the busy vibe means people won't be paying attention to everything you're saying. Start with a cocktail from the bar, and then you can move right into a carafe of wine. Heck, have your own. The Italian-meets-bistro menu will feel like your favorite snuggly sweater: mussels and frites, a satisfying burger, a lovely salmon-meets-Niçoise salad, and pappardelle Bolognese (conveniently available in two sizes). Oh yes, and desserts like crème caramel, apple galette, and house-made gelato help make it all better. Florio has so much charm that once you start dating again, it'll be your new secret weapon for a first date.

TIP: Got a birthday coming up? There's a great private table here with room for eight. There are two seatings for it: 6 p.m. and 8:30 p.m.

Umami $$–$$$ *2909 Webster St. at Union St., 415-346-3431, umamisf.com*
This trendy Cow Hollow *izakaya* (p. 18) has an equal number of young male and female fans and gets pretty hectic downstairs. Start your meal upstairs, where it's a little mellower, so you can go over the list of infractions and why s/he was such a monster. Umami regulars would say get the edamame hummus with flatbread, ahi tacos, miso cod, and beef sliders, and there's a sushi bar with all kinds of rolls and nigiri. Once you're done wolfing down the cookie dough ice cream sushi roll (hey, you can eat whatever the hell you want right now), head downstairs for some sake shots, or drinks like the Hello Kitty (which is geared toward the ladies, but is exactly what most single guys would like to say here).

TIP: Since you could use a laugh, be sure to go to the restroom to hear the Japanese language lessons playing.

OTHER IDEAS: Absinthe (p. 7), The Alembic (p. 16), Beretta (p. 4), Betelnut (p. 82), CIRCA (p. 77), Destino (p. 24), farmerbrown (p. 64), Heaven's Dog (p. 74), Houston's (p. 23), Kokkari (bar; p. 103), Laïola (p. 30), nopa (p. 17), Oola (p. 55), Pesce (p. 51), Pier 23 (Pier 23, The Embarcadero at Broadway, 415-362-5125), Range (bar; p. 59), Ristorante Ideale (p. 50), Salt House (545 Mission St., 415-543-8900), Slow Club (p. 30), The Tipsy Pig (p. 94), Tommy's Mexican Restaurant (p. 60), Town Hall (p. 103), Tres Agaves (130 Townsend St., 415-227-0500), Zaré at Fly Trap (p. 112), Zuni Café (p. 52)

Dinner with the Ex-/Old Flame

There are two kinds of dinners with the ex: either you want them back, or enough time has passed and you're just going to hang out and catch up (and show them how fabulously you're doing without them, don't lie!). Below are sections for each state of affairs.

NICE TO SEE YOU; I'M QUITE FINE WITHOUT YOU

These places have enough activity going on so any awkward pauses aren't too noticeable, and, hey, you look cool for picking a happenin' spot. Even better: go to a restaurant where the staff knows you, so you look like a baller. Make a reservation ahead of time so you don't have to stand around too long waiting for a table and run out of things to talk about. (How the hell were you ever in love with this person?)

A16 $$–$$$ *2355 Chestnut St. at Scott St., 415-771-2216, a16sf.com*

When is this place not busy? When it's closed, that's about it. The Marina/"On Campus" address does not deter people from all over the city who trek here for the Campania-goes-to-California menu of oozy *burrata* (a dairy ball of crack), the Neapolitan pizzas (try the Romana with arugula; I like to drizzle it with chili oil), tender ricotta gnocchi, and meaty main dishes. It's worth sharing one of the *favoloso* desserts, even if it makes it a little awkwardly romantic for a second. The front bar area (a.k.a. the wino waiting room) is where walk-ins hang out and swirl some Vermentino until their table is up. The attentive staff is well schooled on the deeeeep Italian wine list, so you won't look like a dummy if you don't know what Fiano di Avellino is. The room crackles with energy and feels chic and urban—just like you.

TIP: Lunch is served Wednesdays through Fridays. Monday is their famous meatball night, so be prepared for a full house. And if you even remotely like tripe, order the *trippa alla napoletana* here—one of my top ten favorite dishes in the city. I even have a money-back guarantee on this dish for my dining cohorts. You don't like it? I pay for it and take the leftovers home to eat the next day, thankyouverymuch. Just try it.

OTHER IDEAS: Beretta (p. 4), COCO500 (p. 90), Dosa (Fillmore; p. 4), Farina (p. 127), flour + water (p. 61), Laïola (p. 30), nopa (p. 17), Pesce (p. 51), RN74 (p. 128), Salt House (545 Mission St., 415-543-8900), South (p. 74), Starbelly (3583 16th St. 415-252-7500), Town Hall (p. 103)

These places are a wee bit cozy or romantic, but not toooo much, in case things don't go exactly as planned (like, uh, what, she's engaged now? Aw hell.). Proximity to the hard stuff and good wine is also necessary to lessen any inhibitions. Bottoms up. (Heh.) See "Date One," p. 30, for more recommendations (I know, it's like starting all over again).

Range $$–$$$ *842 Valencia St. at 19th St., 415-282-8283, rangesf.com*
A cocktail from this Mission fave is definitely in order. In fact, I'd even come early for your reservation to enjoy a drink at the bar first (you know, to get things rolling). The lighting is flattering, the décor is kind of rustic-deco-modern, and it's comfortable. Phil West's Cali menu features quality ingredients, so the prices are a wee bit higher than some people expect from the Mission. Standbys include the goat cheese and sorrel ravioli, and coffee-rubbed pork shoulder; roast chicken is also well executed. Dessert is gonna seal the deal like no one's business. Check out the boozy nightcaps for the *pièce de (no) résistance*, if you know what I'm sayin', and I think you do.

Serpentine $$–$$$ *2495 3rd St. at 22nd St., 415-252-2000, serpentinesf.com*
Just getting out to this remote Dogpatch restaurant is an adventure—and once you slip into the shadowy and atmospheric industrial-chic space, you can't help but feel totally in the know. Yeah, that's how you roll. Start with a well-crafted cocktail at the bar (with the many bottles seductively flickering in the candlelight). Once you get your table, the eclectic Cal-Med-American menu has seasonal salads, and heartier main dishes all made with good ingredients, like a flatiron steak or house-made linguine. And you can never go wrong with oysters on the half shell.

TIP: This neighborhood joint is also a primo location for a sexy lunch or a weekend brunch—or even a solo burger at the bar. Head to Yield across the street beforehand for a glass of organic/biodynamic/guilt-free wine.

OTHER IDEAS: Bar Jules (p. 31), Bar Tartine (p. 33), Blue Plate (p. 19), Café Claude (p. 31), CAV Wine Bar & Kitchen (p. 14), Contigo (although the name is almost ironic for this occasion; p. 24), Delfina (p. 137), Florio (p. 57), Foreign Cinema (p. 32), Gitane (p. 24), Loló (p. 32), Namu (p. 65), Slow Club (p. 30), South Park Cafe (p. 155), Terzo (p. 5), Ti Couz (3108 16th St., 415-252-7373), Universal Cafe (p. 26), Zaré at Fly Trap (p. 112), Zuni Café (p. 52)

Just Laid Off
(What Color Is Your Parachute, Yo?)

This is happening way too often these days. When I lost my last full-time job, back in 2000, it happened at the inconvenient time of 3:30 p.m. Thank you, Mission mainstay Dalva, for being open at 4 p.m., and Puerto Alegre for getting me all crunk (crazy + drunk) and passed out by 9 p.m. (or so I was told). Little did I know that that day was going to become Marcia Liberation Day, so who knows, your layoff might prove to be a good thing. Hang tuff. Be sure to tell everyone you just got laid off—you deserve all the free drinks you can handle. If you got canned early in the day, look at the bars in "Open Early (Dawn Patrol)," p. 204.

Tommy's Mexican Restaurant $–$$ *5929 Geary Blvd. at 23rd Ave., 415-387-4747, tommysmexican.com*

Awww, this place has been run by the welcoming Bermejo family since 1965. And it's known for making the best damned margaritas in the city. No crappy mix here, *mi amigo*. Julio is going to be your doctor this evening. Yeah, you're getting pitchers tonight. That's what it says right here on your prescription. I also see you have unlimited refills of chips and salsa. And please ensure your friend the (dis)orderly forces you to order something off the Yucatecan menu (like the *pollo pibil*, savory chicken with orange and achiote, or *poc chuc*, marinated pork), or at least some chiles rellenos, because we don't want to find you all curled up in the fetal position on Geary, *claro*?

OTHER IDEAS: Beretta (p. 4), The Front Porch (p. 65), Houston's (p. 23), The Irish Bank Bar & Restaurant (10 Mark Lane, 415-788-7152), Jay'n Bee Club (pub grub and margies; 2736 20th St., 415-824-4190), Olive (p. 194), Park Chalet (p. 133), Puerto Alegre (546 Valencia St., 415-255-8201), The Ramp (855 Terry Francois St., 415-621-2378), Tres Agaves (130 Townsend St., 415-227-0500), Velvet Cantina (p. 6)

Strong and cheap drinks: The Attic (3336 24th St., 415-643-3376), Dalva (3121 16th St., 415-252-7740), Finnegan's Wake (what an appropriate place for you to drink at right now; 937 Cole St., 415-731-6119), Latin American Club (p. 206), Li-Po Cocktail Lounge (p. 204), Mission Bar (2695 Mission St., 415-647-2300), The Orbit Room (1900 Market St., 415-252-9525), Pier 23 (Pier 23, The Embarcadero at Broadway, 415-362-5125), The Royal Exchange (301 Sacramento St., 415-956-1710), Schroeder's (240 Front St., 415-421-4778), Tunnel Top (p. 195), Vertigo Bar (p. 195)

FLYING SOLO

Good (or Hip) Spots for Solo Dining

The city is kind to single diners, chock-full of bars and counters and communal tables. No need to bring a book or twiddle with your iPhone all night—there's plenty to watch at the places below, and you'll most likely end up chatting with your neighbor, if not your bartender. ("Quirky alone" doesn't have to mean asocial.) Oh yeah, and most sushi bars are ideal for solo flights (you get both pieces of hamachi all to yourself).

54 Mint $$–$$$ *16 Mint Plaza at Jessie St., 415-543-5100, 54mint.com*
Ciao bella! Yup, the staff here can be friendly, funny, and flirty, so you'll feel right at home. Then again, service can be totally absent or weird. Huh. This Italian newcomer brings a one-of-a-kind look to San Francisco: the design is airy and rustic-meets-industrial (pottery here, and concrete floors there), plus a touch of butcher-shop style, with white subway tile and marble. The counter offers plenty of action to watch, like the staff making drinks, pouring wine, cutting cheese (I'm talking about the Parmesan wheel, don't be rude), and slicing meats. Almost everything is handmade, like the wonderful bread that reminds me of Italia, plus pastas that include a garlicky Trapanese (Sicilian) pesto over trenette (but the ravioli gets the most raves), and a delicious porchetta. A few items feel overpriced for what you get, however. There's quite the variety of quality products, like the salumi, and cheeses, and you can actually buy and bring home items such as salt, olive oil, and vinegar.

TIP: The downstairs is designed for large groups, and there's a spacious outdoor area on the slightly sketchy plaza for lunch or warm nights.

flour + water $$–$$$ *2401 Harrison St. at 20th St., 415-826-7000, flourandwater.com*
Yet another popular Italian restaurant run by non-Italians, drawing people from all over town to its off-the-beaten-path location. The space is full of reclaimed wood, with good lighting, an original mural on the back wall, and one of the best bathrooms in the city (wait until you see the "curio cabinet" display). Singles can park it at the bar or communal table and tuck into a seasonal salad, and then a bowl of homemade pasta (just don't expect a *big* bowl), or a rather perfect thin-crust pizza, or perhaps

61

something meaty, like pork cheek or chicken *al mattone* (under a brick). The pizza margherita is delicious, with a nicely chewy and blistered crust (and it's one of the more affordable choices). All the wines are under $60 (but you're not drinking a whole bottle, right?—you might want to watch that), with plenty by the glass. The vibe is definitely Mission-y, with a hip crowd, and the late-night hours are a bonus.

SEE "OTHER IDEAS," PAGE 216.

Midweek/Casual Counter Dining

You're not really looking for a scene, just a counter or bar where you can eat your dinner alone and not feel like a total loser or leper.

Gialina $$ *2842 Diamond St. at Kern St., 415-239-8500, gialina.com*

I can't begin to count how many times I have craved this pizza. Sharon Ardiana's cozy Glen Park pizzeria gets packed with couples, families, and friends addicted to her pizza, which has such a flavorful and—dare I say—toothsome crust (I hate that "food writer word," but there it is). The toppings can be very California, like wild nettles, but the Atomica, with mushrooms, mozzarella, spicy chiles, and red onions, or the Puttanesca, with anchovies, olives, and capers, reign supreme in my book. Singles can park at the petite counter in the back overlooking the kitchen and tuck into their very own pizza. For dessert, the grapefruit Italian ice with Campari is the *perfetto* finish.

TIP: Come back on a date and share a chocolate hazelnut dessert pizza.

Hayes Street Grill $$–$$$ *320 Hayes St. at Franklin St., 415-863-5545, hayesstreetgrill.com*

A San Fran stalwart (twenty-five years and counting), Patty Unterman's comfy restaurant needs no introduction. It can get crazy with the opera and symphony crowd, so it's worth timing your visit around that if possible. The bar in the front fills up during the day with Hayes Valley shopkeepers having lunch, while dinnertime means jockeying for a space with folks who just want a cocktail. It feels very neighborhoody. The fries here are some of the city's best, and I also heart the flavorful burger with Grafton cheddar (lunch only). Fresh seafood with a conscience, attentive staff that has been here for years, and it's a good place to bring the grandparents—nothing flashy, just nice.

OTHER IDEAS: Baby Blues BBQ (get the burger; p. 23), Bill's Place (p. 144), Chez Maman (p. 50), Chow (215 Church St., 415-552-2469), The Corner (2199 Mission St., 415-875-9258), Crave (2164 Polk St., 415-440-3663), Gamine (p. 70), Genki Ramen (p. 119), Just For You Café (732 22nd St., 415-647-3033), Kasa Indian Eatery (4001 18th St., 415-621-6940; 3115 Fillmore St., 415-896-4008), Katana-ya (p. 151), Limón Rotisserie (p. 49), Monk's Kettle (p. 23), Mo's Grill (1322 Grant Ave., 415-788-3779), Nopalito

(p. 130), Out the Door (various locations; outthedoors.com), Park Chow (1240 9th Ave., 415-665-9912), Phat Philly (p. 21), Pizza Nostra (p. 134), The Pizza Place on Noriega (3901 Noriega St., 415-759-5752), Pizzeria Delfina (p. 66), Pizzetta 211 (p. 49), The Plant Café Organic (p. 144), Poleng Lounge (p. 72), Pomelo (p. 35), Regalito Rosticeria (3481 18th St., 415-503-0650), Rosamunde Sausage Grill (545 Haight St., 415-437-6851), Schmidt's Deli (p. 12), St. Francis Fountain (p. 34), Tanpopo (1740 Buchanan St., 415-346-7132), Ti Couz (3108 16th St., 415-252-7373), Truly Mediterranean (p. 149), Tu Lan (just get the fried rice, or the vermicelli with imperial spring rolls and pork or chicken; 8 6th St., 415-626-0927), The Taco Shop at Underdogs Sports Bar & Grill (p. 159), Woodhouse Fish Company (1914 Fillmore St., 415-437-2722; 2073 Market St., 415-437-2722), Yamo Thai (3406 18th St., 415-553-8911)

Midweek Casual and Cheap Eats: No Counter Needed

Now, this list is in no way exhaustive, but here are some local faves for cheap solo dining. (You can also have someone come with you—no need to show up alone.)

The Little Chihuahua $ *292 Divisadero St. at Page St., 415-255-8225, thelittlechihuahua.com*

Great neighborhood taqueria that is one step above the usual quality level, with Niman Ranch meats, sustainable seafood, and fresh ingredients. The cult burrito here is the fried plantain with black beans, and I love that I can order a super baby size, which is still pretty *grande*. Tortilla soup is quality, ditto on the kickass salsas (the habanero rules). Vegetarians are happy here. Bonus: you can return for weekend brunch (Mexican French toast!) from 10 a.m.–2 p.m.

Sapporo-ya $ *Kinokuniya Bldg., 1581 Webster St. at Post St., 415-563-7400*

It's hard to beat the 1970s time warp here, with bad overhead lighting, a weird greenish hue to the room, dingy furnishings, and even grass-cloth wallpaper. And Muzak! This noodle house has been around for thirty years, so the décor is too legit to quit. I'm a fan of the kimchi ramen here because, hey, I like some kick, and it comes with their pork that for some reason has this homey taste to it—almost like it's a pork roast your grandma would make—a little fatty, too. One of my preferred hideouts on a chilly night or before a movie at the Kabuki.

Turtle Tower

SEE "OTHER IDEAS," PAGE 217.

OUT WITH A FRIEND

Hip and Moderately Priced

Looking for a happenin' place for dinner with a friend or two? Want some buzz (and want to pack on a buzz)? At most of these hotspots, you can get out for less than $100 for two if you keep things within reason (just don't be ordering bottles of champers or too many cocktails). FYI, I have geared these recommendations for the under-thirty-five set.

Ebisu $$–$$$ *1283 9th Ave. at Irving St., 415-566-1770, ebisusushi.com*
This was totally where I went to for sushi in my twenties. I have since graduated to advanced sushi (I like it sustainable, and no rolls), but it's easy to see how this family-run place (thirty years and counting) will continue to be popular with a younger crowd. The fish is fresh and comes in a variety of approachable presentations, from traditional nigiri to creative rolls to cooked dishes. The Ebisu classics have wacky names, like the dinosaur feet (chopped shrimp and mayo shiso tempura)—not really a dish for a purist, but whatever. There is always a line of people waiting for seats—you'd think they were giving away sushi (they're not). The crowd is a combo of dates at the long sushi bar facing a brigade of friendly sushi chefs, or smaller groups getting red-cheeked on sake at the closely packed tables. The remodeled space has retained its casual feeling but is now quite sleek, with wood walls and modern tables and chairs. It's also quite loud, so don't say I didn't warn you. What did you say?

farmerbrown $$ *25 Mason St. at Market St., 415-409-3276, farmerbrownsf.com*
Located on the corner of crack and wack, this down-home Tenderloin joint is known for attracting an energetic but odd mix of theatergoers, neighborhood partiers, weekend brunch buffet fans, and happy hour hawks. Although the food can sometimes be inconsistent, when it's on, the pulled pork sandwich, shrimp and grits, and the fried chicken (you can specify dark or white meat only) with collards and mac and cheese can really hit the mark. Mmmm, bourbon pecan pie. All the ingredients follow the seasonal/local/organic credo, and many come from African-American farmers. Hott-cool music, funky DIY-rustic interior, and the bar menu includes a refreshing Dark and Stormy (rum and ginger beer), and beers served in Mason jars.

TIP: The bar has special deals, so ask, and the popular weekend all-you-can-eat brunch buffet has live music. There's discounted parking next door (just mention you're a patron).

The Front Porch $$ *65A 29th St. at San Jose Ave., 415-695-7800,*
thefrontporchsf.com

This is a total Outer Mission hipster clubhouse, with a slew of customers sippin' sangria at the bar and chowing down with friends at tables while trying to have conversations over the mariachi bands that pass through. The menu is hearty, with the standout fried chicken served in a popcorn bucket, plus Louisiana shrimp (flown in daily) and grits with a little kick. Friendly servers and a hospitable neighborhood vibe—there's even complimentary cornbread shaped like little ears of corn (awwww, so cute, now is the time when I eat you). I dig the black-and-red checkered floor and eclectic music, and the corner booth tables are pimpin'. Oh yeah, and some of the bench seats have seatbelts—quite handy if your friend is getting out of control.

TIP: Come back for happy hour Mon.–Fri. 5:30 p.m.–7 p.m.

Namu $$ *439 Balboa St. at 6th Ave., 415-386-8332, namusf.com*

I don't think it's possible for me to love this place more. Well, if they were a couple of blocks away from my house, that would be rad. Just the same, Namu is an Inner Richmond gem, a small and chic little spot with scrumptious Japanese-meets-Korean dishes. Plus it has a cool interior (wait until you see the bathroom), and a trio of really nice brothers runs it. And since they're open late Thursday through Saturday, it's a good restaurant industry hangout. Drool-worthy dishes include the spicy pork ribs, *kalbi*-style skirt steak (the marinade is their mom's recipe), the black cod, and the oysters with a spicy *chojang* chili sauce. They also do Korean tacos, KFC (Korean Fried Chicken), and weekend brunch (with a tasty burger). Check their site for happy hour and DJ updates.

nopa

OTHER IDEAS: The Alembic (p. 16), Basil Canteen (1489 Folsom St., 415-552-3963), Beretta (p. 4), Blue Plate (p. 19), Chez Maman (p. 50), Dosa (p. 4), flour + water (p. 61), Heaven's Dog (p. 74), Koo (408 Irving St., 415-731-7077), Laïola (p. 30), Loló (p. 32), Magnolia (p. 30), Mamacita (p. 16), Maverick (3316 17th St., 415-863-3061), Monk's Kettle (p. 23), nopa (p. 17), Ottimista Enoteca-Café (1838 Union St., 415-674-8400), Slow Club (p. 30), Spork (p. 20), The Tipsy Pig (p. 94), Tsunami Sushi (1306 Fulton St., 415-567-7664), Umami (p. 57)

Fun, Cool, and Cheap Eats

Would you rather keep that bill under $50? I hear ya. Here are some spots where you and your under-thirty-five friends can hang out in a fun scene while still keeping things affordable.

Burma Superstar $$ *309 Clement St. at 4th Ave., 415-387-2147, burmasuperstar.com*

Not to fan the flames further on the fame—er, hype—of this place, but it definitely lives up to its name in terms of its citywide popularity. Sure, there are some other excellent Burmese restaurants in town, but none have the same buzz and crowd. When you finally get your table after an hour or so, you'll want to get the catfish chowder, tea leaf or rainbow salad, samusa soup, *poodi* (potato) curry, samosas, and coconut fritters. Oh yeah, and the coconut drink. Great for vegetarians.

TIP: No reservations are accepted, but they will call you when your table is ready, so head down the street to wait at the Bitter End bar (441 Clement St., 415-221-9538). Go early, and avoid the weekend unless you have the patience of a saint. Also open for lunch, with less chaos. Or you can go to its sister restaurant, B Star Bar (p. 19), which has a lot of the same menu items, a back patio, and rarely a wait.

Pizzeria Delfina $$ *3611 18th St. at Guerrero St., 415-437-6800; 2406 California St. at Fillmore St., 415-440-1189, pizzeriadelfina.com*

While the original Mission location draws a hipper crowd, the Pac Heights location is more spacious (and the menu is bigger, too). Either way, the thin-crust pizzas rule, especially the clam pie (although that one is expensive, darn it), the occasional special with eggs in purgatory (it's a spicy tomato sauce), and the panna (with cream). Small plates to share, like the spicy cauliflower and salads, round out the meal. The tripe rocks. Oh yeah, and the California Street location makes their own gelato daily (try it in brioche!). There can be a bit of a wait, but it makes for a good social scene. There are a few really affordable Italian wines by the glass if you're trying to save some dough so you can spend it on your pizza instead.

OTHER IDEAS: B Star Bar (p. 19), Baby Blues BBQ (p. 23), Cha Cha Cha (1801 Haight St., 415-386-5758; 2327 Mission St., 415-648-0504), Charanga (p. 96), Citrus Club (1790 Haight St., 415-387-6366), El Metate (p. 70), Gamine (p. 70), Genki Ramen (p. 119), Hotei (1290 9th Ave., 415-753-6045), Lahore Karahi (p. 41), Lers Ros (p. 75), Limón Rotisserie (p. 49), The Little Chihuahua (p. 63), Little Star Pizza (p. 115), Nopalito (p. 130), Poleng Lounge (p. 72), Regalito Rosticeria (3481 18th St., 415-503-0650), Rotee (400 Haight St., 415-552-8309), San Tung (p. 150), Udupi Palace (1007 Valencia St., 415-970-8000), Weird Fish (p. 111)

So you're not looking for the very latest big thing among the twentysomethings, but you would still like a bit of buzz. And maybe you're not watching your pennies quite so closely. Here are a few slightly spendy urban outposts to check out.

Canteen $$$ *817 Sutter St. at Jones St., 415-928-8870, sfcanteen.com*
Chef-owner Dennis Leary is one of the hardest-working chefs in the biz—he also makes sublime sandwiches all day during the workweek at The Sentinel (p. 141) downtown, his other petite pet project. This former diner is short on seats, so you have to book dinner at one of three brisk seatings (6 p.m., 7:30 p.m., and 9:15 p.m.); Tuesday features an affordable prix-fixe menu with two seatings at 6 p.m. and 8 p.m. Request a booth, unless you want to rubberneck and watch the kitchen show while seated at the grass-green counter (which you kind of do—chef Leary is an intense one to watch). The menu is compact, but chef has major cookin' chops—the New American food is as much a pleasure to look at as it is to eat, making this one of the city's great culinary secrets. The vanilla soufflé has got it going on, and you'll also get all fired up over the complimentary rolls.

TIP: Weekend brunch here rules the school—the pancakes, eggs Benedict, coffee cake, and *chupacabra* (soft scrambled eggs with chorizo or pulled pork and black beans) are all best in class. Do not resist the tractor beam pull of the house-baked brioche (available as a side). Also open for lunch on Fridays, which means you want to cross your fingers for the steak tartare.

Conduit $$–$$$ *280 Valencia St. at 14th St., 415-552-5200, conduitrestaurant.com*
The gleaming copper-conduit interior by Stanley Saitowitz can be a little too contrived for some (one friend called it a "gay prison"), but this modern Mission restaurant is trying to bring some chic and urban style to this, er, kinda shady stretch of Valencia. The contemporary American menu reads a bit minimalist (e.g. "Crab: watermelon, coconut, basil"), so it's kind of a guessing game what a dish actually is (just ask). The refined preparations and seasonal/local ingredients overdeliver for the price, and some of the flavor combos and presentations are quite creative (like the trademark "onion soup" with the gruyère crisp). The large open kitchen commands attention. The kinda kinky coed bathroom is jarring for some (the walls are only somewhat opaque). The bar is a star, and there are plenty of boutiquey wines to try.

TIP: For some reason, parking really sucks in this neighborhood. The pay lot across the street is convenient, and also safer.

OTHER IDEAS: A16 (p. 58), Anchor & Hope (p. 94), Bar Crudo (p. 121), Bar Jules (p. 31), Bar Tartine (p. 33), Bocadillos (p. 102), CAV Wine Bar & Kitchen (p. 14), Chez Papa Resto (4 Mint Plaza, 415-546-4134), COCO500 (p. 90), Contigo (p. 49), Delfina (p. 137), Dosa (Fillmore; p. 4), Farina (p. 127), flour + water (p. 61), Foreign Cinema (p. 32),

Gitane (p. 24), La Mar (p. 134), nopa (p. 17), Orson (p. 15), Range (back room; p. 59),
RN74 (p. 128), Salt House (545 Mission St., 415-543-8900), sebo (p. 53), Serpentine
(p. 59), South (p. 74), SPQR (p. 51), Terzo (p. 5), Town Hall (p. 103), Universal Cafe (p. 26),
Zuni Café (p. 52)

Catch Up with a Good Friend (Less Ruckus)

*Haven't seen your friend in a while? Want to be able to hear each other
without yelling like you're mad at each other? These restaurants have
quiet tables (always ask!), but, unfortunately, quiet often calls for more
moolah, so bring the plastic. For additional ideas, take a look at
"Quiet Dinner with the Grandparents," p. 89 (don't worry, that section
isn't just for AARP magazine subscribers).*

Maki Restaurant $$$ *Kinokuniya Bldg., 1825 Post St. at Webster St., 415-921-5215*

Though it's often criticized for being so expensive, it's a worthwhile spend in my
book. This tiny spot tucked away upstairs in Japantown is ideal for a quiet lunch or
dinner (you can make a reservation), with lovely steamed dishes. I'm a fan of the
chilled *chawan mushi* custard (it can come with chicken or potato) and the salmon and
ikura (salmon roe) *wappa meshi* (rice and seafood or meat that is steamed and comes
in a little box), plus the handmade noodles (sublime udon and soba—especially the
shrimp tempura udon). Grilled hamachi *kama* (collar) and *tonkatsu* (deep-fried pork
cutlet) are also notable; I come here more for the cooked items, not sushi. Everything
tastes quite pristine, and can be a bit subtle—it's not for folks who crave big monster
truck flavor or waves of wasabi. Vegetarian/vegan friendly, too.

TIP: Just call in the late afternoon for your reservation (don't leave a message) and
request a table inside. Otherwise you may end up sitting outside in the mall.

Moss Room $$$ *55 Music Concourse Dr., 415-876-6121, themossroom.com*

Hidden downstairs under the California Academy of Sciences is this latest restaurant
from Loretta Keller (of COCO500; p. 90). You'd never know it's there, and once you're
in it, it's like being in a quiet cave, albeit a well-appointed one (too bad the crowd
isn't always that way—some of the postmuseum folks at lunchtime could use a
little styling). There's a living wall of moss and ferns, a large fish tank, and subdued
lighting, plus some arty design touches (request a booth). The Cal-Med menu is the
picture of seasonality, and super-SLO (seasonal, local, organic). It's not the place to
bring a big eater, since portions are a bit on the "just right" side of things. Interesting
wine choices, with all of them organic, sustainable, or biodynamic (also a bit on the
spendy side), plus some special small-production spirits that go into the cocktails.
Random aside: the restroom has the coolest hand dryer in town.

Sociale

OTHER IDEAS: Absinthe (request a quieter table; p. 7), Ame (p. 88), Ariake Japanese Restaurant (go early; 5041 Geary Blvd., 415-221-6210), Aziza (p. 79), Campton Place Bar and Bistro (p. 11), Chez Spencer (p. 9), Crown & Crumpet (p. 12), Da Flora (p. 25), Dragonfly Restaurant (420 Judah St., 415-661-7755), Eiji (p. 41), Fifth Floor (p. 101), Firefly (p. 9), Hayes Street Grill (p. 62), Incanto (ask to sit by the wine storage; p. 92), Ino (p. 42), Koo (408 Irving St., 415-731-7077), La Ciccia (p. 138), Maykadeh Persian Restaurant (p. 71), Olea (p. 85), Perbacco (p. 102), Piccino (p. 52), Piperade (p. 87), Quince (p. 137), Seasons (757 Market St., 5th Floor, 415-633-3737), sebo (p. 53), Sociale (patio; p. 37), Terzo (p. 5), Zaré at Fly Trap (p. 112), Zuni Café (request a nook; p. 52)

GROUPTHINK

I get a lot of requests for this occasion. It seems most people who want to do big group birthday dinners are in their twenties and thirties, so here's a mini-roundup of restaurants that are ready to handle your party posse in stride (say, eight folks or more). And they're not tooooo expensive, in case you don't want to force your guests to blow a lot of dough. See also "Fun, Cool, and Cheap Eats," p. 66, "Midweek Casual and Cheap Eats: No Counter Needed, p. 63, "Offbeat or Ethnic Group Dinner Locations," p. 75, and "Rehearsal Dinner (Private Rooms/Areas)," p. 83.

Bodega Bistro $–$$ *607 Larkin St. at Eddy St., 415-921-1218, bodegabistrosf.com*
Hit the Tenderloin for this local gem for quality Franco-Vietnamese. It's a bit low-key décor-wise, but the food is what shines (see p. 40 for more details). Really kind people work here, too. There are lots of seating options for group dining.

TIP: You can meet up with your friends for cocktails before or after dinner at Olive (p. 194), just up the street.

El Metate $–$$ *2406 Bryant St. at 22nd St., 415-641-7209*
Sure, it's a taqueria, but it's much more than that, serving some of the tastiest pork chile verde in town, plus commendable carnitas, *chile colorado* (a tasty red chile sauce), and fish tacos—everything tastes really fresh. Here's the best part: you can totally do a cheapity-cheap group dinner in the cheerful back room, and talk to the guys about bringing in your own wine (the staff is super-friendly). It's fiesta time!

TIP: There are a few tables out front, totally *bueno* on a hot day with an agua fresca, and you can walk to Humphry Slocombe (p. 142) for ice cream afterward!

Gamine $$ *2223 Union St. at Fillmore St., 415-771-7771, gaminesf.com*
This Frenchie bistro has one of the best secret tables in the city: in the back is a private booth with room for ten. On the menu: mussels with frites, burgers (beef, salmon, chicken, or veggie), grilled salmon, pork chops . . . you get the drift. Leisurely service means you don't have to eat and run.

Lichee Garden $$ *1416 Powell St. at Broadway, 415-397-2290*

I can't believe the banquet dinner feast I was able to arrange for my friends at this long-respected Cantonese restaurant. I killed my friends with food, and it was only something like $25 a head—and we even got a deal on bringing in our own wine. Imagine a big round table (or two: each table can fit eleven) packed with your friends, and lazy Susans loaded with delicious eats that spin their way around the table (watch your drink!). Just arrange your menu a week ahead of time and you're all set. Some highlights: spicy salted squid, minced squab in lettuce cups, stuffed chicken, the house special pork chop, and the egg foo yung. They have the *nicest* service, and a pleasant room, too, so for a big group, you really can't ask for much more.

TIP: The parking lot around the corner next to the police station on Vallejo Street between Powell and Stockton Streets is oddly reasonably priced.

Maykadeh Persian Restaurant $$–$$$

470 Green St. at Grant Ave.,415-362-8286,
maykadehrestaurant.com
This attractive North Beach restaurant hosts large groups of families and friends all the time. It's been a home away from home for local Persians for more than twenty years, so you know the food is good. Your group will chow down on a tasty array of appetizers, like the garlicky *kashke bademjan* (roasted eggplant

Sociale

with mint) and warm pita, and there are plenty of vegetarian dishes to keep any non-meat eaters content (try the *khoresht fesenjoon* vegetables, almost like a Persian mole of walnuts and pomegranate). The out-of-this-world dish is the *joojeh kebab,* tender and tangy chicken that has been marinated overnight with saffron, onion, and lime, served with long-grain basmati and charred tomatoes. (I am craving it as I write about it.) Plus there's valet parking for only $10 (bonus!), and a full bar.

TIP: Well, a fun fact, anyway: this was the former site of the Old Spaghetti Factory, for you North Beach bohemian history buffs.

Mums $$–$$$$ *1800 Sutter St. at Buchanan St., 415-931-6986, mumssf.com*
Totally fun and total mayhem, just how you like it. All-you-can-eat *shabu-shabu* (p. 72) ($24.95) and optional all-you-can-drink sake and beer ($42.95 for everything). (Note: the all-you-can-drink has a two-hour limit, so take it easy, tiger.) Long waits, noisy as hell, and it gets stuffy with all those bubbling pots of broth, so don't wear a turtleneck or your glasses. There's also a private room available. Make a reservation!

TIP: Eating here gets you one free hour of validated parking at the Japantown garage (but you really shouldn't be driving if you're doing the all-you-can-drink thing).

Shabu-Shabu A Japanese dish that consists of thin slices of raw meat (traditionally tender rib eye) and vegetables that you briefly cook with your chopsticks in a hot broth *(dashi)*. The name is short for "swish-swish," the sound of your chopsticks in the broth. You then dip your cooked meat or vegetables in a variety of sauces that come to the table, served alongside a bowl of steamed rice.

Pauline's Pizza $$–$$$ *260 Valencia St. at 14th St., 415-552-2050,*
paulinespizza.com

When do we outgrow pizza parties? Never. Especially when it's gourmet (the pesto pizza is legendary—and I like their fresh salads, with such good produce). The upstairs room is a perfect party HQ, with all kinds of space (room for up to eighty-five peeps). If your group is eighteen or larger, there's a handy prix-fixe option for $31 per person, with wine and beer (two drinks per person), and service all included. Suhweet! You can also hang out in the wine bar next door.

Poleng Lounge $$ *1751 Fulton St. at Masonic Ave., 415-441-1751,*
polenglounge.com

Three magic words: adobo chicken wings. Your table will attack them like hungry jackals. The savory Filipino-esque fare here is affordable, totally group-ready (they have special party menus), and so delicious (it's street food–inspired). Loungey Indonesian style and a full bar. Check the music lineup, because this place books all kinds of acts in the back room (hey b-boys, hey b-girls)—it's a one-stop-party. (I like dining at the bar here.) Good happy hour deals Tues.–Fri. 4 p.m.–7 p.m.

TIP: Poleng Lounge serves a tasty (and cheap!) take-out lunch Tues.–Fri.

Suppenküche $$–$$$ *525 Laguna St. at Hayes St., 415-252-9289,*
suppenkuche.com

Thank god this perennially busy and energetic German restaurant accepts reservations for groups of six or more (but please note that an 18 percent gratuity will be tacked on your bill). You and your beer-swilling posse will be seated at a large communal table (there are many), and you can start with the charcuterie plate and some potato pancakes, and then move on to heartier fare. You can get bratty with some wurst or Wiener schnitzel, while vegetarians actually have more than one choice. *Jawohl!* Undoubtedly, your group will order *das boot,* a glass boot of beer you can all share (hopefully, no one in your group has something communicable). Hic.

TIP: If you're coming with just one friend, be prepared for a long wait (but the bar is a fun area to hang out). Lunch is only served on Fridays, and the weekend brunch is exactly the kind of restorative fare your boot-drinking self needs.

Tortilla Heights $$ *1750 Divisadero St. at Bush St., 415-346-4531,*
tortillaheights.com

Looking for something to fit your broke-ass postcollege budget? Tortilla Heights is mos def better than Chevy's and has some wicked cheap fiesta menus ($18–$24) that

even include a shot of tequila. *Arriba, abajo* . . . It's not a place where you'll find me
for dinner, but for a big party group of twentysomethings, it makes sense. Be sure to
try the tacos Nick's Way (one crispy, one soft).

OTHER IDEAS: B Star Bar (p. 19), Cha Cha Cha (1801 Haight St., 415-386-5758; 2327
Mission St., 415-648-0504), Charanga (p. 96), E&O Trading Company (314 Sutter St.,
415-693-0303), Eric's Restaurant (1500 Church St., 415-282-0919), farmerbrown (p. 64),
Fattoush Restaurant (1361 Church St., 415-641-0678), The Front Porch (p. 65), Loló
(p. 32), Los Jarritos (p. 145), Mamacita (p. 16), Medjool (2522 Mission St., 415-550-9055),
Nopalito (p. 130), Osha Thai (various locations; p. 120), The Pizza Place on Noriega
(3901 Noriega St., 415-759-5752), Puerto Alegre (546 Valencia St., 415-255-8201), Radio
Africa Kitchen at Coffee Bar (p. 109), Saha (1075 Sutter St., 415-345-9547), Tommy's
Mexican Restaurant (get the back room; p. 60), Velvet Cantina (p. 6), Walzwerk
(family-style menu; 381 S. Van Ness Ave., 415-551-7181)

Twenty- to Fortysomething Group Dinner (Hip/Spendy)

Let's get down to it: you want to go to a hotspot with some slick design, good cocktails or wines by the glass, and some buzz. And you don't really care about blowing some dough, or actually your guests' dough, since they're the ones paying for you tonight.

Aziza $$$ *5800 Geary Blvd. at 22nd Ave., 415-752-2222, aziza-sf.com*
Your group can feast on exquisite Cal-Moroccan fare, made with the freshest seasonal ingredients while seated in a private room that can hold thirty-two. There's also the side room that is good for smaller groups, or, weekdays only, you can buy out the front room (which seats fifty-four). Note that parties of eight or more have to all get the $62-per-person tasting menu; it's a barrage of wonderful food, so come hungry. (Read more about Aziza on p. 79.)

Dosa $$–$$$ *1700 Fillmore St. at Post St., 415-441-3672, dosasf.com*
One of the better prix-fixe menus in town: four courses with a variety of choices off the flavoriffic South Indian menu, which means vegans and meat eaters can coexist in a friendly fashion ($39 per person, plus $20 per person for wine pairings, with
three half glasses preselected for each dish). (Read more about Dosa on p. 4.
The Valencia location also offers a prix-fixe menu, but doesn't serve cocktails.)

Heaven's Dog $$–$$$ *1148 Mission St. at 7th St., 415-863-6008, heavensdog.com*

Totally random location, but dang, the expertly crafted cocktails alone are worth a trek crosstown. This addition to the Charles Phan culinary empire actually offers northern Chinese cuisine, but like the Vietnamese Slanted Door, it's all about using excellent ingredients, many of them organic. There's a semi-private room that can hold up to fourteen guests, and the prix-fixe menu for family-style dining starts at $38. Make sure your menu includes the edamame salad with bean curd, the pork ribs in black bean sauce, ma po tofu, and the spicy chicken. Cool loungey style, late late hours (try 1 a.m. most nights) so you won't be rushed out, and a lively urban scene.

TIP: Heaven's Dog is also perfect for pre- or post-theater if you're seeing something at the Orpheum or Golden Gate Theatre, with good parking deals.

South $$–$$$ *330 Townsend St., No. 101, at 4th St., 415-974-5599, southfwb.com*

The city's sole Aussie restaurant, this SoMa southern hemisphere outpost is tucked away in a commercial building, but is worth the search. It has a cheerful style, plenty of Aussie and Kiwi wines to choose from, and a good communal table for groups to take over. Order up a bushman's plate for the table, the flavorful kingfish sashimi, and of course, some barramundi and New Zealand lamb. The dishes have unique ingredients and flavors, a welcome changeup from the usual California fare. Friendly vibe and a good happy hour. Cute staff that you want to say g'day to.

TIP: If it's a game day, call the restaurant for info on their deal with a nearby parking lot.

Zarzuela $$–$$$ *2000 Hyde St. at Union St., 415-346-0800*

So, it's not exactly new (cough), but this español neighborhood favorite is so worth a mention. It has a warm and rustic atmosphere, with a back room that has space for twenty (the banquette fabric is a little tired, but once you're sitting down, who cares?). The extensive menu of Spanish tapas and larger plates has some definite standouts, like the tender *salpicon de marisco* (seafood salad), the *jamón serrano* with *pan y tomate* (bread with a tomato spread), grilled mushrooms, poached octopus and potatoes, sublime grilled squid (*sí señor!*), and a flavorful white bean stew. Servers are charming—many have been there for a long time. Parking is a *puta, me lo siento . . .*

OTHER IDEAS: 1300 on Fillmore (p. 128), A16 (p. 58), Anchor & Hope (p. 94), Bar Bambino (p. 6), Beretta (p. 4), Betelnut (p. 82), BIX (p. 20), Bossa Nova (139 8th St., 415-558-8004), butterfly (p. 138), Chez Papa Resto (4 Mint Plaza, 415-546-4134), COCO500 (p. 90), Conduit (p. 67), Contigo (p. 49), Farina (p. 127), farmerbrown (p. 64), Florio (p. 57), Foreign Cinema (p. 32), Laïola (p. 30), La Mar (p. 134), Local (p. 29), Nettie's Crab Shack (clambake or crab Sundays; 2032 Union St., 415-409-0300), nopa (p. 17), Orson (p. 15), RN74 (p. 128), Serpentine (p. 59), Slanted Door (p. 98), Terzo (p. 5), Tokyo Go Go (3174 16th St., 415-864-2288), Town Hall (p. 103), Zaré at Fly Trap (p. 112)

Looking for something a little bit funky or different for your group gathering? Maybe you're just down for some delicious ethnic food. It's time to act like Joe Alioto and "order some food for the runway" (that would be the center of the table—famiglia style, baby!). Be sure to look at "Affordable Birthday Group Dinner," p. 70, for additional places.

CHEAP $–$$

Five Happiness $–$$ *4142 Geary Blvd. at 6th Ave., 415-387-1234*

For a shockingly affordable and totally memorable spread, book a banquet dinner at this thirty-five-year-old gem. It's comfortably appointed, with big round tables with lazy Susans, carved wood panels, and Pepto pink tablecloths. Be sure to speak in advance with the very kind manager, Bill Yang, and request a Shangaiese banquet menu. Your group will feast on a parade of dishes, like a cold appetizer plate (a bonanza of flavors, including "drunken" rice wine–marinated chicken and five-spice beef shank); Peking duck; the triple delight of shrimp, the red pork shank, and more.

Depending on the dishes and size of your group, you could get out of here for under $30 per person— unheard of for so many courses of elegant food. Ask about bringing in your own bubbles and wine, too!

Lers Ros $–$$ *730 Larkin St. at Ellis St., 415-931-6917, lersros.com*

It's the Thai restaurant of your dreams, with the most authentic Thai dishes I've ever had in San Francisco. This is a casual spot, so get the gang together and order up while you play name that tune with the cheesy music: think Backstreet Boys and Michael Bolton, eep. The dishes will all come out at once unless you tell them you want things to come out slowly, which you do. Also, be sure to order your food medium spicy if you like a little heat; otherwise, expect it to be seriously spicy twicey. Here's what to get: the Thai herb sausage, pork belly/*pad kra prow moo krob* (say that three times fast) with crispy rind and basil leaves (this dish is a must), the duck/larb

salad, the papaya salad with salty crab (ask for it without sugar, medium spicy—it will be sour and spicy, just like your cranky aunt!), and *yum woon sen* (the glass noodle salad, which can be made vegetarian), plus a side of sticky rice. This place is total flavor country. The prices are unbelievably cheap, and the late hours (open until 12 a.m.) are a bonus. Free delivery until 10 p.m., too; hot damn.

OTHER IDEAS: Brothers Restaurant (4128 Geary Blvd., 415-387-7991), Lichee Garden (p. 71), Lotus Garden (3216 Mission St., 415-282-9088), My Tofu House (4627 Geary Blvd., 415-750-1818), Pagolac (seven-course beef dinner; 655 Larkin St., 415-776-3234), Pot de Pho (p. 152), Sai Jai Thai (p. 117), San Tung (p. 150), Shalimar (532 Jones St., 415-928-0333), Spices II (p. 42), Toyose (p. 151), Yummy Yummy (1015 Irving St., 415-566-4722)

MODERATE $$–$$$

One Market $$$ *1 Market St. at Spear St., 415-777-5577, onemarket.com*
Tucked in the back of the kitchen is a booth you can reserve for the whole night, and it will fit up to seven of your peeps (a minimum of four is required). It's smack dab in the kitchen next to the huge stockpots, and there's even a view of the Ferry Building. The seven-course dinner tasting menu is $85 per person Monday through Thursday, $95 per person Friday and Saturday. You also get a tour of the wine cellar and kitchen, and can help prepare a dish (watch your bangs with the crème brûlée torch)—they will even give you some chef whites to wear. (For more, see p. 99.)

PPQ Dungeness Island $$ *2332 Clement St. at 24th Ave., 415-386-8266, ppqdungeness.com*
Seriously now, where are you going to find dinner for four for less than $125? PPQ Dungeness Island, baby! This Vietnamese place is packed with groups of people, *packed* (you made your reservation, right?) sporting oh-so-practical bibs that charmingly say, "Let's get cracking." Your group will snarf on imperial rolls, chicken salad, roasted crab, garlic noodles, and fried bananas with ice cream. There is nothing quite like a room full of people attacking some crab; it's almost like a variation of the Roman Colosseum. You will end up with crab bits in your hair, and some crab shrapnel will most likely fly into your beer glass, your lap, and your neighbor's lap, so leave the dry-clean-only fashions at home. If you're ordering the set dinner, I think you can substitute the kind of crab you want—just ask nicely. It comes with the roasted crab, but the salty peppercorn version (coated in garlic and a black pepper batter) is the well-known crowd pleaser here, or there's also the spicy crab (coated with jalapeño, basil, garlic, scallions, and black pepper). It's not *great* crab, but put enough garlic on anything and it's certainly enhanced. And, speaking of garlic, no kissing people outside your crab circle for twenty-four hours.

TIP: Parking is the pits, so park your ride in the lot (on Clement Street between 23rd and 24th Avenues) where the first hour is validated, and after that it's something like $3 an hour. So worth it.

Sotto Mare $$–$$$ *552 Green St. at Grant Ave., 415-398-3181, sottomaresf.com*
This joint is totally keeping the old-school North Beach Italian vibe alive, with fresh seafood and more memorabilia than you can shake a fishing pole at. Sound fun? Then you gotta check out the bonus room downstairs. It's begging for a guys' poker night, or a bachelorette get-together for ladies who know how to party and crack crab. (Read more about Sotto Mare on p. 42.)

415-392-1700), Oyaji (p. 18), R & G Lounge (Cantonese; 631 Kearny St., 415-982-7877),
Ryoko's (p. 40), Suppenküche (p. 72), Thanh Long (Vietnamese crab feast; 4101 Judah St.,
415-665-1146), Wooden Charcoal Barbecue House (Korean barbecue; 4611 Geary Blvd.,
415-751-6336)

SPENDY $$$–$$$$

Boulettes Larder $$$$ *Embarcadero Plaza, 1 Ferry Bldg., 415-399-1155,*
bouletteslarder.com
This Ferry Building gourmand outpost for breakfast, lunch, spices, and stocks
transforms into the ultimate private room in the evening. If money is no object,
there's room for up to twenty-four to have a multicourse meal fresh from the farmers'
market cooked just for you—you're literally flanking the European kitchen (and there
to take in all the nice smells). The tables are set with twinkling candles, perfect linens,
and there's a view of the Bay Bridge in the distance. It's all so bougie.

Incanto $$$ *1550 Church St. at Duncan St., 415-641-4500, incanto.biz*
It's no surprise that a restaurant that prides itself on using the whole animal has a
special Whole Beast option for large groups. With a minimum of two weeks' notice,
up to seventeen carnivores can feast on a roasted suckling pig that's carved tableside
(or a lamb or goat, served as a roulade). It all goes down in the Dante Room, a PDR
(private dining room) that's all yours. (There's also the option to order a tasting menu
for the group if the whole beast idea doesn't appeal.)

OTHER IDEAS: Ame (the red table: chef Hiro Sone cooks for you, up to seven people;
p. 88), Jai Yun (p. 126), Kappou Gomi (authentic Japanese; 5524 Geary Blvd., 415-221-
5353), Kyo-ya (*kaiseki*/multicourse dinner/$100 per person; 2 New Montgomery St.,
415-546-5090), Supperclub (dine in bed; 657 Harrison St., 415-348-0900)

Just Drinks and Bites (Private Rooms/Areas)

Don't want to do a seated dinner? Okay, let's mingle and do canapés.
Prices vary. In case you're looking for private rooms in bars, be sure to
peek at "Private Party Rooms" in the cocktail section, p. 195.

CIRCA *2001 Chestnut St. at Fillmore St., 415-351-0175, circasf.com*
This Marina hotspot/cougar den features an upstairs mezzanine with room for
standing receptions up to fifty.

Crimson Lounge *687 McAllister St. at Gough St., 415-673-9353,*
crimsonlounge.com
This bar tucked away beneath Indigo in Hayes Valley, outfitted in racy red (hence
the name), is a total party hideaway. There's room for twenty to seventy-five guests,
and there's a full bar, and approachable (but definitely not groundbreaking) passed
appetizers are available.

The Liberty Café *410 Cortland Ave. at Bennington St., 415-695-8777,*
thelibertycafe.com
A Bernal Heights mainstay. There's a back patio and wine bar rentable for private
events on Tuesday, Wednesday, and Sunday evenings.

Press Club *20 Yerba Buena Lane at Market St., 415-744-5000, pressclubsf.com*
A slick subterranean wine-tasting room underneath the Four Seasons Hotel. Features
a couple of different areas available for private parties (the reserved lounge area is a
great way for sixteen people to be seated and hang out).

Solstice *2801 California St. at Divisadero St., 415-359-1222, solsticelounge.com*
The lounge is rentable for parties of up to forty—all you have to do is spend $300
an hour with your group. The menu includes crab and artichoke dip, carnitas tacos,
sliders, and other kinds of party-ready fare. Not available on Friday or Saturday nights.

It's not a restaurant, but the Hotel Vitale (8 Mission St., 415-278-3700) has a few
terrace suites and studios with "no effen way!" views. They can also help make
arrangements for food and more.

OTHER IDEAS: Andalu (3198 16th St., 415-621-2211), Basil Canteen (1489 Folsom St.,
415-552-3963), Beretta (p. 4), BIN 38 (3232 Scott St., 415-567-3838), Bossa Nova
(139 8th St., 415-558-8004), Bubble Lounge (714 Montgomery St., 415-434-4204),
Cha Cha Cha (2327 Mission St., 415-648-0504), Cigar Bar & Grill (850 Montgomery St.,
415-398-0850), The Cosmopolitan (121 Spear St., 415-543-4001), District
(216 Townsend St., 415-896-2120), Dosa (Fillmore; p. 4), E&O Trading Company
(314 Sutter St., 415-693-0303), La Mar (p. 134), Laszlo (2526 Mission St., 415-401-0810),
Mexico DF (139 Steuart St., 415-808-1048), Nihon Whisky Lounge (private room fits
20–30; 1779 Folsom St., 415-552-4400), Paragon (701 2nd St., 415-537-9020), Pauline's
Pizza (wine bar; p. 72), Pisco (p. 196), Sauce (p. 120), The Spot Lounge (2325 Taraval St.,
415-564-4464), Tres Agaves (130 Townsend St., 415-227-0500), Velvet Cantina (p. 6),
Yoshi's (1330 Fillmore St., 415-655-5600), Zinnia (500 Jackson St., 415-956-7300)

Good thing you like your best friend's boyfriend (just don't like him toooo much, ahem). Looks like the two cutest couples wanna hit the town: here are some nicer places where a party of four will have fun dining together on shareable portions.

Aziza $$$ *5800 Geary Blvd. at 22nd Ave., 415-752-2222, aziza-sf.com*
It's time you knew: this is one of my top three all-time favorite SF restaurants. Chef-owner Mourad Lahlou's modern Cal-Moroccan food is creative and so craveable, made with über-fresh ingredients (he goes to upward of three farmers' markets a week). His food just keeps getting better and better; it kind of blows my mind. Aziza is a perfect location for a variety of occasions (date night, birthday, parents in town, the list goes on), partly because the food is such a pleasure to share (and ooh and ahh over). Start with any of the seasonal vegetables, the goat cheese with tomato jam, and the meatballs, and what's next is up to you, but you absolutely have to try the couscous, the best in town. The rabbit is also exquisite. Desserts are inventive and refreshing—ditto on the savory cocktails, made with ingredients like tarragon, harissa, and black pepper. I prefer the exotic front room (especially the booths). Getting to this part of town is a bit of a haul, but there's valet parking, so here's hoping one of you has wheels.

OTHER IDEAS: 1550 Hyde Café and Wine Bar (1550 Hyde St., 415-775-1550), 54 Mint (p. 61), A16 (p. 58), Anchor & Hope (p. 94), Bar Jules (p. 31), Blue Plate (p. 19), CAV Wine Bar & Kitchen (p. 14), Chapeau! (126 Clement St., 415-750-9787), COCO500 (p. 90), Contigo (p. 49), Delfina (p. 137), Destino (p. 24), Dosa (p. 4), flour + water (p. 61), Frascati (ask for table 22 or 23; 1901 Hyde St., 415-928-1406), Heaven's Dog (p. 74), Laïola (p. 30), La Mar (p. 134), Maykadeh Persian Restaurant (p. 71), nopa (p. 17), Orson (p. 15), Oyaji (p. 18), Poleng Lounge (p. 72), Range (p. 59), Ristorante Ideale (p. 50), RN74 (p. 128), Slanted Door (p. 98), Slow Club (p. 30), South (p. 74), SPQR (p. 51), Terzo (p. 5), Zaré at Fly Trap (p. 112), Zuni Café (p. 52)

Big Birthday Group Dinner (Private Rooms)

Getting a group together to pop open a Nebuchadnezzar of something special? Here are private rooms worthy of your milestone birthday. It's all about having some fun where no one can hear you get toasted, and roasted. By the way, you look great.

Boulevard $$$$ *1 Mission St. at Steuart St., 415-543-6084, boulevardrestaurant.com*

A big birthday calls for a special room, and the wine cellar room at Boulevard is just that, with a churchlike arched ceiling, stone walls, and wine racks surrounding a table that can fit up to twelve. (Private dining rooms really don't get much better.) Nancy Oakes's vision for American cuisine here highlights the finest ingredients available, from red abalone to what's in season at the farmers' market just across The Embarcadero. Inspired flavor combinations, and one of the longest lists of (utterly delicious) starters in the city—you'll want to order one of everything, but your stomach and pocketbook will keep you in check. The wine list means business. Even if you don't score the private room, a meal here is always memorable, and the service is so warm and well-mannered. A total San Francisco favorite year in and year out for a reason.

TIP: This is also a classy place to take someone for a special lunch, a business lunch, and a date at the bar. I love dining at the counter that overlooks the kitchen, either solo or with a hot date.

OTHER IDEAS: Absinthe (40 people; p. 7), Acquerello (14–20 people; p. 89), Aziza (32 people; p. 79), Coi (8 people; p. 135), Fifth Floor (14 people; p. 101), Foreign Cinema (rooms for 10–70 people; p. 32), Gary Danko (7 people; p. 37), Jardinière (rooms for 16 and 50 people; p. 13), Kokkari (rooms for 10 and 30 people; p. 103), La Folie (30 people; p. 38), Masa's (14 people; p. 136), Palio d'Asti (50 people; p. 107), Perbacco (rooms for 18 and 40 people; p. 102), Quince (16 people; p. 137), Spruce (rooms for 14 and 40 people; p. 100), Town Hall (40 people; p. 103), Waterbar (50 people; p. 105)

Spruce

Awwww, little Timmy is turning four. Are you sure he and his friends are ready for a step up from Chuck E. Cheese's? Below are places where it's okay if someone gets cake in their hair. Just be sure to speak with a manager beforehand—consider hosing the party after the lunch rush or earlier than dinner. (These are also kid-friendly places in general.)

Chenery Park $$ *683 Chenery St. at Diamond St., 415-337-8537, chenerypark.com*
It's worth trying to schedule the get-together on a Tuesday night here, because it's Kid's Night. The special kid's club menu includes hot dogs, mac and cheese, Chenery chicken nuggets with French fries, plain pasta with cheese, and root beer floats.

TIP: Since there are a limited number of high chairs and booster seats available, you can call ahead and reserve them.

Giorgio's Pizzeria $–$$ *151 Clement St. at 3rd Ave., 415-668-1266,*
giorgiospizza.com
The owners here are smart: they offer pizza-making parties for kids at only $13 per head (with a minimum of ten tyke pizza makers). The kids get to play with their own dough and add their own toppings, and the finished pizza is served back to them (awwww, look at that, your little Chase is so talented!). But book ahead of time, because there's only one two-hour reservation per day (11 a.m.–1 p.m.).

TIP: When you want to come back again, there's a "Kids Make Their Own Pizza Happy Hour" every Wednesday from 4 p.m. to 6 p.m.

Max's Opera Cafe $$ *601 Van Ness Ave. at Golden Gate Ave., 415-771-7300,*
maxsworld.com
No, I wouldn't normally recommend this place (uh, it's a chain)—and besides, I like my Reuben to come from Morty's (p. 21). But for a kid's birthday party? It's perfect. There is a dedicated kid's menu with items like chicken tenders and three kinds of macaroni, as well as a flowerpot sundae complete with gummy worms. Ew!

OTHER IDEAS: Barney's Gourmet Hamburgers (various locations; barneyshamburgers.com), Bill's Place (p. 144), Boogaloos (do a buyout and host it after they close at 3 p.m.; 3296 22nd St., 415-824-4088), Dino's Pizza (2101 Fillmore St., 415-922-4700), Gaspare's Pizza House & Italian Restaurant (p. 154), Memphis Minnie's (576 Haight St., 415-864-7675), Pizza Inferno (1800 Fillmore St., 415-775-1800), Q (225 Clement St., 415-752-2298), Secret Garden (721 Lincoln Wy., 415-566-8834), South Beach Café (800 Embarcadero St., 415-974-1115), Toy Boat Dessert Café (401 Clement St., 415-751-7505)

Sweet Sixteen Birthday Dinner

*Here are some fun places for the 'rents to take the sixteen-year-old—
who will assuredly have some of his or her friends along—out for a
very special dinner. Just make sure to stop by the BMW dealership
on the way there, right, Daddy?*

Betelnut Pejiu Wu $$$ *2030 Union St. at Buchanan St., 415-929-8855,
betelnutrestaurant.com*
A San Francisco stalwart that continues to appeal to a wide audience. (I'm back in
love with this place after a long hiatus.) The Cow Hollow location draws an energetic
crowd, and the red and rattan interior feels Indo-chic. Alex Ong's Pan-Asian menu
has some classics (like the lettuce cups and the Szechuan green beans), but I'd rather
order tender lamb skewers, *shui jiao* (spicy pork dumplings, and they're not kidding
about the spicy!), the oven-smoked sea bass, and the big wow Hanoi *Cha Ca La Vong*
(fish and noodles). I also love the turmeric goat belly. Be sure to ask about the off-the-
menu beggar's chicken—there are only a few available each night. It's an infinitely
tender chicken that comes baked in lotus leaves and clay—the birthday boy or girl can
work out any "I didn't get the diamond earrings that I wanted" frustration and crack
its clay exterior with a mallet at the table.

TIP: Come for the Tuesday night "Pig Out" menu featuring roasted suckling pig.

Farallon $$$$ *450 Post St. at Powell St., 415-956-6969, farallonrestaurant.com*
There aren't many times in life when you want to lay out this kind of dough (well,
unless you're loaded and you don't care), so let's warm up the credit card. It's a total
seafood fantasyland, from the upscale *20,000 Leagues Under the Sea* décor (think
jellyfish chandeliers) to the stellar raw bar (oysters galore). The "coastal cuisine" here
is fresh, sustainable, and elegant. There's also lamb and beef for the non-seafood
fans. Sure, there are a lot of tourists, but it's a fitting location for a special occasion.

TIP: The winehold is a semiprivate room in case you have a bigger group (up to
twelve). And I'm a fan of the Oyster Bar in the front, a swank spot for a quick date.

OTHER IDEAS: Ana Mandara (891 Beach St., 415-771-6800), BIX (p. 20), Boulevard
(p. 80), Foreign Cinema (p. 32), The Garden Court (Palace Hotel, 2 New Montgomery St.,
415-546-5089), Jardinière (p. 13), Kokkari (p. 103), Le Colonial (p. 84), Slanted Door
(p. 98), Town Hall (p. 103), Waterbar (p. 105), XYZ (181 3rd St., 415-817-7836), Yank Sing
(daytime; p. 97)

So Aunt Enid from Nebraska, your well-heeled cousin from Manhattan, and your vegetarian sister-in-law are all converging for your wedding. Below are a few locations for rehearsal dinners based on a midsized group of diners (say, around twenty). Everyone has their own style, so these suggestions are not one size fits all, but will hopefully fit a few. (See also "Conventioneers/Large Groups: Banquet Dinner," p. 105, and "Popular Private Rooms," p. 106).

I also think a Chinese banquet dinner could be a fantastic option for a large group—it's a very San Francisco thing to do, and it's affordable. And besides, who doesn't love Peking duck? Look into Five Happiness (p. 75), Gold Mountain (644 Broadway, 415-296-7733), Hong Kong Lounge (5322 Geary Blvd. 415-668-8836), Lichee Garden (p. 71), Mayflower Seafood Restaurant (6255 Geary Blvd., 415-387-8338), and R & G Lounge (631 Kearny St., 415-982-7877).

A16 (p. 58) You can get the back atrium room all to yourself (good for groups of 9–20). You decide a set menu, which would smartly include salumi, the famed burrata, pizza, and excellent pastas, like the ricotta gnocchi.

Avedano's *235 Cortland Ave. at Bonview St., 415-285-6328, avedanos.com*
Adjoining Avedano's Holly Park Market (a butcher shop and market) in Bernal Heights is the Udder Room (har, but seriously), a private dining room with space for twenty-five seated, forty standing. Guests can have a family-style or plated meal, and the menu is custom-made using seasonal ingredients. $1,200 minimum. Bonus: no corkage for beer or wine.

Blue Plate (p. 19) This eclectic restaurant in a former house in the Outer Mission is a fun space to throw a funkier party (read: Aunt Enid wouldn't be so comfortable here). There's a spacious back room (seats 16–18) with the ability to buy out the lush garden, which seats twenty (best in the late summer and fall, obviously). Or you can do a complete buyout, which would fit fifty to sixty people.

Foreign Cinema (p. 32) This spacious Cal-Med Mission spot has a lot of space, so it offers a variety of options, including an urban private gallery space, a romantic patio, a mezzanine area, and a full-service bar next door (Laszlo). Chic décor and style, too. Not cheap, so don't get your hopes up.

Isa *3324 Steiner St. at Lombard St., 415-567-9588, isarestaurant.com*
You can take over the romantic heated patio at this contemporary French-fusion restaurant in the Marina—there's room for up to sixty seated. It's a total date place, so it's not short on atmo. Popular dishes include the Maine lobster broth, sweetbreads, potato-wrapped sea bass, pan-roasted chicken, and foie gras.

Le Colonial *20 Cosmo Pl. at Taylor St., 415-931-3600, lecolonialsf.com*
This atmospheric French Colonial–Vietnamese restaurant (it was once a Trader Vic's)
has private terraces, rooms, and a lounge. Your event can be scalable, from passed
apps to a family-style sit-down meal. Popular dishes include the shaking beef, sea
bass, and lamb chop.

luella *1896 Hyde St. at Green St., 415-674-4343, luellasf.com*
The handy back room can hold up to twenty-eight, with a prix-fixe menu of hearty
Cal-American cuisine that will make any Midwestern relatives happy. The quaint
Russian Hill location (complete with cable cars going by and twinkling lights) totally
scores points with out-of-towners.

Palio d'Asti *640 Sacramento St. at Montgomery St., 415-395-9800, paliodasti.com*
Smart Financial District Italian restaurant with pizzas, house-made pastas, and meaty
entrées that will please everyone in the family. The front private dining room has
room for forty, and the one in the back (fits fifty) has an outdoor patio, too.

Perbacco (p. 102) Italian is one of those cuisines that appeals to most, so take
advantage of it and book one of the two private rooms here (eighteen or forty
seated) for a Piemontese feast of house-made salumi, sublime pastas, and more. Chic
Financial District location, and features an excellent wine list.

Town Hall (p. 103) This Southern beauty has a perfect private dining room
upstairs that fits forty seated or eighty for cocktails—and you get your own bar.

SEE "OTHER IDEAS," PAGE 217.

Good for Buyouts

*Sometimes it's worth doing a buyout so you'll have a place all to yourself
(and what happens in the restaurant, stays in the restaurant). Below are
places you can make your own for all kinds of events. If you really, really
love a restaurant, you can always call and see if you can negotiate a
buyout. See also "Rehearsal Dinner (Private Rooms)," p. 83.*

Axis Cafe *1201 8th St. at 16th St., 415-437-2947, axis-cafe.com*
A somewhat unknown café at the base of Potrero Hill, with a spacious industrial
style and an outdoor patio—it's a larger event space with room for up to 175. Bonus
features: easy parking, a kitchen (so you don't have to bring in catering), and an
indoor fireplace.

Bar Jules (p. 31) This Hayes Valley bistro is just the right size (and atmosphere) for private events like a ladies' lunch or baby shower. There's room for thirty-eight seated or sixty-five standing.

Candybar *1335 Fulton St. at Divisadero St., 415-673-7078, candybarsf.com*
This Western Addition "dessert lounge" is a good space for a cocktail party (with sparkling wine–based drinks) and passed apps, with room for seventy. There's a kitchen, rotating art, and an urban and laid-back vibe. Oh yeah, and desserts. Inquire about renting the Kung Fu Tacos truck.

Namu (p. 65) This Inner Richmond restaurant serves its unique hybrid of Japanese-Korean fare in a stylish natural-modern setting. The restaurant can fit up to forty people seated, and sixty standing.

Olea *1494 California St. at Larkin St., 415-202-8521, oleasf.com*
An intimate Californian restaurant at the base of Nob Hill, it has a warm and welcoming vibe—it almost feels like you're in someone's apartment. Room for twenty-seven seated.

Piccino (p. 52) Definitely off the beaten path, and rates high on charm. A buyout can be cheaper on Monday, when the restaurant is closed, and the sweet spot is eighteen guests. You can have your menu customized, ranging from special pizzas to a whole suckling pig, plus custom wine pairings, and some badass coffee to finish (they have a special relationship with Blue Bottle Coffee).

Slow Club (p. 30) This place is no stranger to buyouts, so your event will run smoothly, from the passed apps to when it's time for a sit-down dinner. Full bar, and they can customize the cocktail menu for your soiree. Sundays are the best night to do it because they're closed, so it tends to cost less. Can seat a max of fifty-five, and ninety for heavy apps and drinks.

Terroir (p. 205) This SoMa French wine shop with a cool rustic-industrial look is available for complete buyouts (with room for a standing reception of fifty people). Talk to the owners for recommendations on chefs to cater the party vittles for you. Or inquire about hiring the Spencer on the Go truck, the Chez Spencer (p. 9) taco truck that serves French bistro fare.

OTHER IDEAS: Boulettes Larder (p. 123), butterfly (p. 138), Delfina (p. 137), Ristorante Ideale (p. 50), Sociale (p. 37), Yield Wine Bar (2490 3rd St., 415-401-8984)

Congrats—you got hitched. Here are a few places near City Hall in Hayes Valley where you can pop some bubbly and have a celebratory lunch or dinner with your nearests and dearests. Call as far in advance as possible to book and make arrangements.

If you want to venture farther from the Civic Center area, see "Food that Rates as Good as the View," p. 138, and "Rehearsal Dinner (Private Rooms)," p. 83, for other dinner options.

Absinthe Brasserie & Bar $$$ *398 Hayes St. at Gough St., 415-551-1590, absinthe.com*

Lively brasserie with great group dining options (including private areas), plus cocktails and well-chosen wines to fuel the celebration. Read more on p. 7. (Closed Mondays.)

Citizen Cake $$–$$$ *399 Grove St. at Gough St., 415-861-2228, citizencake.com*

Artsy-industrial interior, a sunny corner location, and fresh California cuisine. Since the restaurant is popular with wedding crowds, the staff will work with you to craft a special menu to help make the event go seamlessly. You know the desserts will be faaaabulous (the owner is Elizabeth Falkner). (Closed Mondays.)

Jardinière $$$$ *300 Grove St. at Franklin St., 415-861-5555, jardiniere.com*

A perfect Cal-French headquarters for celebrations, and it's not just because the ceiling above the bar was designed to look like the bottom of a Champagne glass. A variety of private dining options, or perhaps just bites and cocktails in the downstairs J Lounge. (Lunch is served Fridays only during the holiday season.)

Zuni Café $$$ *1658 Market St. at Franklin St., 415-552-2522, zunicafe.com*

Urbane location, a local fave. Conveniently open continuously from lunch; book later in the afternoon to avoid the lunch rush. Parties of ten or fewer are ideal. Start at the bar for champers and cocktails. (Closed Mondays.)

OTHER IDEAS: Bar Jules (p. 31), Bodega Bistro (inexpensive; p. 40), Hayes Street Grill (p. 62)

ALL IN THE FAMILY

Ahhh, the 'rents are in town. Here's hoping they'll be picking up the check, but, of course, you need options spanning the spendy to the cheap (well, not too cheap—let's say moderate). Here are some parental unit–approved places where you can make reservations in advance, you don't have to yell to be heard, and there's valet parking, or at least parking nearby—we all know how much your father loves circling for parking. (See also "Meet the Parents/Future In-Laws," p. 92.)

CONSERVATIVE 'RENTS

Piperade $$$ *1015 Battery St. at Green St., 415-391-2555, piperade.com*
Chef-owner Gerald Hirigoyen's Basque cooking is authentic, flavorful, and unique. And how charming, chef Hirigoyen is in the restaurant and on the floor greeting guests all the time. His friendly presence only increases the already cozy atmosphere, with rustic beams, tables set with traditional Basque striped runners of red and blue, and wood plank floors. But make no mistake: service is refined, matching the well-appointed tables and crisp linens. The menu has some can't-miss items, including the *calamari a la plancha* (grilled on a hot metal plate), cold foie gras, garlic soup (an effective hangover cure—but really, don't tell mom you're hungover), the namesake piperade, lamb chop, and for dessert, the famed orange blossom beignets, gateau basque, and cornmeal cake (you kind of have to get all three; seriously). There are also different Basque specials served each day. Explore the wine list by Emmanuel Kemiji—and get ready to pronounce some funky Basque names.

TIP: This restaurant is a perfect business lunch location, and there's a great round table for larger groups, plus a communal table. Full bar, too, so it's a good one to hang out at after work. In the evening there is plentiful parking available in the neighborhood, so don't be deterred by the lack of valet service.

OTHER IDEAS: Absinthe (p. 7), Acquerello (p. 89), Big 4 (p. 89), BIX (p. 20), Boulevard (p. 80), EPIC Roasthouse (p. 91), Farallon (p. 82), Fifth Floor (p. 101), Garibaldi's (get the lamb; 347 Presidio Ave., 415-563-8841), Gary Danko (p. 37), Harris' Restaurant (p. 18), House of Prime Rib (p. 158), Jardinière (p. 13), Kokkari (p. 103), Lark Creek Steak (p. 11), LuLu (816 Folsom St., 415-495-5775), Michael Mina (p. 53), North Beach Restaurant (1512 Stockton St., 415-392-1700), One Market (p. 99), Perbacco (p. 102), Quince (p. 137), Rose Pistola (532 Columbus Ave., 415-399-0499), Scala's Bistro (p. 92), Silks (222 Sansome St., 415-986-2020), Sociale (p. 37), Spruce (p. 100), Waterbar (p. 105)

COOL 'RENTS

Are your parents a little quirky, cool, or adventurous? Or maybe they're from Manhattan? Here are restaurants with a little more urban flair and funk (and some are definitely casual, and will therefore take a little less money away from your inheritance).

If your parents are super-cool and just love a total urban vibe with lots of young people around (or mom just recently divorced her third husband and wants to "check out the city" with you), take a look at "Hip but Not a Total Scene (Slighty Spendy)," p. 67, and "Girls' Night Out," p. 4. Or, if they're still paying off your college bills, just go to Ti Couz (3108 16th St., 415-252-7373).

Ame $$$$ *689 Mission St. at 3rd St. (in the St. Regis Hotel), 415-284-4040, amerestaurant.com*
Quite the chic and sleek number, the dining room here may be a bit too minimalist for some, but others will find its Zen–Calvin Klein aesthetic delightfully soothing. Chef-owners Hiro Sone and Lissa Doumani have a refined and seasonal Franco-Japanese style that even integrates Italian influences—but it never feels weirdly fusiony. Dishes on the seafood-centric menu (don't worry, there's meat, too) include a daily crudo; the memorable "Lissa's staff meal" with cuttlefish; *chawan mushi* (custard with sea urchin and more); smoked ocean trout; and the signature sake-marinated cod with shrimp dumplings in shiso broth. The wine list includes some very special sakes, and service is dialed in.

TIP: If you're on a date or dining solo, the sexy petite sushi bar is your spot.

OTHER IDEAS: A16 (p. 58), Aziza (p. 79), Canteen (p. 67), Chapeau! (126 Clement St., 415-750-9787), Chez Spencer (p. 9), COCO500 (p. 90), Coi (p. 135), Conduit (p. 67), Contigo (p. 49), Delfina (p. 137), Dosa (Fillmore; p. 4), Farina (p. 127), flour + water (p. 61), Foreign Cinema (p. 32), La Ciccia (p. 138), La Mar (p. 134), Laïola (p. 30), Le Colonial (p. 84), Moss Room (p. 68), Orson (p. 15), Range (p. 59), RN74 (p. 128), Slanted Door (p. 98), Terzo (p. 5), Town Hall (p. 103), Woodward's Garden (back room; 1700 Mission St., 415-621-7122), Zaré at Fly Trap (p. 112), Zuni Café (p. 52)

The last place you want to bring your grandparents is a super-noisy restaurant. Here are a few ideas for quieter spots where they'll be comfortable. And when making a reservation, always request a quieter table, because grandchildren should be seen and heard.

Acquerello $$$$ *1722 Sacramento St. at Polk St., 415-567-5432, acquerello.com*
This high-end Italian restaurant definitely appeals to the older set, partly because not a lot of twentysomethings can afford it. Chef/co-owner Suzette Gresham-Tognetti and co-owner Giancarlo Paterlini have been delighting diners for twenty years with dishes like the totally wicked, dear-lord-just-hold-me Parmesan *budino* (custard), beef or seafood carpaccio, and decadent pastas like *panzarotti* stuffed with lobster and another with foie gras, truffle, and Marsala (yes, they're rich—I hope grandpa didn't forget his Lipitor). You can order à la carte, or a three-, four-, or five-course dinner, or the chef's tasting menu ($94) with wine pairings (+$68). The cheese cart is no slouch, so try to make that happen. Stellar Italian-focused wine list—destination-worthy in and of itself. The formal European-style service here never goes out of style.

TIP: The gelato drizzled with aged balsamic is spectacular, and the biscotti have their own following as well.

Big 4 Restaurant $$$$ *1075 California St. at Taylor St., 415-771-1140, big4restaurant.com*
I love to park myself at the bar at the Big 4, located in The Huntington Hotel on the top of Nob Hill; there's a hearty bistro menu, with chicken potpie, pot roast, and a lamb burger. While the restaurant is primarily known for its annual Wild Game Dinners (yak or piranha, anyone?), chef Gloria Ciccarone-Nehls (a dead ringer for Liza Minnelli, by the way), who has been the chef here for twenty-five years and counting, offers approachable American fare, like chicken under a brick, filet mignon, and a tasty petrale sole. The New American fare will make grandpa happy, and the portions aren't tiny. The old-fashioned and stately décor (forest green banquettes, lots of dark wood, vintage framed pictures, white tablecloths on tables with a single rose bud and a candle) makes the room appear older than it actually is. The piano playing in the background completes the classy San Francisco vibe (nightly 5 p.m.–10 p.m.).

TIP: Be sure to get a cocktail from Ty at the bar before dinner. And request to be seated in Ron's section for dinner if you're a history buff; he's full of incredible San Francisco historical facts.

OTHER IDEAS: Alioto's (8 Fisherman's Wharf, 415-673-0183), Campton Place Restaurant (340 Stockton St., 415-955-5555), Dining Room at the Ritz-Carlton (p. 38), EPIC Roasthouse (p. 91), Greens (p. 112), Harris' (p. 18), Hayes Street Grill (p. 62), House of Prime Rib (p. 158), Incanto (p. 92), Jardinière (p. 13), Katia's Russian Tea Room (come for lunch; p. 12), La Folie (p. 38), Magic Flute Garden Ristorante (p. 132), Masa's

(p. 136), North Beach Restaurant (1512 Stockton St., 415-392-1700), Piperade (p. 87), Quince (p. 137), The Rotunda (lunch; p. 10), Scoma's (request a quieter table; p. 139), Seasons (757 Market St., 5th Floor, 415-633-3737), Shanghai 1930 (during the week; 133 Steuart St., 415-896-5600), Silks (222 Sansome St., 415-986-2020), Sutro's at the Cliff House (p. 139), Tadich Grill (get a booth; p. 101), Venticello (1257 Taylor St., 415-922-2545), Waterbar (p. 105)

Cool (or Bad or Gay) Aunt or Uncle in Town

Let's hear it for the bad aunt who drives too fast and gives you good advice on how to deal with your mother, or your uncle who gave you your first beer and sold you his El Camino for $400. And then there's always the gay uncle. Here's where to go when your auntie or uncle is in town and they want to take you out somewhere fun.

BAD AUNT

COCO500 $$–$$$ *500 Brannan St. at 4th St., 415-543-2222, coco500.com*
It's no secret your auntie likes her cocktails (we see who you took after), so she should be pleased with the refreshing ones here (the daiquiri is a champ). She'll also like the modern styling and urban vibe—it's chic but comfortable. And since Loretta Keller's SoMa corner restaurant always seems to draw an eclectic crowd spanning all ages, she shouldn't feel too old, or too young if she's a MILF sporting a tramp stamp. The flatbread is recommended, ditto on the fried green beans, and speaking of vegetables, there are a bunch of vegetarian choices—usually some of my favorite dishes—on the seasonal Cali menu. Looks like it's gonna be the chocolate and peanut butter COCOcup for dessert (the fifty-fifty dessert with fruit and buttermilk panna cotta is another star).

OTHER IDEAS: A16 (p. 58), Bar Jules (p. 31), Betelnut (p. 82), Contigo (p. 49), District (wine and bites; 216 Townsend St., 415-896-2120), Dosa (Fillmore; p. 4), Foreign Cinema (p. 32), Gitane (p. 24), Laïola (p. 30), Range (p. 59), RN74 (p. 128), SPQR (p. 51), Spruce (p. 100), Zuni Café (p. 52)

EPIC Roasthouse $$$–$$$$ *369 Embarcadero at Folsom St., 415-369-9955, epicroasthousesf.com* Somehow a Sazerac and a dry-aged steak seem right for dinner with yer uncle, no? Might as well throw in a spectacular view of the Bay Bridge, a pleasure cruise of a wine list, and a variety of options for meaty indulgence, like marrow bones, a porterhouse pork chop, prime rib, and five styles of potatoes (chef Jan Birnbaum means business). There's also plenty of seafood in case Uncle John is coming in from a landlocked state and wants some oysters and crab.

TIP: If you want to meet up for a drink and a bite instead of a full-tilt dinner, the upstairs Quiver Bar has an extensive bar menu, including an array of sliders—like vinegar barbecue pork shoulder—and more of that view. (There's a great deal on a burger, beer, and brownie for $20, plus happy hour Mon.–Fri.)

OTHER IDEAS: A16 (p. 58), The Alembic (p. 16), Anchor & Hope (p. 94), BIX (p. 20), Florio (p. 57), Harris' (p. 18), House of Prime Rib (p. 158), Kokkari (p. 103), Magnolia (p. 30), Ozumo (p. 105), RN74 (p. 128), Salt House (545 Mission St., 415-543-8900), Town Hall (p. 103), Waterbar (p. 105)

GAY UNCLE

Every family has to have at least one gay uncle, and since you live in San Francisco, you'll probably get to see him quite a bit. Here are a few stylish places where you can take your uncle (these spots also tend to draw a good-looking crowd—hey, he knows what he likes).

2223 Restaurant $$$ *2223 Market St. at 15th St., 415-431-0692, 2223restaurant.com* Naturally, your gay Uncle Rick will be thrilled to be in the Castro for dinner, so let's indulge him. "No name" (as many locals call it) is not the trendiest location per se, but it's definitely a neighborhood standby. Start with a cocktail or glass of chard at the fun and social bar, and then you can sit down for some comforting classics on the New American menu, like the crispy calamari salad or the tower (of chicken power): an herb-roasted chicken on a bed of garlic mashed potatoes, blue lake green beans, and onion rings on top. Save room for dessert: the sour cherry bread pudding has been on the menu for years for a reason.

TIP: The $12 Tuesday menu is one of the city's better meal deals (hello Southern fried chicken salad), but it gets packed, FYI. The weekend brunch is as popular as it is tasty.

CASTRO LOCATIONS: Anchor Oyster Bar (p. 48), Chow (215 Church St., 415-552-2469), Destino (p. 24), L'Ardoise (p. 36), Poesia (4072 18th St., 415-252-9325)

OTHER IDEAS: Absinthe (p. 7), Canteen (p. 67), Chez Spencer (p. 9), Citizen Cake (p. 86), Contigo (p. 49), Dosa (Fillmore; p. 4), Farina (p. 127), Fifth Floor (p. 101), Firefly (p. 9), Foreign Cinema (p. 32), Gitane (p. 24), Jardinière (p. 13), Orson (p. 15), Perbacco (p. 102), Quince (p. 137), RN74 (p. 128), Spruce (p. 100), XYZ (181 3rd St., 415-817-7836), Zuni Café (p. 52)

Meet the Parents/Future In-Laws

So, mumsie and daddy are coming to town, and it's time to finally meet them. Here are nice places where you should be all lined up to have a pleasant meal. You just worry about not spilling anything or saying something inappropriate about having hot sex with their son or daughter, mmmkay?

Incanto $$$ *1550 Church St. at Duncan St., 415-641-4500, incanto.biz*
First things first: while chef Chris Cosentino is known for his use of offal and unusual cuts (what I like to call meatses partses), there is plenty on the menu that won't freak out the 'rents, like seasonal salads, risotto, handkerchief pasta with pork ragu, and seafood. But if you're feeling a bit more adventurous, you'll be rewarded for trying dishes like tripe, beef heart, lamb neck, and more. A bottle off the thoughtful wine list will help get everyone relaxed. The room is comfortable and has a rustic sensibility (no tablecloths), and the Noe Valley location means you won't have much "urbanity" to deal with (read: no panhandlers out front). Parking isn't too taxing either.

TIP: Don't get huffy over the additional 5 percent service charge for the kitchen; it's used to offer medical benefits to all employees, and as a boost for nontipped employees.

Scala's Bistro $$$ *432 Powell St. at Sutter St., 415-395-8555, scalasbistro.com*
Perhaps the parents are coming in from the Midwest, or they don't want to leave the vicinity of their Union Square hotel. If so, then this San Francisco standard is your spot. It's not a place I necessarily seek out as a local, but it's definitely well suited for out-of-town guests who will enjoy the Italian brasserie atmosphere (try to get a booth for your group). And since it's in a hotel (the Sir Francis Drake), it has an approachable menu designed for a broad audience. The fritto misto and salads made with seasonal ingredients are a good beginning, and the pastas feature savory combinations, like orecchiette with spicy Calabrian sausage. Mains include steak frites and a hearty

cassoulet. There are occasionally small mistakes, like items being oversalted or overcooked, but the pleasant atmosphere, California-centric wine list, and attentive service help smooth over any bumps.

TIP: A classic dessert here is the Bostini cream pie, a trio of vanilla custard, chiffon cake, and chocolate sauce. They serve a full menu until late (midnight Thurs.–Sat.), which is useful for theatergoers and folks arriving into town late (I recommend the pizzettas and a cocktail).

OTHER IDEAS: Absinthe (p. 7), Acquerello (p. 89), Big 4 (p. 89), BIX (p. 20), Boulevard (p. 80), EPIC Roasthouse (p. 91), Fifth Floor (p. 101), Firefly (p. 9), Garibaldi's (get the lamb; 347 Presidio Ave., 415-563-8841), Gary Danko (p. 37), Harris' (p. 18), Jardinière (p. 13), Kokkari (p. 103), La Ciccia (p. 138), Lark Creek Steak (p. 11), LuLu (816 Folsom St., 415-495-5775), North Beach Restaurant (1512 Stockton St., 415-392-1700), One Market (p. 99), Perbacco (p. 102), Piperade (p. 87), Quince (p. 137), RN74 (p. 128), Rose Pistola (532 Columbus Ave., 415-399-0499), Sociale (p. 37), Spruce (p. 100), Town Hall (p. 103), Venticello (1257 Taylor St., 415-922-2545), Waterbar (p. 105), Zuni Café (p. 52)

Kid-Friendly (Other Kids Will Be Throwing Food)

Here are casual places where you won't get the stink eye when you show up with your little one in tow. Remember that ethnic places are almost always a good bet.

Green Chile Kitchen $ *1801 McAllister St. at Baker St., 415-440-9411, greenchilekitchen.com*
At 5 p.m. this place is toddler HQ. Plenty of booster seats, casual décor, approachable Mexican food (including a kid's burrito or a breakfast taco), and there's enough ruckus generated by other kids so the occasional happy screech by your little Caitlin won't raise any eyebrows.

luella $$ *1896 Hyde St. at Green St., 415-674-4343, luellasf.com*
Schedule dinner on a Sunday evening (when it opens at 5 p.m.), since it's kids' night! The "little luella" menu is geared toward diners under the age of ten and includes chicken potpie, pasta, pizza, mac and cheese, and broccoli and cheese, so they get their vegetables. Plus there are ice cream sundaes for dessert. Adults, meanwhile, can tuck into some brandade, a variety of salads, and substantial entrées like the classic Coca-Cola–braised pork shoulder.

The Tipsy Pig $$–$$$ *2231 Chestnut St. at Avila St., 415-292-2300, thetipsypigsf.com*
Sure, this spacious tavern is a Marina hotspot in the evening, but when it opens up at 5 p.m., you'll see plenty of parents dining with their offspring. There's a child-friendly

menu, plus crayons and a connect-the-dots game are provided. Parents can get their gastropub groove on with the Tipsy burger or a pork chop, and, of course, an adult beverage. Parents and kids alike will love the cheddar and thyme biscuits. There's a back patio in case little Hunter wants to walk around and check things out.

SEE "OTHER IDEAS," PAGE 218.

Cool Parents (and Well-Behaved Kids)

So you still want to eat somewhere decent, or at least a place that isn't a burger joint. Many of the spots below are perfect when they first open for dinner service, and you'll find kid-friendly options on the menu.

When mommy and daddy finally get a night to themselves, check out "Date Two," p. 31, "Date Three," p. 33, and "Romantic Date," p. 36, for a dinner devoid of booster seats.

Anchor & Hope $$$ *83 Minna St. at 2nd St., 415-501-9100, anchorandhopesf.com*
Plenty of parents bring their little ones to this seafood restaurant (the owners have kids, so they're not fazed one bit), and the playful maritime décor will keep your

tykes distracted. Many kids seem to enjoy the fish-and-chips, but the kitchen will happily whip up some grilled cheese sandwiches if that's what's needed. Meanwhile, the adults get to get their seafood on, with oysters on the half shell, angels on horseback (meaty Blue Point oysters wrapped in smoky bacon with arugula and a tangy remoulade, and nope, they don't suck, not one bit), "fries with eyes" (fried smelts), seafood salads, fried Ipswich clams, and one of my favorite dishes in the city: warm sea urchin still in its shell, resting on a base of mashed potatoes, Dungeness crab, tomato, cream, and a verjus beurre blanc—it's so good you want to swear at it. The wine list and beer list are notable, making it a perfect postwork destination (good happy hour).

TIP: Anchor's sister restaurant, Town Hall (p. 103), is happy to do up some chicken strips, and the fried mac and cheese, meatballs, fries, and burger are very "Hey Mikey, he likes it!"

nopa

Foreign Cinema $$–$$$ *2534 Mission St. at 21st St., 415-648-7600,*
foreigncinema.com
Probably one of the best kids' menus in town: three courses for $7–$11, which includes
crudités, pasta, and homemade ice cream; there's also the option for some chicken
(fried or roasted), steak, and red sauce on the pasta. The outdoor patio provides
enough room for little ones to walk around in case they start squirming out of their
chair. Thank heavens, mommy can enjoy a cocktail. (For more on why adults will love
this place, go to p. 32.)

OTHER IDEAS: Absinthe (p. 7), Aperto (1434 18th St., 415-252-1625), Bacco
Ristorante (737 Diamond St., 415-282-4969), Blue Plate (p. 19), The Butler & The Chef
(p. 131), Chez Spencer (there's a sandbox on the patio; p. 9), Chouchou (400 Dewey Blvd.,
415-242-0960), Contigo (p. 49), Delfina (p. 137), Dosa (p. 4), Firefly (p. 9), Florio (p. 57),
The Front Porch (p. 65), Houston's (p. 23), Kokkari (p. 103), Laïola (p. 30), Lark Creek
Steak (p. 11), Luna Park (p. 54), Lupa (4109 24th St., 415-282-5872), Magic Flute
Garden Ristorante (p. 132), Mamacita (p. 16), nopa (p. 17), Nopalito (p. 130), Perry's
(1944 Union St., 415-922-9022; 155 Steuart St., 415-495-6500), Pizzeria Delfina (p. 66),
Rose Pistola (532 Columbus Ave., 415-399-0499), Rose's Café (p. 10), Scoma's (p. 139),
sebo (on Sun. for *izakaya* night; p. 53), Slanted Door (p. 98), Sociale (p. 37), SPQR
(p. 51), Suppenküche (p. 72), Ton Kiang (5821 Geary Blvd., 415-752-4440), Town Hall
(p. 103), Walzwerk (381 S. Van Ness Ave., 415-551-7181), Yank Sing (p. 97)

Dinner with Teenagers

*Is your fifteen-year-old niece visiting? Perhaps your younger cousin and
his best friend are in town for the weekend. Here are some lively places
to take teens that will make you look kind of cool for knowing about
them. (Yup, I'm here to make you look good.) But if your teen is a total
gourmand and watches the Food Network instead of Gossip Girl, take
a peek at "Hip and Moderately Priced," p. 64.*

Dim sum is a blast with teenagers for lunch; Ton Kiang (5821 Geary Blvd., 415-752-4440)
and Yank Sing (p. 97) are dependable places. If you want to do more of an authentic
(and a less spendy) adventure, hit Chinatown's City View Restaurant (662 Commercial
St., 415-398-2838) or Dol Ho (808 Pacific Ave., 415-392-2828), or S&T Hong Kong
Seafood (p. 147) in the Outer Sunset.

Charanga $$ *2351 Mission St. at 20th St., 415-282-1813, charangasf.com*
Hopefully your teenager is more adventurous than picky, because the Pan-Latin fare
here might be a touch "challenging." The menu features dishes like *patatas bravas*
(fried potatoes), *tostones* (green plantains), grilled steak with chimichurri sauce, and

lechon asado (Cuban-style roast pork leg). The atmosphere is artsy, colorful, and lively, with music and a sangria-fueled vibe (you better not be adding to that, ahem). Service can be a little harried, so don't be in a rush if you're eating here. A fun slice of Mission life.

TIP: It gets packed, so make a reservation. And the $15 parking lot next door is really useful instead of circling for 30 minutes.

Khan Toke Thai House $–$$ *5937 Geary Blvd. at 24th Ave., 415-668-6654*

This is one of those places where people keep returning because the atmosphere is so unique, even if the food isn't. (When your teens get older and more discerning, you can take them to Lers Ros [p. 75]). You take your shoes off in the foyer, and then you're led to a sunken table with even deeper sunken seating—your feet go down into a pit under the table, but don't worry, there aren't any snakes. (Request a table in the back for a view of the garden.) Adding to the charm: lots of wood carvings, and the attentive staff is in traditional Thai outfits. Pass on the prix-fixe menu deal and just order à la carte off the extensive menu (you get more food that way).

TIP: Wear nice socks. And when it's time to go to the restroom, you are given sandals (so don't fret about your stockinged feet).

Tony's Pizza Napoletana $$ *1570 Stockton St. at Union St., 415-835-9888, tonyspizzanapoletana.com*

Hey, all teenagers love pizza, so they might as well find out what a damned good pizza tastes like instead of the crap they're going to have delivered to their college dorm room soon. The list of pizza choices is extensive, from the spectacular tomato pie (New Jersey style), to an award-winning pizza margherita and other Italian types, to Sicilian pizzas for two, to a classic pepperoni. Fun old-school look, with wood floors, marble tables, big band and swing music, booths, and a full bar. The location is ideal: a corner right on Washington Square in North Beach, so you can walk around before and after dinner (maybe get a gelato from Naia around the corner at 520 Columbus Ave.). Chef-owner Tony Gemignani might even do some impressive pizza tossing (he's a pizza acrobat—really!).

OTHER IDEAS: Betelnut (p. 82), Blue Plate (p. 19), Cha Cha Cha (1801 Haight St., 415-386-5758; 2327 Mission St., 415-648-0504), Chow (215 Church St., 415-552-2469), Destino (p. 24), Dosa (p. 4), Ebisu (p. 64), Front Porch (p. 65), Le Colonial (p. 84), Limón Rotisserie (p. 49), LuLu (816 Folsom St., 415-495-5775), Luna Park (p. 54), Mamacita (p. 16), nopa (p. 17), Nopalito (p. 130), Park Chow (1240 9th Ave., 415-665-9912), Pizzeria Delfina (p. 66), Rose Pistola (532 Columbus Ave., 415-399-0499), Slanted Door (p. 98), St. Francis Fountain (p. 34), Ti Couz (3108 16th St., 415-252-7373), The Tipsy Pig (p. 94)

I totally remember having lunch in the city with my grandparents—it was a big deal. Here's where to have a lunch date with your (young) grandkids, plus a few casual everyday spots, too. Places with a fish tank are a bonus. For more ideas, see "Kid-Friendly (Other Kids Will Be Throwing Food)," p. 93, and "Cool Parents (and Well-Behaved Kids)," p. 94.

Yank Sing $$–$$$ *One Rincon Center, 101 Spear St. at Howard St., 415-957-9300; 49 Stevenson St. at 2nd St., 415-541-4949, yanksing.com*

Dim sum is perfect for grandkids—whether they are four or fourteen, they are bound to find some dumplings on those carts that they'll enjoy. The excitement of carts wheeling around, the steaming baskets containing the surprise of dumplings, the hustle of the room—heck, even as an adult I get a kick out of it. Just wait until they see the goldfish dumplings, so cute, and the pork *siu mai* or barbecue pork buns are a slam dunk for younger kids. Yank Sing may be one of the spendier dim sum parlors in town, but unless you're an adventurous grandma who likes trucking around Chinatown, this place has everything you need. It's comfortable, efficient, and a family-run business with amazing quality control—they taste all of their dim sum each and every day. They also make excellent *xiao long bao* (Shanghai soup dumplings, which will be a better choice for the adults, since they contain hot soup inside).

TIP: Visit the Rincon Center location. There's validated parking, and while you're waiting for your table, the kids can check out a cool atrium with a waterfall.

OTHER IDEAS: Academy Café (55 Music Concourse Dr., 415-876-6124), Anchor & Hope (p. 94), Aperto (1434 18th St., 415-252-1625), Beach Chalet (1000 Great Hwy., 415-386-8439), Bill's Place (p. 144), Chow (215 Church St., 415-552-2469), Cliff House Bistro (1090 Point Lobos Ave., 415-386-3330), The Garden Court (Palace Hotel, 2 New Montgomery St., 415-546-5089), Great Eastern (dim sum *and* fish tanks; 649 Jackson St., 415-986-2500), Houston's (p. 23), Lovejoy's Tea Room (p. 13), Park Chow (1240 9th Ave., 415-665-9912), R & G Lounge (631 Kearny St., 415-982-7877), Rose Pistola (532 Columbus Ave., 415-399-0499), S&T Hong Kong Seafood (dim sum *and* fish tanks; p. 147), Scala's Bistro (p. 92), Scoma's (p. 139), Taylor's Automatic Refresher (p. 144), Ton Kiang (dim sum all day; 5821 Geary Blvd., 415-752-4440)

Great Eastern

Graduation Dinner

Looks like someone got their diploma. Was it your high school diploma or your Masters? Whatever it is, it's time for the fam to get together for a nice meal and to celebrate the end of your financial bleed of the family coffers. BIX (p. 20) and Boulevard (p. 80) are two of the best places for a graduation meal, but here are a few more special places that are appropriate for the grandparents (but still aren't tooooo formal or quiet).

The Slanted Door $$$ *1 Ferry Building #3, 415-861-8032, slanteddoor.com*
This is one of the most hyped restaurants in the city, which only adds to the feeling of success you'll get when scoring a table. If your group is big enough, there's a private room with space for twenty, which is definitely what you'll want if the grandparents are in tow; otherwise, it will be too loud. There are large round tables that are ideal for groups, and if your group is larger than seven, you'll have to preorder the prix-fixe menu ($38 per person at lunch, $48 per person at dinner). Personally, I prefer The Slanted Door at lunch because of the lovely view of the water (especially from a table on the outside patio), so if you're here for dinner, try to come early to enjoy it. Favorite dishes on the Vietnamese menu include the daikon rice cakes, caramelized catfish claypot, shaking beef, and the cellophane noodles with Dungeness crab. Everything is made with quality and seasonal ingredients—you can really taste it.

TIP: I like swinging by the bar later in the evening for a bite and, of course, one of their stellar cocktails.

OTHER IDEAS: Aziza (p. 79), Big 4 (p. 89), BIX (p. 20), Boulevard (p. 80), EPIC Roasthouse (p. 91), Farallon (p. 82), Foreign Cinema (p. 32), Jardinière (p. 13), Kokkari (p. 103), Le Colonial (p. 84), Perbacco (p. 102), Piperade (p. 87), Quince (p. 137), Spruce (p. 100), Town Hall (p. 103), Waterbar (p. 105), Zuni Café (p. 52)

SUPER-FANCY: Acquerello (p. 89), Dining Room at the Ritz-Carlton (p. 38), Gary Danko (p. 37), La Folie (p. 38), Michael Mina (p. 53)

ALL BUSINESS

Some of San Francisco's finer restaurants are open for lunch on Fridays, so maybe you can schedule your meeting then. You know, it's Friday, so loosen that tie or undo the top button of your blouse and order another martini. Examples: BIX (p. 20) and Jardinière (p. 13). For more, see "Nice Friday Lunch," p. 123. If you want to do a business breakfast, try Café de la Presse (352 Grant Ave., 415-249-0900), Campton Place Restaurant (340 Stockton St., 415-955-5555), Seasons (757 Market St., 5th Floor, 415-633-3737), Silks (222 Sansome St., 415-986-2020), and Vitrine (St. Regis, 125 3rd St., 415-284-4049).

One Market $$$ *1 Market St. at Steuart St., 415-777-5577, onemarket.com*
The big windows looking upon the Ferry Building, the splash of natural light, the proximity to downtown, and the classic yet comfortable style all make for a pleasant business dining atmosphere. Oh yeah, and there's the delicious food by chef Mark Dommen. *Do not* pass up the smoked trout with the rösti and egg—almost like brunch for lunch. All the ingredients are farmers' market fresh (heck, it's just across the street), and there are good choices off the grill, too. Seal the deal on a house classic for dessert: the butterscotch pudding. Service is professional, tables are full of deal-making diners, and there's a full bar in case you feel like something stiffer than wine with lunch. A total after-work scene blows up in the bar.

TIP: See p. 76 for details about the chef's table in the kitchen.

Spruce $$$ *3640 Sacramento St. at Spruce St., 415-931-5100, sprucesf.com*
One of the spiffier restaurants to open in San Francisco of late, this well-appointed number is pure class. Everything is tenderly curated, from the linens to the drool-worthy wine list, and service is on point. The dining room doesn't pack a super-businessy crowd during the day since it's not in the FiDi, but it's still one of the better power lunch locations in the city. Chef Mark Sullivan's menu features ingredients that are as rich as the clientele; some stars include the superlative boudin blanc and one hell of a luxurious burger on the bar menu. Perk up with the house-roasted coffee.

TIP: I think dining at the bar here (or just cocktails) is one of the sexier nighttime spots for a date, oh yesiree.

OTHER IDEAS: Absinthe (p. 7), Ame (p. 88), Boulevard (p. 80), Campton Place Restaurant (340 Stockton St., 415-955-5555), Farallon (p. 82), Kokkari (p. 103), Kyo-ya (2 New Montgomery St., 415-546-5090), Michael Mina (p. 53), Ozumo (p. 105), Palio d'Asti (p. 107), Perbacco (p. 102), Piperade (p. 87), RN74 (p. 128), The Rotunda (p. 10), Scala's Bistro (p. 92), Seasons (757 Market St., 5th Floor, 415-633-3737), Silks (222 Sansome St., 415-986-2020), Vitrine (St. Regis, 125 3rd St., 415-284-4049), Waterbar (p. 105)

Old-School Power Lunch

There are servers, and then there are servers in white jackets who have seen it all, heard it all, and know a thing or two about discretion and making a proper cocktail. Sadly, these places are going the way of bluefin tuna, but here are a few spots keepin' the old-school dream alive.

Le Central $$–$$$ *453 Bush St. at Grant Ave., 415-391-2233, lecentralbistro.com*
Claiming to be San Francisco's first French bistro (since 1974), this restaurant adjacent to the FiDi draws plenty o' power brokers and society shakers (think Wilkes Bashford and his customers), and is basically former mayor Willie Brown's living room. Get ready to swim through a sea of suits. Known for its cassoulet, roast chicken and frites, and Alsatian *choucroute garnie* (a hearty dish of sauerkraut and sausages), it otherwise has a pretty straightforward and limited menu.

TIP: Ask for Herb Caen's table for complete San Francisco nostalgia.

Sam's Grill $$–$$$ *374 Bush St. at Belden Pl., 415-421-0594, belden-place.com/samsgrill*
Service can be brusque, the food can be kind of plain, and the wood chairs can be a little hard on the tuchus, but hey, who said the 1940s were easy? The menu is a definite throwback—one of the few places in town still serving celery Victor (and Hangtown fry, too). It's all about seafood at this FiDi institution, or for those preferring something meaty, get the sweetbreads or veal porterhouse with bacon.

Full of wood "private rooms" with curtains for maximum wheelin' and dealin' secrecy, or having lunch with your secretary. Trust, the career waiters in this joint won't say a peep.

Tadich Grill $$–$$$ 240 California St. at Battery St., 415-391-1849, tadichgrill.com

A true San Francisco original. Heck, it's only San Francisco's oldest restaurant (since 1849), which is why generations of families keep returning here. Seafood is the thing to order, from the pan-fried sand dabs or rex sole to the cioppino (broiled items are good, and the daily specials are the freshest things to get). You can also get closer to having a heart attack with the Hangtown fry. Servers are a bit crusty, like the sourdough. The long bar is the best place to soak it all up, including a few Herb Caen martinis. The private booths are perfect for larger groups (four or more).

TIP: No reservations are taken, so come early, or dine late in the afternoon, since it's open continuously.

OTHER IDEAS: Alfred's Steakhouse (659 Merchant St., 415-781-7058), Maxfield's (The Palace Hotel, 2 New Montgomery St., 415-512-1111), North Beach Restaurant (1512 Stockton St., 415-392-1700), Scoma's (p. 139)

Power Dinner

Is the boss in town from New York? Want to take your high-profile client or shareholders out to dinner? Here are dining destinations that are urbane, classy, delicious, and will make you look good.

Fifth Floor $$$–$$$$ 12 4th St. at Stevenson St., 415-348-1555, fifthfloorrestaurant.com

Damn, this restaurant is chic (*j'adore* the low-slung white chairs, which make it feel a bit like a Parisian atelier). It's good for business (or those who like mixing business with pleasure, ahem). The New American menu features dishes ranging from tea-smoked duck breast to pork belly to New York strip steak, and there's a tasting menu for those who want to up the ante. The wine list is curated with love, care, and knowledge by Master Sommelier Emily Wines, and the service is thoughtful and attentive.

TIP: There's also a comfortable café/lounge that is just right for a quick meeting over a cocktail and a few bites (or a burger).

Perbacco $$$ *230 California St. at Battery St., 415-955-0663, perbaccosf.com*
One of those chameleon FiDi places that works for business, dates, or family dinners.
Rustic Italian décor, no. The interior here is spacious, stylish, and sleek, almost a
Milano-Swedish hybrid (funny, the chef is Swedish—but don't do any Swedish Chef
imitations, okay?). The front bar can pack a crowd after the whistle blows—blame
it on the truffled egg toast and refreshing cocktails. Chef Staffan Terje's menu is
focused on Piemontese cuisine, with house-made salumi and pastas that will blow
your mind, like the signature *agnolotti dal plin,* plump pillows of pasta stuffed with
roasted veal breast and Savoy cabbage (just do it). The menu is surprisingly affordable
considering the quality of the ingredients and portions. Barolo and Barbaresco
abound on the Italian-accented wine list.

TIP: Perbacco is a top choice for a business lunch as well. The two upstairs rooms are
well suited for larger groups (of suits). (Sorry, didn't mean to hit you over the head
with that one.)

OTHER IDEAS: Ame (p. 88), Boulevard (p. 80), Campton Place Restaurant
(340 Stockton St., 415-955-5555), EPIC Roasthouse (p. 91), Farallon (p. 82), Gary Danko
(p. 37), Masa's (p. 136), Michael Mina (p. 53), One Market (p. 99), Piperade (p. 87),
Quince (p. 137), Seasons (757 Market St., 5th Floor, 415-633-3737), Spruce (p. 100),
Waterbar (p. 105)

"Fun Client" Business Dining

*So you still need your meal to be dialed in, but the vibe can be a bit less
formal and more energetic. Basically, this is a client you can drink with and
say the "F" word in front of. (Most of these places are close to Downtown.)*

LUNCH

Bocadillos $–$$$ *710 Montgomery St. at Washington St., 415-982-2622, bocasf.com*
This cozy little Basque spot on the outskirts of North Beach and the Financial District is
full of punchy color. FiDi workers come out in droves for lunch here, which is primarily
about the $9 special: two bocadillos (mini-sandwiches) with stuffings like roast beef,
onion marmalade, and goat cheese; or the Catalan sausage with Manchego and
arugula; or the very popular lamb burger. You can also carb up with a side of *patatas
bravas* (fried potatoes) and romesco sauce. Take your seat at the counter, tall tables,
or communal table. Every neighborhood could use a destination like this for coffee
and egg dishes in the morning, an inexpensive lunch, a chic happy hour, and a primo
date destination for a dinner of tapas (share the "arm of a gypsy," a rolled cake with
hazelnut mousse for dessert).

OTHER IDEAS: Amber India (25 Yerba Buena Lane, 415-777-0500), Anchor & Hope (p. 94), Betelnut (p. 82), butterfly (p. 138), Café Tiramisu (28 Belden Pl., 415-421-7044), COCO500 (p. 90), Dosa (Fillmore; p. 4), Garibaldi's (347 Presidio Ave., 415-563-8841), Hog Island Oyster Co. (p. 151), Houston's (p. 23), Kokkari (p. 103), La Mar (p. 134), Lark Creek Steak (p. 11), LuLu (816 Folsom St., 415-495-5775), RN74 (p. 128), Salt House (545 Mission St., 415-543-8900), Slanted Door (p. 98), Sociale (p. 37), South (p. 74), Town Hall (p. 103), Yank Sing (p. 97), Zuni Café (p. 52)

DINNER

Kokkari Estiatorio $$$ *200 Jackson St. at Front St., 415-981-0983, kokkari.com*
Sadly, San Francisco doesn't have many Greek restaurants, but fortunately the one we do have is major. *Opa!* Chef Erik Cosselmon is a master o' meats, so pray for spring lamb or goat, or go for some pig. Which is better, the smooth *taramosalata* spread, or the house-made pita it comes with? The grilled octopus is one of the best in the city (so tender), and ditto on the lamb chops with damn-near-perfect potatoes. The rustic-elegant space is comfortable and quite huge, including the ever-busy bar, tables near the large fireplace, and a back room with an open kitchen. Big windows overlook the street outside, and the upbeat atmosphere is perfect for out-of-towners.

TIP: Is it just the two of you on date night? Table 2 by the windows is a touch quieter and more secluded, which makes for easier conversation. There's also a great private room downstairs for twelve (but no plate breaking!).

Town Hall $$$ *342 Howard St. at Fremont St., 415-908-3900, townhallsf.com*
A favorite of hearty eaters (and fried chicken lovers) across town, this spot always has a *laissez les bons temps rouler* feel to it, full of a buzzing crowd getting saucy on Sazeracs and margaritas at the long bar. The American menu isn't shy on bold flavors (or fat grams): you might as well start with Faith's Cheese Toast (ham, poached egg, jalapeño cream—uh huh), veal meatballs, and house-smoked ribs . . . and did I mention the fried chicken? (Bwok!) The historic space has a rich Arts and Crafts–meets–East Coast style, with dark-stained wood floors, exposed brick walls, and wood tables. There's also a huge private dining room upstairs.

TIP: Town Hall hosts a popular barbecue lunch during the week on the outdoor patio in the summer; call for details.

OTHER IDEAS: Anchor & Hope (p. 94), Betelnut (p. 82), BIX (p. 20), butterfly (p. 138), COCO500 (p. 90), Dosa (Fillmore; p. 4), Gitane (p. 24), Heaven's Dog (p. 74), Houston's (p. 23), La Mar (p. 134), LuLu (816 Folsom St., 415-495-5775), Ozumo (p. 105), Plouf (40 Belden Pl., 415-986-6491), RN74 (p. 128), Salt House (545 Mission St., 415-543-8900), Scala's Bistro (p. 92), sebo (p. 53), Slanted Door (p. 98), South (p. 74), Zuni Café (p. 52)

"Just the Guys" After-Work/Business Dinner

So you still need to impress, or maybe you're on a nice expense account, but it's not a super-stuffy close-the-deal kind of meal. It's more like a "let's order a few drinks and eat some dude food and talk about the hot new receptionist" kind of meal. (See "Bachelor Party Patrol," p. 17, for additional ideas—no joke.)

5A5 Steak Lounge $$$–$$$$ *244 Jackson St. at Battery St., 415-989-2539, 5a5stk.com*

Now, I wouldn't recommend this place for a Friday or Saturday night (when the vibe is more of a club than a restaurant), and even during the week it veers toward the (truth be told) cheesy. But you get to watch all kinds of entertaining people: hot Russian women with sculpted guys, groups of Asian women out on the town . . . you get the idea. It's actually not a standard San Francisco crowd, which is why it's fun to rubberneck here. You can start with shishito peppers, salads, or a variety of "shooters," but the main event is the A5 Wagyu beef, the highest grade of beef in the world. Yeah, a four-ounce steak will put you back $80, but since it really is one step away from meat custard (it's the richest beef you'll ever taste—you barely need a knife), you won't want much more than that. This beef is so special that when the restaurant buys A5 steak, the distributor provides a certificate of authenticity that includes the cow's nose print and family lineage (too bad they don't do that with spouses). Oh yeah, and they pour Krug by the glass. Have fun burning up the company card.

Wexler's $$–$$$ *568 Sacramento St. at Montgomery St., 415-983-0102, wexlerssf.com*

A newcomer to the Financial District, this American restaurant features Southern flavors and comforting fare with a pedigree, like barbecue Scotch eggs, a smoky chicken liver mousse with green tomato chutney, and short ribs. The small space is a bit modern and spare, with room for groups in the front, and notably good service. Cocktails are also top-drawer.

TIP: You can finish the night in a bourbon haze just a few blocks away at Rickhouse (p. 211). Wexler's is also a popular lunch spot.

OTHER IDEAS: Amber India (25 Yerba Buena Lane, 415-777-0500), Big 4 (p. 89), BIX (p. 20), EPIC Roasthouse (p. 91), Harris' (p. 18), House of Prime Rib (p. 158), Lark Creek Steak (p. 11), Ozumo (p. 105), Perbacco (p. 102), Salt House (545 Mission St., 415-543-8900), Town Hall (p. 103), Tres Agaves (130 Townsend St., 415-227-0500)

CONSERVATIVE

These restaurants don't serve anything too "weird," so your guests won't be wrinkling their noses at the menu.

Waterbar $$$$ *399 The Embarcadero at Folsom St., 415-284-9922, waterbarsf.com*

If your group has the ducats, this is *the* place to host an event. There's a ridiculous multimillion-dollar view of the bay, and there's even a private dining room with its own terrace (as well as an outdoor patio you can take over). The focus here is on, you guessed it, seafood—from briny raw or baked oysters to shellfish platters to delicious fish-and-chips (you've never seen anything like it). For groups, you could do a clambake or a lobster feast. I also enjoy Waterbar for lunch (I brought grandma here and it was a hit); happy hour really is ($1 local oysters every day 11:30 a.m.–6 p.m.); and, if you are in a small group, you can request one of the power booths facing the bay for one of the best views in the city. Sunny days mean the patio gets packed—you can ogle runners on The Embarcadero while you throw back $20 Bloody Marys at brunch (it comes with bacon and prawns in it). Be sure to check out the nineteen-foot aquarium columns inside, which contain two of the ugliest and utterly fascinating Wolf eels (Wolfie and Barbara), that sometimes come out for a spin.

OTHER IDEAS: 1300 on Fillmore (p. 128), Absinthe (p. 7), Americano (8 Mission St., 415-278-3777), Boulevard (p. 80), EPIC Roasthouse (p. 91), Farallon (p. 82), Harris' (p. 18), LuLu (816 Folsom St., 415-495-5775), North Beach Restaurant (1512 Stockton St., 415-392-1700), One Market (p. 99), Palio d'Asti (p. 107), Spruce (p. 100), Town Hall (p. 103)

ADVENTUROUS

Think your group is up for a little something different? Here are restaurants that will show off some different flavors, execution, and styles.

Ozumo $$$–$$$$ *161 Steuart St. at Howard St., 415-882-1333, ozumo.com*

You have that AmEx corporate card ready? Good, because it will get a workout at this spendy modern Japanese restaurant, *hai*. Its location near the Financial District and Downtown means it blows up after work, so expect a little mayhem of suited and stockinged cohorts at the front bar. Retire to the sushi bar, dining room, or the *robata* grill bar for less chaos—they have a variety of options for large groups. Speaking of the robata, the meats and vegetables that come off the grill will make you say *domo arigato* (Mr. Roboto!). Big sushi selection, extensive sake list, Kobe beef . . . hell, there are all kinds of ways to blow some yen. It sports a sleek and modern look, and there's a view of the water that will please any out-of-towners you may have with you.

OTHER IDEAS: Amber India (25 Yerba Buena Lane, 415-777-0500), Ame (p. 88), Ana Mandara (891 Beach St., 415-771-6800), Dosa (Fillmore; p. 4), E&O Trading Company (314 Sutter St., 415-693-0303), Foreign Cinema (p. 32), Incanto (p. 92), La Mar (p. 134), Le Colonial (p. 84), Orson (p. 15), Perbacco (p. 102), Shanghai 1930 (133 Steuart St., 415-896-5600), Slanted Door (p. 98)

LAST-MINUTE BIG GROUP DINNER

Got a big group and need a table fast? Be willing to do something early, like 6 p.m., or later, like 9 p.m. (it can be hard to score prime-time seating at 7 p.m.). It's also easiest to do a prix-fixe menu, or share some mixed apps and limit the main-dish choices to a few items. Be sure to ask about minimum guarantees or deposits, and have that credit card ready to hold the reservation.

Absinthe (p. 7), Amber India (25 Yerba Buena Lane, 415-777-0500), Americano (8 Mission St., 415-278-3777), Big 4 (p. 89), butterfly (p. 138), Chaya (132 The Embarcadero, 415-777-8688), Conduit (p. 67), Dosa (Fillmore; p. 4), E&O Trading Company (314 Sutter St., 415-693-0303), EPIC Roasthouse (p. 91), Franciscan (Pier 43½, Fisherman's Wharf, 415-362-7733), Il Fornaio (1265 Battery St., 415-986-0100), Khan Toke (p. 96), La Mar (p. 134), Lark Creek Steak (p. 11), Le Colonial (p. 84), Luce (888 Howard St., 415-616-6566), luella (p. 84), LuLu (816 Folsom St., 415-495-5775), Maya (303 2nd St., 415-543-2928), Maykadeh Persian Restaurant (p. 71), Mexico DF (139 Steuart St., 415-808-1048), New Delhi (160 Ellis St., 415-397-8470), North Beach Restaurant (1512 Stockton St., 415-392-1700), One Market (p. 99), Orson (p. 15), Palio d'Asti (p. 107), Poleng Lounge (p. 72), Saha (1075 Sutter St., 415-345-9547), Shanghai 1930 (133 Steuart St., 415-896-5600), Silks (222 Sansome St., 415-986-2020), Tres Agaves (130 Townsend St., 415-227-0500), Waterbar (p. 105), Yoshi's (1330 Fillmore St., 415-655-5600), Zaré at Fly Trap (p. 112), Zazil (Westfield Centre, 845 Market St., 4th Floor, 415-495-6379), Zinnia (500 Jackson St., 415-956-7300)

Popular Private Rooms

Here you go: a list of the some of the city's most popular private rooms.

A16 (p. 58), Absinthe (p. 7), Aziza (p. 79), Betelnut (p. 82), Boulevard (p. 80), Coi (p. 135), Dining Room at the Ritz-Carlton (p. 38), E&O Trading Company (314 Sutter St., 415-693-0303), EPIC Roasthouse (p. 91), Farallon (p. 82), Farina (p. 127), Fleur de Lys (777 Sutter St., 415-673-7779), Florio (p. 57), Foreign Cinema (p. 32), Gary Danko (p. 37),

Heaven's Dog (p. 74), Incanto (p. 92), Jardinière (p. 13), Kokkari (p. 103), La Folie (p. 38), Local (p. 29), Masa's (p. 136), Moss Room (p. 68), Nihon Whisky Lounge (loungey setup; 1779 Folsom St., 415-552-4400), Orson (p. 15), Palio d'Asti (p. 107), Perbacco (p. 102), Quince (p. 137), Slanted Door (p. 98), Spruce (p. 100), Terzo (p. 5), Town Hall (p. 103), Waterbar (p. 105), Yoshi's (1330 Fillmore St., 415-655-5600)

Get Happy after Work

The whistle has blown, so it's time to wet your whistle. Let's stop talking deals and enjoy some happy hour deals instead. Here's where you can unwind at the bar, have some bites, and not look like a total geek for being in your Banana Republic clothes and schlepping your computer bag.

Americano $–$$ (during happy hour) *8 Mission St. at The Embarcadero, 415-278-3777, americanorestaurant.com*

It's like this place invented happy hour. The spacious and heated outdoor patio (it's tented during the winter) explodes after work into a sea of blue shirts (you know, the classic blue work shirt). It's not a spot to relax, really—it's more about getting loaded on cocktails and flirting while eating off the affordable *enoteca* menu, with snacky bites, plus panini and flatbread pizzas.

Palio d'Asti $–$$ (during happy hour) *640 Sacramento St. at Montgomery St., 415-395-9800, paliodasti.com*

The only thing better than pizza is free pizza. This is truly one of the city's best happy hour deals: free pizza with two drinks weekdays from 4 p.m. to 7 p.m. Plus $7 house cocktails and $9 seasonal cocktails (well-made ones, too). Grab a friend, and cheers.

OTHER IDEAS: 21st Amendment Brewery (563 2nd St., 415-369-0900), Amber India (cool lounge and deals; 25 Yerba Buena Lane, 415-777-0500), Anchor & Hope (p. 94), Basil Canteen (1489 Folsom St., 415-552-3963), BIX (p. 20), Chaya (132 The Embarcadero, 415-777-8688), Cigar Bar & Grill (850 Montgomery St., 415-398-0850), The Cosmopolitan (121 Spear St., 415-543-4001), District (216 Townsend St., 415-896-2120), Ducca (50 3rd St., 415-977-0271), E&O Trading Company (314 Sutter St., 415-693-0303), Eastside West (3154 Fillmore St., 415-885-4000), EPIC Roasthouse (p. 91), farmerbrown (p. 64), Grand Cafe (501 Geary St., 415-292-0101), Iluna Basque (701 Union St., 415-402-0011), Liverpool Lil's (2942 Lyon St.,

415-921-6664), LuLu (816 Folsom St., 415-495-5775), Maya (303 2nd St., 415-543-2928), Mexico DF (139 Steuart St., 415-808-1048), midi (185 Sutter St., 415-835-6400), Olive (p. 194), One Market (p. 99), Orson (p. 15), Ozumo (p. 105), Pied Piper Bar at Maxfield's (p. 210), Ponzu (401 Taylor St., 415-775-7979), RN74 (p. 128), Roots Restaurant (466 Bush St., 415-659-0349), The Royal Exchange (301 Sacramento St., 415-956-1710), Schroeder's (240 Front St., 415-421-4778), Shanghai 1930 (133 Steuart St., 415-896-5600), Taverna Aventine (582 Washington St., 415-981-1500), Thirsty Bear (661 Howard St., 415-974-0905), Tokyo Go Go (3174 16th St., 415-864-2288), Tsunami Sushi (1306 Fulton St., 415-567-7664; 301 King St., 415-284-0111), Waterbar (p. 105)

Co-Worker Birthday Lunch

So it's time to take Susan in accounting or Dave in the mailroom out to lunch (how old is he, anyway?). Here are a few affordable spots that are good for lunchtime groups.

Henry's Hunan Restaurant $–$$ *Various locations,*
henryshunanrestaurant.com
With five locations around the city, this place is a champ for big group lunches (and has been doing it right since the early 1970s). Some of my favorites on the menu are Diana's meat pie, Marty's special (or the smoked ham dish), the hot and sour beef or chicken, Hunan house bean curd in black bean sauce, string beans with smoked ham, and shredded pork with eggs. You like it hot? You better if you're coming here.

Primo Patio Cafe $–$$ *214 Townsend St. at 3rd St., 415-957-1129,*
primopatiocafe.com
Fun hole-in-the-wall that serves no-frills and affordable Caribbean fare, from jerk chicken to blackened snapper (sandwiches, too). Be sure to get extra "primo sauce" on the side—awesome with fries. Share a pitcher of Buli-Buli, a Cuban house specialty of beer, lime, sugar, and ice (don't knock it until you try it). It's all about the covered patio in the back (simply go down the long walkway) with colorful umbrellas. The patio is a treat on sunny days, and fine on foggy ones, too (just not recommended on cold or wet days. There's also not much of a sign, so look for the address.

OTHER IDEAS: Amber India (buffet lunch; 25 Yerba Buena Lane, 415-777-0500), Bodega Bistro (p. 40), Brickhouse Café and Bar (426 Brannan St., 415-369-0222), Café Bastille (22 Belden Pl., 415-986-5673), Chaat Cafe (320 3rd St., 415-979-9946), Crossroads Café (p. 27), Golden Flower Vietnamese Restaurant (667 Jackson St., 415-433-6469), Lers Ros (p. 75), Manora's Thai Cuisine (p. 8), Mi Lindo Yucatan (401 Valencia St., 415-861-4935), The Plant Café Organic (p. 144), Pot de Pho (p. 152), Slow Club (p. 30), South Park Cafe (p. 155), Taylor's Automatic Refresher (p. 144), Tropisueño (75 Yerba Buena Lane, 415-243-0299)

Need to meet up with someone for coffee and looking for a spot that feels more Fast Company than, say, Playboy, but still has a cool vibe? If you're meeting up after work and have your heart set on a glass of wine instead of coffee, some places below serve vino; otherwise take a look at "Let's Meet Up: Online Dating ;-)," p. 27.

Coffee Bar $ *1890 Bryant St. (located at the corner of Florida St. at Mariposa St.), 415-551-8100, coffeebar-usa.com*
I think it would be a better world if every city had at least five of these concepts. This two-level corner space in the Media Gulch has it all: a slick look with cool art and photographs; good coffee (wait until you try a coffee off the Clover); free Wi-Fi (with outlets everywhere—how civilized); dig-able music; natural light; hot and cold sandwiches, Dynamo donuts, pastries, and 4505 *chicharrones;* communal tables; an outdoor patio; a groovy calendar of events (including the Radio Africa Kitchen dinners every Thurs.–Fri.); a nice selection of beers and wine; and easyish parking. (Speaking of easy, a lot of the people here are rather easy on the eyes. I'm just sayin'.) It can sometimes be Mac laptop central, but it will help make your business meeting look less out of the ordinary. I heart this place.

OTHER IDEAS: Armani Café (1 Grant Ave., 415-677-9010), Blue Bottle Mint Plaza (66 Mint St., 510-653-3394), Café de la Presse (352 Grant Ave., 415-249-0900), Café du Soleil (p. 27), Café Reverie (848 Cole St., 415-242-0200), The Corner (2199 Mission St., 415-875-9258), Crossroads Café (p. 27), Epicenter Cafe (764 Harrison St., 415-543-5436), Four Barrel Coffee (p. 148), The Grove Fillmore (2016 Fillmore St., 415-474-1419), Haus (3086 24th St., 415-374-7353), La Boulange (various locations; baybread.com), Rulli Gran Caffè (2300 Chestnut St., 415-923-6464), Samovar Tea Lounge (p. 8), Stable Café (tapas served Thurs.–Fri. 4 p.m.–9 p.m.; 2128 Folsom St., 415-552-1199), Sugarlump Coffee Lounge (2862 24th St., 415-826-5867)

Piccino

Playing Hooky

Ahhh, someone doesn't feel like being on the clock, eh? Here's what people who don't have nine-to-five jobs get to enjoy during the week. Things like brunch or a late lunch. Or dim sum (see p. 147)! See, this is how the self-employed class lives. (See "'Morning After' Breakfast," p. 34, for more ideas.)

Dottie's True Blue Café $–$$ *522 Jones St. at Geary St., 415-885-2767*

The lines at this homey breakfast place verge on utter insanity. As crazy as the people roaming around outside. And weekends? Fuhgettaboutit. Which is exactly why Dottie's is perfect for a late hooky brunch (it's open until 3 p.m., but closed on Tuesdays, FYI). Here's why people will wait in line for an hour: fluffy omelets, whole wheat–buttermilk or blueberry–cornmeal pancakes, griddled chile cornbread with pepper jelly (you can buy jars to take home), thick French toast, tasty links and sausages, great daily specials, and the list goes on. The line does, too—please note that you'll be standing outside on a sketchy Tenderloin street while waiting for your table, but you'll be fine. You'll just be watching some very kooky characters in life's rich pageant. Cute details inside, too, like vintage salt-and-pepper shakers and a lamp made from an Italian stovetop espresso pot.

Outerlands Café $–$$ *4001 Judah St. at 45th Ave., 415-661-6140, outerlandssf.com*

I like riding my bike out to Ocean Beach through Golden Gate Park just so I can visit this café for lunch once I get out there. It blows me away with its house-made levain bread that is the stuff of dreams—good soups and salads, too. Cool beachy design, with awesome use of driftwood, and pleasant natural light. A true Outer Sunset gem. Come back for dinner (it's a small but delicious menu) and Sunday brunch.

Brenda's French Soul Food

TIP: Head next door for an espresso at Trouble Coffee Company (4033 Judah St., 415-682-4732), equally a quirky visual feast. The "Build Your Own Damn House" combo of cinnamon toast, a whole young coconut, and coffee is a holy trinity of taste—and, yes, totally random.

OTHER IDEAS: Brenda's French Soul Food (p. 34), The Butler & The Chef (p. 131), Cane Rosso (open for lunch at 11 a.m. Mon.–Fri.; 1 Ferry Bldg., 415-391-7599), Chloe's Café (p. 132), The Grove Fillmore (2016 Fillmore St., 415-474-1419), Hog Island Oyster Co. (p. 151), Mama's (1701 Stockton St., 415-362-6421), O'Reilly's (622 Green St., 415-989-6222), Park Chalet (p. 133),

Piccino (p. 52), Pizzetta 211 (p. 49), The Ramp (855 Terry Francois St., 415-621-2378), Rose's Café (p. 10), S&T Hong Kong Seafood (dim sum; p. 147), St. Francis Fountain (p. 34), Swan Oyster Depot (p. 123), Universal Cafe (lunch Wed.–Fri. 11:30 a.m.–2:15 p.m.; p. 26), Zazie (p. 35), Zuni Café (p. 52)

SPECIAL DINERS
(READ: I HAVE NEEDS)

Inexpensive Vegetarian

Below are some inexpensive places that are either strictly vegetarian or are least very vegetarian, since you hippies never seem to have any money anyway (kidding!). And just because a restaurant only serves vegetables doesn't get them listed here: it has to be pretty good. Be sure to check the "Veganomics" section, p. 113, for additional ideas.

Weird Fish $–$$ *2193 Mission St. at 18th St., 415-863-4744, weirdfishsf.com*
Weird name, funky Mission crowd, and a quirky menu to please an army of vegetarians. It may have fish in the title, and plenty of fish dishes, but vegetarians can take their pick from salads, vegan tacos, the "buffalo" seitan or tofu, and even a vegetarian fish-and-chips (made with seitan, tofu, or in a combo with zucchini). And, of course, there are the yo-yos (fried pickles). Plenty of vegetable side dishes as well, and gambling vegetarians can order the "Suspicious Vegetarian Dinner," but fear not, they won't sneak anything meaty in it—it's really just a surprise dish. This joint is small so there's usually a line, but you can wait it out next door in The Corner, the sister café and wine bar. The staff is friendly, just like the vibe. (Vegans are also happy here.)

SEE "OTHER IDEAS," PAGE 218.

Moderately Priced Vegetarian

For such a produce-loving town, it's sad that there are only two strictly vegetarian restaurants that veer toward the spiffier side of things décor-wise. That said, most top restaurants in San Francisco offer vegetarian tasting menus, so you can even go out for a super-posh dinner experience (take a peek at "Meat Eater and Vegetarian Coexistence," below).

Greens $$–$$$ *Building A, Fort Mason, 415-771-6222, greensrestaurant.com*
I'll never forget taking a carrot-eatin' friend to chef Annie Somerville's vegetarian trailblazer, who sighed audibly while looking at the menu, saying, "Wow, I can order everything on the menu." Awwww! (Although fear not: meat eaters will enjoy the preparations as well.) Seasonality is the name of the game here, so if there's any way to time your visit, summer is when the menu is especially magical (grilled peaches, anyone?). You'll find salads (naturally), pastas, pizza, curries, and other vegetable dishes (everything can be made vegan as well). It's not cheap for what you think is going to be hippie grazing, but there are no $48 steaks either. The view of the water is a treat, so it's especially popular at sunset, and for weekend brunch and lunch. The interior is natural/simple-meets-warehouse, with wood tables (no tablecloths), some cool redwood sculptures and tables, and candlelight at night. The carpeted floor helps absorb sound, so it's not too noisy (helps if you're on a date).

TIP: Look at the website closely to find out how to get to the restaurant because it can be a little tricky, but parking is easy. And if you're hosting a meatless wedding party, there's a spacious private room for events.

OTHER IDEAS: Millennium (580 Geary St., 415-345-3900)

Meat Eater and Vegetarian Coexistence

Wouldn't it be swell if meat eaters and vegetarians could dine out together? Well, they can. Below are nicer places that aren't total holes-in-the-wall but are vegetarian-friendly or have special vegetarian menus.

Zaré at Fly Trap $$–$$$ *606 Folsom St. at 2nd St., 415-243-0580, zareflytrap.com*
One of San Francisco's oldest restaurants (since 1906) is now in the hands of Hoss Zaré, an affable chef who is big on personality, hospitality, and flavor. His Mediterranean-Persian menu features savory fare like a lamb shank, braised duck legs with candied citrus, and a smoked pheasant salad, but vegetarians will be thrilled with their own separate menu, with roasted beets, mushroom kebab, and the special vegetarian *kufteh* (meatball) Zaré has created. The look is vibrant (bright persimmon pillars) and

comfortable (no tablecloths), but some historical elements remain, like the pressed tin ceiling and antique prints on the walls. Expect a well-composed wine program and farm-fresh cocktails (see, that's something meaties and vegetarians can share).

TIP: It opens early for dinner (4 p.m.), so it's an ideal postwork and happy hour destination. And your meat-eating friends will dig meatball Mondays, when Zaré cooks up giant meatballs with meaty surprises inside.

OTHER IDEAS: A16 (p. 58), Aziza (p. 79), Betelnut (p. 82), COCO500 (p. 90), Contigo (p. 49), Dining Room at the Ritz-Carlton (call ahead; p. 38), Dosa (p. 4), E&O Trading Company (314 Sutter St., 415-693-0303), Firefly (p. 9), Fleur de Lys (call ahead for the vegetarian menu; 777 Sutter St., 415-673-7779), La Folie ("Menu Jardinière"; p. 38), Luce (vegetable tasting menu on request; 888 Howard St., 415-616-6566), Maki (p. 68), Mamacita (p. 16), Masa's (call ahead for the vegetarian menu; p. 136), Maykadeh Persian Restaurant (p. 71), Michael Mina (vegetarian menu; p. 53), Minako (order handmade udon a day in advance; 2154 Mission St., 415-864-1888), nopa (the vegetable tajine rocks; p. 17), Oyaji (p. 18), Piccino (p. 52), The Plant Café Organic (p. 144), Range (p. 59), Saha (1075 Sutter St., 415-345-9547), Slanted Door (p. 98), Tataki (2815 California St., 415-931-1182), Yank Sing (p. 97)

Piccino

Veganomics

Below are vegan-friendly places, but don't forget that most Thai and Indian places offer a number of good options, too. Be sure to check "Inexpensive Vegetarian," p. 111, for additional ideas. Also see "'Morning-After' Brunch with a Vegan," p. 36.

Cha-Ya Vegetarian Japanese Restaurant $–$$ *762 Valencia St. at 18th St., 415-252-7825*

This offshoot of the original Berkeley location specializes in Japanese *shojin* cuisine (basically, Buddhist monk food), so you know that it's gonna be healthy. Zero animal products. Small space, sparsely decorated, packed full of Mission hipsters and hemos (emo homos) and Technicolor-dressed vegan-kidz. Even the servers are cute with their kerchiefed heads. The menu is huuuuuge, full of anything your heart could desire from a Japanese menu: curry, udon or soba bowls, vegetable sushi, gyoza, tempura, and standouts like the "moon garden" (steamed tofu custard with a slew of vegetables). You'll find some good deals on some dinner "sets," and it's fun food to share with a group. Vegan desserts, too! Just be prepared to wait for a table.

OTHER IDEAS: Borobudur (700 Post St., 415-775-1512), Café Gratitude (2400 Harrison St., 415-824-4652), Dosa (p. 4), Golden Buddha (832 Clement St., 415-668-4888), Golden Era (572 O'Farrell St., 415-673-3136), Helmand Palace (2424 Van Ness Ave., 415-345-0072), Judahlicious (3906 Judah St., 415-665-8423), Karma (200 6th Ave., 415-831-1088), Luna Park (p. 54), Minako (2154 Mission St., 415-864-1888), Pauline's Pizza (call 24 hours in advance for vegan pizza; p. 72), The Plant Café Organic (p. 144), Shangri-La (2026 Irving St., 415-731-2548), Thai House Express (901 Larkin St., 415-441-2248; 599 Castro St., 415-864-5000), Weird Fish (p. 111)

Gluten-Free Eats

It's tough to eat gluten free (I tried it for three weeks, and it was rough).
But with a little communication ahead of time and some server education
(like, no soy sauce!), many places, like the ones listed below, can try to
accommodate your needs.

Thai places can be good gluten-free destinations to consider because of the rice noodles they use.

Zadin $$ *4039 18th St. at Noe St., 415-626-2260, zadinsf.com*
This contemporary Vietnamese restaurant in the Castro with a modern and pleasant interior has been a godsend to gluten-free diners because the waitstaff really understands the needs of those with celiac disease. On the menu: traditional Vietnamese dishes like imperial or fish rolls, shaking beef, plus salt-and-pepper calamari fried in a gluten-free batter, delicious pho, and there's even gluten-free beer! Non-celiacs also dine quite fine.

OTHER IDEAS: Amici's East Coast Pizzeria (a gluten-free pizza; various locations; amicis.com), Betelnut (p. 82), Burma Superstar (p. 66), The Butler & The Chef (p. 131), Café Gratitude (2400 Harrison St., 415-824-4652), Chow (215 Church St., 415-552-2469), COCO500 (p. 90), Dosa (p. 4), Eiji (p. 41), Espetus (p. 17), Fattoush Restaurant (1361 Church St., 415-641-0678), Foreign Cinema (p. 32), Greens (p. 112), Ike's Place (3506 16th St., 415-553-6888), Just for You Cafe (oatmeal pancakes; 732 22nd St., 415-647-3033), Millennium (580 Geary St., 415-345-3900), Park Chow (1240 9th Ave., 415-665-9912), The Plant Café Organic (p. 144), Regalito Rosticeria (3481 18th St., 415-503-0650), Slanted Door (ask to see the ingredient binder; p. 98), Thai House Express (901 Larkin St., 415-441-2248; 599 Castro St., 415-864-5000), Weird Fish (p. 111)

We know them well. (Perhaps you're one of 'em.) Below are ideas on where to find menus that include the comfortable, the safe, and the "normal."

Little Star Pizza $$ *846 Divisadero St. at McAllister St., 415-441-1118; 400 Valencia St. at 15th St., 415-551-7827, littlestarpizza.com*

Pleasing children, stoners, and deep-dish lovers citywide, this pie parlor has a total laid-back atmo, with a choice jukebox and plenty of beers on tap (and good wines, too). I know it's a pizza joint, but the spicy chicken wings here are killer. There are thin-crust pizzas for folks who really don't like to change things up, but the deep-dish pizzas are where it's at; they have a substantial and buttery cornmeal crust that takes a while to bake (about twenty-five minutes). The deep-dish pies are super-hefty, so you're done at the end of slice two (unless you're baked). Picky eaters won't like the Little Star since it has two classic offenders in it (spinach and mushrooms), but I think it's the best pie: it also comes with ricotta, feta, onions, and garlic (I ask them to take it easy on the vampire's enemy). Cheesecake for dessert, hells yeah.

TIP: The Divisadero location is (in)famously cash only.

Street $$ *2141 Polk St. at Vallejo St., 415-775-1055, streetonpolk.com*

A Russian Hill neighborhood standby for homey and straight-ahead New American fare, like calamari, a popular ground sirloin burger and fries, a pork chop (with the bone taken out—rejoice, squeamish ones!), and Sunday night buttermilk fried chicken. It also has a bar scene (it's open until 2 a.m.), but the kitchen closes earlier. The down-home vibe means it's very "come as you are" instead of "dress to impress."

OTHER IDEAS: Baby Blues BBQ (p. 23), Blue Plate (p. 19), Chow (215 Church St., 415-552-2469), Home (2100 Market St., 415-503-0333), Just for You Cafe (dinner Wed.– Fri.; 732 22nd St., 415-647-3033), luella (p. 84), Maverick (3316 17th St., 415-863-3061), nopa (p. 17), Park Chow (1240 9th Ave., 415-665-9912), Pauline's Pizza (p. 72), Q (225 Clement St., 415-752-2298), Tony's Pizza Napoletana (p. 96), Venticello (1257 Taylor St., 415-922-2545)

Whoops, it looks like someone hit it too hard. It happens. Here's where you can let the healing begin. And no, I am not going to subject you to some menudo (the Mexican tripe soup that reputedly cures hangovers); that would be mean. (See also "'Morning After' Breakfast," p. 34.)

El Farolito $ *2950 24th St. at Alabama St., 415-641-0758; also 2779 Mission St. at 24th St., 415-824-7877; 4817 Mission St. at Russia Ave., 415-824-7877, elfarolitoinc.com*
Three words for you, partier: super quesadilla suiza. It's a life raft of carne asada, cheese, avocado, salsa, and sour cream, all sandwiched in a flour tortilla. You can even share one with your "2-for-1 shots!" partner in crime since it's the size of Jalisco. Don't forget your cash money.

Phoenix Bar & Irish Gathering House $–$$ *811 Valencia St. at 19th St., 415-695-1811, phoenixirishbar.com*
Thank god, this place is actually kind of dark, so that vise around your head will feel less piercing. And Irish people understand what that peculiar color of green of your face means. They are happy to help with all kinds of brunchy stuff here, like waffles, pancakes, and corned beef hash, although you might not be up for a full-on Irish breakfast. (Black pudding for you? I think not. Order the half-Irish breakfast instead.) Hey, now, look who's ready for an Irish coffee!

Taqueria Can-cún $ *3211 Mission St. at Valencia St., 415-550-1414; also 2288 Mission St. at 19th St., 415-252-9560; 1003 Market St. at 6th St., 415-864-6773*
One of my favorites for burritos, for sure, but it wasn't until the magic of their nachos saved me one day that I realized how special this taqueria really is. Get ready for a montaña of meat, refried beans, avocado, cheese, sour cream, jalapeños, and their crappy grainy chips that I barely pay attention to anymore. Crack open a cold Pacifico and you should be tight. Just hope the jukebox isn't blaring its usual mariachi medley dialed to 11.

Zeitgeist $ *199 Valencia St. at Duboce Ave., 415-255-7505*
Since you're probably getting up late anyway, you just might make it right on time for lunch. There's a daily barbecue on the patio here that kicks off at 11 a.m. (ish), including a handmade Niman Ranch patty or a garden burger, with some kick-ass potatoes. They serve a decent Bloody Mary, but don't mess with the surly bartenders, or they will cut you. There's plenty of fresh air (it's a beer garden), and once you start drinking again (you're surrounded by pitchers of beer—it's bound to happen), you'll be extra-excited when the Tamale Lady shows up with some hot porky treats for you (get her spicy salsa). Whoa, what time is it? Yup, it's 4:20.

OTHER IDEAS: Art's Cafe (p. 141), Barney's Gourmet Hamburgers (various locations; barneyshamburgers.com), Flipper's (p. 130), Ironwood BBQ (p. 133), Just for You Cafe (732 22nd St., 415-647-3033), Kate's Kitchen (471 Haight St., 415-626-3984), The Little

Chihuahua (p. 63), little skillet (p. 149), Los Jarritos (p. 145), Maverick (3316 17th St., 415-863-3061), Pastores (p. 145), Phat Philly (p. 21), Pork Store Café (16th St. has full liquor and outdoor seating; p. 34), Turtle Tower (pho or chicken soup, and lemon soda; p. 153)

Hungover (Can't Leave Bed)

What the hell were you thinking? Dude, I haven't seen anyone drink like that since I was in Ensenada partying with Chuy back in 1987. Let's get you out of ICU and on the road to recovery.

Mozzarella di Bufala $–$$ *69 West Portal Ave. at Vicente St., 415-661-8900, dibufala.com*

Once you manage to keep some crackers down (if you even have any around the house), it's time to make the move. It's time to call and order a pizza and a Coca-Cola (always works for me). Start with the Coke. Then, a little later, it's time for pizza. Sure, you can do just plain cheese, but once you try a slice of the thin-crust Brazilian pizza, you will become part of my posse o' pizza converts. This pizza has saved my hungover ass so many times I should create a shrine to it made of bottles of Jack. Black olives, linguiça, onion, and hard-boiled egg that is all crumbled up. Get the thin crust (very important)! Don't be afraid, it's amazing, my own personal Lourdes of pizzas. And nab one of their coupons off their website to save some money, honey. Good luck.

Sai Jai Thai $ *771 O'Farrell St. at Hyde St., 415-673-5774*

From this place I only do delivery, which can sometimes take a while, FYI. I actually ate at the restaurant once and it was like a bad Internet date—the real thing was not as cute as I thought it was going to be. It's a good menu of authentic Thai dishes, including the winner of the Mr. FIx-It delivery dish title, the *kor moo yang,* a whomping pile of fatty and grilled pork shoulder with the most awesome (yes, awesome) nutty fried rice and a spicy chili and fish sauce you dunk your pork into. Hold me. My other hangover special is the *kao rad nah gai,* sautéed chicken, mushrooms, and onions in gravy, with Chinese sausage and a fried egg on top. Healed! I also like the beef salad, and the *pad kee mao,* which is totally meow: stir-fried rice noodles with carrot, cabbage, broccoli, basil, and a spicy sauce, with your pick of pork, chicken, or beef.

OTHER IDEAS: La Canasta (burritos delivered, hallelujah; 3006 Buchanan St., 415-474-2627, lacanastasf.com), Genki Ramen (fried chicken and ramen, evenings only; 3944 Geary Blvd., 415-752-2663), Phat Philly (delivery in the Mission area only; 3388 24th St., 415-550-7428), Tai Chi (braised string beans; 415-441-6758), Thai Place II (get the Thai-style barbecue chicken or beef noodle soup; 312 Divisadero St., 415-552-6881), Ton Kiang (dim sum all day; 5821 Geary Blvd., 415-752-4440), Yum Yum Hunan (super-fast, and decent kung pao chicken; 1828 Divisadero St., 415-346-8235), Zante Pizza & Indian (do not fear Indian pizza, it's brilliant; 3489 Mission St., 415-821-3949)

RESTAURANT SPECIAL FEATURES

Late-Night Chow

Yes, it's tragic how few places there are to eat at after 10 p.m. in this town, but here are thirty places where you can get your late-night grub on. Hours are always subject to change, so call first before calling your cab.

A part-time fave is Namu (p. 65) in the Inner Richmond, open until 1 a.m. Thursdays through Saturdays. Korean tacos and fried chicken, yessiree.

15 Romolo $ (p. 209) Hearty bar bites nightly 6 p.m.–1:30 a.m. (bar until 2 a.m.)

The Alembic

The Alembic $$ (p. 16) Dinner nightly 5 p.m.–1 a.m. (bar until 2 a.m.)

Beretta $$ (p. 4) Weekdays 5:30 p.m.–1 a.m., weekends 11 a.m.–1 a.m.

The Brazen Head $$$ (p. 39) Daily 5 p.m.– 1 a.m. (bar until 2 a.m.)

El Farolito $ (p. 116) Daily 10 a.m.–2:45 a.m.

TIP: Line too long? Head across the street to Taqueria San Jose (2830 Mission St., 415-282-0203). And you will pay—the super burritos are weirdly expensive here. Fish tacos and tacos al pastor are good, plus decent carnitas. And great late late hours: open Sun.–Thurs. 8 a.m.–midnight, Fri.–Sat. 8 a.m.–4 a.m.

El Zocalo $ (p. 155) Weekdays 11 a.m.–3 a.m., weekends 9 a.m.–3 a.m.

119

Genki Ramen $ *3944 Geary Blvd. at 4th Ave., 415-752-2663, genkiramen.com*
Sun.–Thurs. 11:30 a.m.–11 p.m.; Fri.–Sat. 11:30 a.m.–1 a.m.
Late-night food at its best: fried dishes (chicken *karaage*—fried chicken nuggets—
croquettes, tempura), plus gyoza, curry, and the namesake ramen. Slow service, FYI, in
case you're hangry (a dangerous combo of hungry and angry). Yay, they deliver.

Globe $$ *290 Pacific Ave. at Battery St., 415-391-4132, globerestaurant.com*
Mon.–Sat. 6 p.m.–1 a.m.; Sun. 6 p.m.–11:30 p.m.
Dark lighting, loud music . . . The food isn't exactly spot on, but you can have yet
another cocktail with your thin-crust pizza.

Grubstake $–$$ *1525 Pine St. at Polk St., 415-673-8268, sfgrubstake.com*
Daily 5 p.m.–4 a.m.
Gotta love the old train-car style. Skip the burgers and go for the simple and belly-
filling Portuguese *caldo verde* (kale, potato, and linguiça soup) or get the Buffalo
chicken wings, which are actually slow roasted instead of fried (be sure to ask for
their homemade hot sauce). But if you really want a burger, go full tilt and order the
Nugget: a bacon cheeseburger with a fried egg on top. Cash only.

Harry's Bar $ *2020 Fillmore St. at California St., 415-921-1000, harrysbarsf.com*
Last call for food is 11:45 p.m. nightly.
Terrifying drunk and horny Pac Heights crowd, but the quality burgers make it worth
navigating the scene. Especially Sundays through Thursdays, when you get a burger
and fries for only $6.95 (10 p.m.–midnight).

Heaven's Dog $$ (p. 74) Mon–Sat. 11 a.m.–1 a.m.; Sun. 4:30 p.m.–9 p.m.

It's Tops Coffee Shop $ *1801 Market St. at Octavia Blvd., 415-431-6395*
Wed.–Sat. 8 p.m.–3 a.m.; Sun. 3 p.m.–11 p.m.; daily 8 a.m.–3 p.m.
Sausage-stuffed waffles and peanut butter and chocolate chip pancakes. 'Nuff said.

Katana-ya $–$$ (p. 151) Weekdays 11:30 a.m.–1:15 a.m.; weekends noon–
1:15 a.m.

Lers Ros $–$$ (p. 75) Daily 11 a.m.–12 a.m. (plus free delivery until 10 p.m.)

Magnolia Gastropub & Brewery $$ (p. 30) Mon.–Thurs. noon–midnight;
Fri. noon–1 a.m.; Sat. 10 a.m.–1 a.m.; Sun. 10 a.m.–midnight

Monk's Kettle $$ (p. 23) Daily noon–1 a.m.

Naan 'N' Curry $ *336 O'Farrell St. at Mason St., 415-346-1443 naancurry.com*
Daily 11 a.m.–4 a.m.
There's much better Indian to be found in SF, but being able to get *tikka masala* and
free chai tea at 3 a.m. is pretty cool.

nopa $$$ (p. 17) Daily 6 p.m.–1 a.m.

Oola $$$ (p. 55) Sun.–Mon. 6 p.m.–midnight; Tues.–Sat. 6 p.m.–1 a.m.

Osha Thai $$ *696 Geary St. at Leavenworth St., 415-673-2368, oshathai.com*
Sun.–Thurs. 11 a.m.–1 a.m.; Fri.–Sat. 11 a.m.–3 a.m.
The original Geary Street location is the only one open this late. Decent and affordable Thai, and quick service once you get your table.

Ozone Thai $–$$ *1160 Polk St. at Post St., 415-440-9663, theozonethai.com*
Weekdays 3 p.m.–1 a.m.; weekends 5 p.m.–1 a.m.
Random location on a second floor above the messy Lower Polk show below. The minced catfish salad rules, as does the Thai salad, but beware, things can be spicy. Bonuses: they deliver until 1 a.m., and there's a coupon online. Oh yeah, and there's late-night karaoke.

Ryoko's Japanese Restaurant and Bar $$ (p. 40)
Daily 6 p.m.–1:30 a.m. (bar closes at 2 a.m.)

Sauce $$ *131 Gough St. at Oak St., 415-252-1369, saucesf.com*
Daily 5 p.m.–midnight (bar closes at 2 a.m.)
Dude, are you high? It'll help you get through the hefty plates of frat-boy comfort food (stick with the apps). Full bar.

Scala's Bistro $$$ (p. 92)
Sun.–Wed. 5:15 p.m.–11 p.m.; Thurs.–Sat. 5:15 p.m.–midnight

Spices! $–$$ (p. 43) Daily 11 a.m.–11 p.m.

Spices II $–$$ (p. 42) Daily noon–11:45 p.m.

Taqueria Can-cún $ (p. 116) Daily 10 a.m.–1:45 a.m.

Teo $ *3741 Geary Blvd. at Arguello Blvd., 415-387-9655*
Weekdays noon–4 a.m.; weekends 5 p.m.–4 a.m.
Total late-night Korean party zone. Fried chicken wings, spicy tofu soup, and more.

Tommy's Joynt $ *1101 Geary Blvd. at Van Ness Ave., 415-775-4216,*
tommysjoynt.com
Daily 11 a.m.–1:45 a.m.
Hofbrau hootenanny. An SF classic. Meat, tons of beers, full bar, self-serve pickles, checkered tablecloths, old-school patrons . . . wrong, but so right. Cash only.

Toyose $$ (p. 151) Daily 6 p.m.–1:20 a.m. (kitchen)

Yuet Lee $ *1300 Stockton St. at Broadway, 415-982-6020*
Mon., Wed., Thurs., Sun. 11 a.m.–midnight; Fri.–Sat. 11 a.m.–3 a.m.
A late-night standard (I call it the green lantern since it's a bright green late-night beacon). Try the salt-and-pepper squid, spareribs, clams in black bean sauce, oyster and pork clay pot, or the *jook* (rice porridges). Cash only.

TIP: If you get to Yuet Lee and forgot that it's closed on Tuesdays, head down the street to Vietnam Restaurant, open daily 9 a.m.–2 a.m., at 620 Broadway at Grant Ave., 415-788-7034.

Monday Dinner/Industry Night

Probably the one night you really don't want to cook is Monday. You just want some food. Good food. And if you work in the industry, doubly so. It also might be the only night you get to dine out with your S.O. (significant other), so some "nicer" places are included as well.

Bar Crudo $$–$$$ *655 Divisadero St. at Grove St., 415-409-0679, barcrudo.com*
Now in its new (and bigger) digs on the Divisadero corridor, this local star is one of the best spots for innovative seafood in the city. Freaking fresh as all get out. Brothers Mike and Tim Selvera have a good eye and artsy aesthetic, from the choice tracks they play on the sound system to the reclaimed fish market style. It all adds up to the energetic crowd they have a knack for attracting. The coveted seats are at the bar—which get you in closer proximity to the choice wines and beers; you're going to have to make some decisions tonight, but at least there aren't any wrong answers. As for the food, the crudos are total flavor journeys—I am such a sucker for the arctic char. Oh, and I love the chowder, the oysters, and the uni and avocado on toast, and the lobster salad, and and and . . . This place rules. Good happy hour, too (Mon.–Fri. 5 p.m.–6:30 p.m.).

TIP: Since they don't serve dessert, head to Candybar (p. 85), just a block away.

OTHER IDEAS: A16 (meatballs!; p. 58), Ame (p. 88), Aziza (p. 79), Beretta (p. 4), The Brazen Head (p. 39), Contigo (p. 49), Delfina (p. 137), Firefly (p. 9), flour + water (p. 61), Gialina (p. 62), Heaven's Dog (p. 74), La Ciccia (p. 138), La Folie (p. 38), Namu (p. 65), nopa (p. 17), Perbacco (p. 102), Piperade (p. 87), Pizzeria Delfina (p. 66), Range (p. 59), RN74 (p. 128), SPQR (p. 51), Spruce (bar; p. 100), Yuet Lee (p. 121), Zaré at Fly Trap (meatball Mondays; p. 112)

Late Lunch during the Week (Open Continuously)

Sometimes you aren't part of the lunch rush. Maybe you're an artiste, so you wake up late and want to eat at three o'clock (bartenders and drunks are like that, too, so watch it). Here are a few places that are open continuously where you can dine later in the day. See "Dim Sum," p. 147, for other great options.

Arlequin Cafe & Food To Go $$ *384 Hayes St. at Gough St., 415-626-1211*
Flanking Absinthe and Arlequin Wine Merchant is this hidden gem for afternoon sandwiches (good Cuban), salads, and coffee (they also serve breakfast items in the morning). As for the hot items, regulars love the lamb burger and the mac and cheese. There are tables and chairs in the front, but you want to be sitting out back in the garden; it's under some trees, so it's not completely sunny, FYI. Oh yeah, there are heaters for when it's chilly, which is often in this foggy town. A commendable selection of beers available by the bottle, free Wi-Fi, and a tasty green iced tea keep locals coming back (especially on the busy weekends). Pricing is a bit of an uptick from most cafes (blame it on the boutiques).

TIP: You can purchase a bottle of wine or champers in the wine shop and bring it over to the café with no corkage.

OTHER IDEAS: Absinthe (day menu; p. 7), Bar Bambino (p. 6), Betelnut (p. 82), Bocadillos (p. 102), Café Bastille (22 Belden Pl., 415-986-5673), Café Claude (p. 31), Café Divine (1600 Stockton St., 415-986-3414), Cane Rosso (1 Ferry Bldg., 415-391-7599), Colibrí Mexican Bistro (438 Geary St., 415-440-2737), Crave (2164 Polk St., 415-440-3663), Heaven's Dog (p. 74), Hog Island Oyster Co. (p. 151), Home (2100 Market St., 415-503-0333), Il Fornaio (1265 Battery St., 415-986-0100), Lark Creek Steak (bar menu; p. 11), Le Central (p. 100), Lemongrass Thai (2348 Polk St., 415-929-1183), Out the Door (various locations; outthedoors.com), Piazza Pellegrini (659 Columbus Ave., 415-397-7355), Piccino (p. 52), Pizzeria Delfina (p. 66), Rose's Café (p. 10), Regalito Rosticeria (3481 18th St., 415-503-0650), The Rotunda (p. 10), Samovar Tea Lounge (p. 8), Sam's Grill (p. 100), Sotto Mare (p. 42), Swan Oyster Depot (p. 123), Tadich Grill (p. 101), Tony's Pizza Napoletana (p. 96), Tres Agaves (130 Townsend St., 415-227-0500), Zazie (p. 35), Zuni Café (p. 52)

Some restaurants are open every day for lunch, while a number of good restaurants open for Friday lunch. Either way, here are a few spots that serve more than just sandwiches for a TGIF lunch.

Boulettes Larder $$ *Embarcadero Plaza, 1 Ferry Bldg., 415-399-1155, bouletteslarder.com*

Actually, it's bougie larder. A local favorite for lunch; it's infinitely better to hit this place during the week than the impossible weekend (although Sundays mean beignets). It's like dining in some Euro-globetrotting friend's kitchen, although you'll be sitting at one of the tables in the adjoining walkway or outside looking out on the water. Everything is prepared with the best ingredients, from roasted chicken to a Middle Eastern salad, but it can border on too artisanal-precious (and pricey) for some. Occasional 'tude as well, so it's not you, it's them. You can also pick up tarts, cookies, rare Japanese ingredients, spices, and stocks to cart home. Ta.

OTHER IDEAS: A16 (p. 58), Absinthe (p. 7), Bar Jules (p. 31), BIX (p. 20), Bocadillos (p. 102), Boulevard (p. 80), Café Claude (p. 31), Café de la Presse (352 Grant Ave., 415-249-0900), Campton Place Bar and Bistro (p. 11), Canteen (p. 67), Citizen Cake (p. 86), COCO500 (p. 90), Farina (p. 127), Fringale (570 4th St., 415-543-0573), Jardinière (p. 13), Kokkari (p. 103), La Mar (p. 134), Luce (888 Howard St., 415-616-6566), LuLu (816 Folsom St., 415-495-5775), Magnolia (p. 30), Mission Beach Café (p. 125), One Market (p. 99), Perbacco (p. 102), Piccino (p. 52), The Rotunda (p. 10), Slanted Door (p. 98), Slow Club (p. 30), Sociale (p. 37), Spruce (p. 100), Suppenküche (p. 72), Tadich Grill (p. 101), Town Hall (p. 103), Universal Cafe (p. 26), Waterbar (p. 105), Yank Sing (p. 97), Zuni Café (p. 52)

Late Saturday Lunch

Sometimes it's hard to get your act together on a Saturday. Maybe you missed the brunch window, but you still want to grab a bite to eat. Here's where you can find a "nicer" meal besides a burrito at a taqueria.

Swan Oyster Depot $$ *1517 Polk St. at California St., 415-673-1101*

Actually, late in the day is a brilliant time to go because of the perpetual nutty lines here—just come to dine after the lunch rush (the last seating is at 5:20 p.m.). The marble counter has only eighteen stools, each one of them precious because you get a ringside seat view of the Sancimino family show (their chatter is as fresh as their fish). Swan has a special place in my heart, offering seafood classics like oysters on the half shell (perfect with a draught Anchor Steam beer), chowdah (a thinner style), house-smoked trout, crab Louie, a combo seafood salad, and the Swan special: shrimp cocktail and a Bud. The nicest damn people work here. Since 1912, much respect.

TIP: Cash only (like the day it opened). Closed Sundays. If you are up for an early lunch and can handle oysters and beer before 11 a.m., come early to beat the crowds (doors open at 8 a.m.).

OTHER IDEAS: Absinthe (day menu; p. 7), Beretta (p. 4), Betelnut (p. 82), butterfly (p. 138), Café Bastille (22 Belden Pl., 415-986-5673), Café Claude (p. 31), Hog Island Oyster Co. (p. 151), Home (2100 Market St., 415-503-0333), Lark Creek Steak (bar menu; p. 11), Le Central (p. 100), Piccino (p. 52), Pizzeria Delfina (p. 66), Rose's Café (p. 10), The Rotunda Restaurant (p. 10), Samovar Tea Lounge (p. 8), Tadich Grill (p. 101), Ton Kiang (dim sum all day; 5821 Geary Blvd., 415-752-4440), Troya (349 Clement St., 415-379-6000), Yank Sing (p. 97), Zazie (p. 35), Zuni Café (p. 52)

Sunday Brunch without Lines (Reservations Accepted)

I don't know about you, but my days of waiting in line for an hour for a table for brunch—clutching my double latte and trying to ignore my headache and grumbling stomach—are kind of over. Here are places where you can reserve a table in advance and waltz on in—especially handy when you have grandma in tow.

Chouquet's $$ *2500 Washington St. at Fillmore St., 415-359-0075, chouquets.com* A sunny corner location plus outdoor seating make this Fillmore Street spot a neighborhood standard. During the week, it's quite the Pac Heights ladies-who-lunch scene, but brunch packs more of a diverse crowd. Quiches and egg dishes galore, plus a decadent croque madame (on Acme bread) fall more on the breakfasty side of things, while the salads include a tasty one of smoked trout, fingerling potatoes, and mâche. There's also a burger (made with good beef) or a club sandwich to consider. Friendly servers with French accents, a bright orange color scheme, and well-made desserts to share.

OTHER IDEAS: 1300 on Fillmore (p. 128), 2223 Restaurant (p. 91), Absinthe (p. 7), Americano (8 Mission St., 415-278-3777), Bar Tartine (p. 33), butterfly (p. 138), Café de la Presse (352 Grant Ave., 415-249-0900), Chouchou (400 Dewey Blvd., 415-242-0960), CIRCA (p. 77), Citizen Cake (p. 86), Dosa (p. 4), EPIC Roasthouse (p. 91), Farina (p. 127), Foreign Cinema (p. 32), Fresca (3945 24th St., 415-695-0549), The Garden Court (Palace Hotel, 2 New Montgomery St., 415-546-5089), Garibaldi's (347 Presidio Ave.,

415-563-8841), Grand Cafe (501 Geary St., 415-292-0101), Greens (p. 112), Home (2100 Market St., 415-503-0333), LuLu (816 Folsom St., 415-495-5775), Magic Flute Garden Ristorante (p. 132), Maverick (3316 17th St., 415-863-3061), Namu (p. 65), Pork Store Café (16th St. location only; you all have to arrive at once; p. 34), Seasons (757 Market St., 5th Floor, 415-633-3737), Serpentine (p. 59), Spork (p. 20), The Tipsy Pig (p. 94), Waterbar (p. 105), XYZ (181 3rd St., 415-817-7836), Zuni Café (p. 52)

Just Dessert

Not looking for a full meal, eh, sugar whore? Craving a little something sweet? (Did you just smoke a bowl? You did, didn't you?) Here are a few dessert places where you can get a sugar high going, too.

Mission Beach Café $ *198 Guerrero St. at 14th St., 415-861-0198, missionbeachcafesf.com*

There are too many scrumptious things at this corner cafe to get you into deep trouble, from the city's best *cannelés* (a very complicated-to-make little Frenchie cake) to my favorite: the banana (and butterscotch) cream pie. Plus there's a wicked lemon velvet cream pie and seasonal fruit pies. Aw hell, my skinny jean dreams just bit the dust (again). You're going to find all kinds of things here to rot your teeth (sorry to do that to you). Has a chic designy interior, with the coffee to match (Blue Bottle, of course).

TIP: It's also known for its potpies (another perfect crusty item), delicious for a cozy midweek dinner, and brunch really packs them in.

Mission Pie $ *2901 Mission St. at 25th St., 415-282-1500, missionpie.com*

Pie. *Pie!* An undeniable pleasure, and, sadly, the options where you can get a good slice these days are few and far between. Enter Mission Pie. Whether you want fruit pie, savory pie, tarts, or even vegan pie, you've found your pie place. Summertime fruit has found one of its better showcases here. It has a rustic and homey interior made from reclaimed materials, and not only does the produce come from nearby farms, but there is also a strong community-minded approach to everything they do here. It's pie you can feel really, really good about eating. Well, kind of.

OTHER IDEAS: Arlequin (p. 122), Beard Papa's Cream Puffs (various locations; beardpapasf.com), Boulettes Larder (p. 123), Candybar (p. 85), Citizen Cake (p. 86), Crown & Crumpet (p. 12), Destination Baking Company (598 Chenery St., 415-469-0730), Kara's Cupcakes (various locations, karascupcakes.com), La Boulange (various locations; baybread.com), Lotta's Bakery (1720 Polk St., 415-359-9039), Miette (various locations; miettecakes.com), Pacific Puffs (2201 Union St., 415-440-7833), Patisserie Delanghe (1890 Fillmore St., 415-923-0711), Patisserie Philippe (655 Townsend St., 415-558-8016), Range (sit at the bar; p. 59), Roland's Bakery (plus excellent bagels; 422 Haight St.,

415-896-4925), Rulli Gran Caffè (2300 Chestnut St., 415-923-6464), Schubert's Bakery (best Swedish princess cake; 521 Clement St., 415-752-1580), Stella Pastry & Café (446 Columbus Ave., 415-986-2914), Sweet (no seating; 218 Church St., 415-552-8992), Tartine Bakery (p. 131), Thorough Bread and Pastry (p. 133), Victoria Pastry Company (1362 Stockton St., 415-781-2015), Zanze's Cheesecake (2405 Ocean Ave., 415-334-2264)

You're Not in Charge (One-of-a-Kind Tasting Menus)

If you don't have a lot of food issues, there's nothing quite like telling the chef "just cook for me." Not a lot of chefs or restaurants like to cook on the fly like that. Well, unless you're at a fine dining or Japanese restaurant, which has its own term for this style of cooking: omakase. Here are a few places where chefs get excited to do it up for you.

Jai Yun $$$–$$$$ *680 Clay St. at Kearny St., 415-981-7438, menuscan.com/jaiyun*
This random little hole-in-the-wall cranks out some rather notable Shanghainese fare (although it sometimes can veer into spicier flavors). You basically call ahead for your reservation (at least two days is ideal, but I also know some folks who have risked it and just walked in), order what price menu you want (the baseline is $55 per person, or you can do $65, $80, or up to $150—I say go for $65), and just make sure you show up on time for your reservation. The no-frills room is great for a group because there are round tables with lazy Susans (and you will end up with more dishes to try). The dishes will sail out, starting with classic chilled ones like smoked fish, cucumber, jellyfish, and beef shank. The warm dishes include whole fish, orange beef, and, my favorites, the crispy eggplant and the ethereal abalone with egg whites. You'll get anywhere from fifteen to twenty-five dishes, and while it sounds like a lot, the portions aren't. Unfortunately, the menu doesn't change very much, so you could come here a year later and still have a similar experience. Which is okay, because the food is that delicious. Here's why it's a deal: you can bring your own wine, and I have never paid corkage (I had a wonderful birthday dinner experience here with twenty friends). Here's why it's challenging: no one speaks English. And here's why it's extra-kooky: cash only, and closed on Thursdays. Who closes on Thursdays? Jai Yun does.

OTHER IDEAS: Ame (p. 88), Aziza (p. 79), Dining Room at the Ritz-Carlton (p. 38), Ino (p. 42), Kappa (1700 Post St., 415-673-6004), Kiss Seafood (p. 33), La Folie (p. 38), sebo (p. 53)

Chef's Table Wanna pretend you're buddies with the chef? Heck, maybe you are already. Anyway, here are a few places where you can get extra-close to the action—definitely worth considering for a memorable group dinner. (Note: some restaurants around town have "chef's tables," but they don't overlook the kitchen, so they are not mentioned here. And no, I am not writing up Benihana.)

LOCATIONS: E&O Trading Company (room for 12–14; 314 Sutter St., 415-693-0303), EPIC Roasthouse (booth that sits 5 facing the kitchen; p. 91), One Market (chef's table in the kitchen; p. 99), Perbacco (chef's table for 8; p. 102)

Rubbernecking

There aren't many jobs you'd want to watch someone do (executive assistant, grave digger, toll-booth worker), but cooking is one worth watching. Take a seat at the counter at these places and you'll get both an eyeful and an earful of kitchen reality as you watch the line do its thing.

Of course, most sushi counters fit the bill, so I won't be listing them all here, although I will mention a few.

Farina $$$ *3560 18th St. at Valencia St., 415-565-0360, farinafoods.com*
One of the splashier imports to the city, this Genovese/Ligurian restaurant delivers on a design and style unlike any other local establishment. It's airy, with an artsy-meets-industrial bakery look. Take a seat on a cherry red lollipop stool at the back marble counter overlooking the pasta-making station; you'll be able to watch a variety of traditional pastas get rolled out and cut during the night. Or sit by the ovens to smell the house specialty of *focaccia di Recco* coming out piping hot (it's a thin sort of focaccia, with a gooey stracchino cheese inside—especially delicious with Rovagnati ham). The pastas here are quite sublime, especially the *mandilli al pesto,* handkerchief pasta with the most magnificent pesto you'll ever taste. Ever. I promise. (The slightly steep price tag feels less painful after your first bite.) Finish the carbo-loading with sweet milk fritters at the end. There's also a full bar, plus plenty of Italian wines to taste.

OTHER IDEAS: A16 (p. 58), Anchor Oyster Bar (p. 48), Bar Crudo (p. 121), Bar Jules (p. 31), Bar Tartine (p. 33), Betelnut (p. 82), Boulevard (p. 80), Canteen (p. 67), Chez Maman (p. 50), Conduit (p. 67), Contigo (p. 49), Heaven's Dog (p. 74), Hog Island Oyster Co. (p. 151), Ino (p. 42), Laïola (p. 30), Lark Creek Steak (p. 11), Local (p. 29), nopa (p. 17), Nopalito (p. 130), One Market (p. 99), Oyaji (p. 18), Ozumo (p. 105), Pizza Nostra (p. 134), nm (p. 6), Rose Pistola (532 Columbus Ave., 415-399-0499), sebo (p. 53), SPQR (p. 51), Swan Oyster Depot (p. 123), Terzo (p. 5), Universal Cafe (p. 26), Zushi Puzzle (1910 Lombard St., 415-931-9319)

Music, Maestro, Please!

*The live music scene isn't what it used to be, but there are still some
local spots where you can hear live jazz and more. Be sure to call
ahead and confirm, because hours can change as quickly as a pianist
changing chords.*

1300 on Fillmore $$$ *1300 Fillmore St. at Eddy St., 415-771-7100,
1300fillmore.com*

As soon as you walk in through the door of this Fillmore District establishment, the
swish jazz vibe wraps around you like a mink stole. The lounge is one of the sexier
venues in the city (open at 4:30 p.m.), with comfortable low chairs and tables where
you can loosen up with cocktails and appetizers; the room warmly glows from the
wall of backlit photos of the Jazz Age in the "Harlem of the West." The dining room
is plush, with dramatic lighting and lots of fabric. David Lawrence's menu of soulful
American cuisine veers toward the elegant, with creamy grits featuring barbecue
shrimp that are already peeled, or a juicy fried chicken that comes deboned. I am more
in love with the appetizers than the entrées, like the bourbon-braised pork belly and
freshwater shrimp hushpuppies, but the short rib and skillet-fried chicken do hold
their own. Kudos for the cornbread with jalapeño jelly, and the chive biscuits. There's
live jazz Mondays through Wednesdays, and a gospel brunch on Sundays. Request a
seat in the back if you want the music to be less prominent during your meal.

SEE "OTHER IDEAS," PAGE 219.

Fit for Cork Dorks

*There are some people who pair their wine with their food, and then you
have those who like to start with their wine first. Here are restaurants with
wine lists that will inspire you to drink your dinner. Let's get swirlin'.*

RN74 $$$ *301 Mission St. at Beale St., 415-543-7474, michaelmina.net/rn74*

The latest offshoot from the Michael Mina culinary empire, this chic SoMa outpost
(tricked out by New York's slick design firm, AvroKO) is a fitting homage to Burgundy.
Raj Parr's wine list is enough to put a mischievous twinkle in most sommeliers' eyes,
while your average drinker gets turned on to some very fine wines indeed. Sure, the
staff is in jeans, but don't let that fool you, because the pedigree of the contemporary
Cal-French cuisine, service, and overall kitted-out style is a far cry from casual Fridays.
Lunchtime, it's the perfect setting for a business lunch with someone in town from
New York. Postwork, the FiDi-heavy crowd is taxed with deciding between sublime
wines or refreshing cocktails over posh bar bites, like maitake mushroom tempura

or sturgeon rillettes. Dinnertime is fair game for dates, business, industry folks, the works. The playful design inspired by a train station (watch the clackity-clacking board listing "last bottles" on the back wall), and inventive dishes (like the barley and duck cassoulet) make this place the dining car of your dreams. All aboard!

TIP: The bar offers late-night bar bites until last call, which can be around 12:30 a.m. or 1 a.m.

OTHER IDEAS: A16 (p. 58), Acquerello (p. 89), Ame (p. 88), Bar Crudo (p. 121), BIN 38 (3232 Scott St., 415-567-3838), Boulevard (p. 80), Campton Place Restaurant (340 Stockton St., 415-955-5555), CAV Wine Bar & Kitchen (p. 14), Coi (p. 135), Dining Room at the Ritz-Carlton (p. 38), District (216 Townsend St., 415-896-2120), Fifth Floor (p. 101), Fleur de Lys (777 Sutter St., 415-673-7779), Gary Danko (p. 37), Incanto (p. 92), Jardinière (p. 13), La Ciccia (p. 138), La Folie (p. 38), Masa's (p. 136), Michael Mina (p. 53), nopa (p. 17), Perbacco (p. 102), Quince (p. 137), Silks (222 Sansome St., 415-986-2020), Slanted Door (p. 98), SPQR (p. 51), Spruce (p. 100), Terzo (p. 5), XYZ (181 3rd St., 415-817-7836)

Food with Yer Pooch

No, we're not talking about your tummy: we're talking about Fifi and Fido. Obviously, outdoor seating is key (see the next section for even more ideas), but here are dog-friendly places where the odds are quite good that your pet will have fellow four-legged furry company.

Atlas Café $ *3049 20th St. at Alabama St., 415-648-1047, atlascafe.net*
A Mission mainstay, this café draws a steady stream of neighborhood folks for its breakfast sandwiches, creative lunchtime offerings (vegetarians love the yam or baked beet sandwiches, while meat eaters dig the smoked turkey and Cuban beef), and easygoing café atmosphere (just ignore the often-cranky cashiers). Plenty of laptop-totin' freelance types, too. Pet owners are able to park it on the patio, and it's usually a pooch party. Since beer is served, Atlas morphs into a fun scene during the early evening, especially on live bluegrass night (Thursdays).

TIP: It's cash only, so bring it.

Flipper's $ *482 Hayes St. at Octavia St., 415-552-8880*
Well, the food is a far cry from what I'd call outstanding here, but sometimes you just want a no-nonsense (and cheap) breakfast, right? Stick with easier items, like omelets. Bonus: breakfast is served all day, so it's hangover HQ. The spacious patio can accommodate a bunch of folks trying to get some fresh air when the weather is nice, so you're not fighting with thirty people over six precious seats. A lot of pooches are in the mix, so it really is quite the SF scene. Bandit! Stop chewing on that lady's bag!

Nopalito $$ *306 Broderick St. at Oak St., 415-437-0303, nopalitosf.com*
There are carnitas, and then there are carnitas from Nopalito, made from some quality pig (that's sooooome pig). In fact, I like to get an extra order to go so I can scramble it up with eggs and cheese the next day, a breakfast I almost wish I didn't create because now I crave it all the time. Anyway, enough about me. Other *estrellas* on this casual nopa (p. 17) offshoot's menu include the ancho chile tamale (the house-made masa is unlike anything you've tasted in SF), my favorite *pozole* (a pork shoulder and hominy stew), and the hearty *birria* (yeah, it's a goat stew, and you should try it). There are a few tacos, but no burritos served, amigo: it's about regional specialties here. The indoor-outdoor patio is unexpectedly dog-friendly, so your pooch is sure to entertain the legions of children here during the day and early evening hours. Speaking of early hours, come by for a brunch of their chilaquiles. You can thank me later.

OTHER IDEAS: Cafe Flore (2298 Market St., 415-621-8579), Chez Spencer (p. 9), Dolores Park Café (501 Dolores St., 415-621-2936), Duboce Park Café (2 Sanchez St., 415-621-1108), Ottimista Enoteca-Café (1838 Union St., 415-674-8400), Park Chalet (p. 133), Park Chow (1240 9th Ave., 415-665-9912), Rose's Café (they have special dog biscuits; p. 10), Sociale (p. 37), Squat and Gobble Café (3600 16th St., 415-552-2125), Universal Cafe (p. 26), Zazie (dogs are allowed on the patio on Mondays; p. 35)

When a random heat wave rolls through town, everyone scrambles to find an outdoor table. Below are locations for each meal (breakfast, weekend brunch, lunch, afternoon beer/wine/happy hour, and dinner) for those joyous days when the fog breaks. Now, whether you score a table or not is up to you and what kind of luck you have. (Note that all the places listed below have more than just two random tables out front on the sidewalk, and covered patios are not included.)

BREAKFAST

The Butler & The Chef Bistro $$ *155A South Park Ave. at 3rd St.,*
415-896-2075, thebutlerandthechefbistro.com

Ooh la la! While this très-Frenchie café is quite the popular weekend brunch spot (they serve brunch all day), it's a purr-fect place to take advantage of for breakfast (or lunch!) during the week. Many items are organic, from the eggs on the eggs Benny to the fresh-made croissants and *pain perdu*. But the star of the show here is the Belgian waffle—it has more fans than Beyoncé, and comes with a variety of toppings, like banana and honey. There are tables with wicker French bistro chairs out front, and while you're sipping your café au lait from a bowl, you'll be overlooking South Park, only adding to the *très charmant* vibe. The interior is no slouch either, a colorful space with eclectic antiques and bistro styling.

TIP: The tiny tables are built for two, so bigger groups won't get a table outside. In fact, even for a table inside, your posee has to be six or less.

Tartine Bakery $–$$ *600 Guerrero St. at 18th St., 415-487-2600,*
tartinebakery.com

Like this bakery needs one more person in line. A kingpin of the 18th Street "gourmet ghetto," the baked goods here do not mess around. Morning buns, croissants, bread pudding—these are the things to make your day start off on the good foot. The somewhat aloof/I-work-in-a-boutique staff attitude, however, has bugged me on more than one occasion. There is a row of tables outside, but if they're all full of bougie breakfasters, get your cappuccino and croissant to go and flounce over to Dolores Park.

TIP: Pick up a cream tart for later—whether it's coconut or banana or lemon (or all three, you hedonist) is entirely up to you. For loaves of just-baked bread, stop by Wed.–Sun. at 5 p.m., when they're fresh out of the oven.

SEE "OTHER IDEAS," PAGE 220.

Chloe's Café $–$$ *1399 Church St. at 26th St., 415-648-4116*

Total Noe Valley neighborhood breakfast/brunch joint, so the waits on the weekend are long. High five on the scrambles (the red potato and cheddar one is good, but be sure to check the board for creative specials)—especially with a side of rosemary or whole wheat–walnut toast. The banana-walnut pancakes are tops, and there's evil cinnamon-croissant French toast with fresh strawberries (or banana, if you ask nicely). Friendly and pro staff, many of whom have worked there for years (Flo, is that you?). The place is eeny meeny teeny tiny, so no big groups.

TIP: Cash only, hon. And if the wait for a table is super-long, walk over to Martha & Bros. (1551 Church St.) for a cuppa coffee first.

Magic Flute Garden Ristorante $$–$$$ *3673 Sacramento St. at Spruce St., 415-922-1225, magicfluteristorante.com*

This WASPy Laurel Heights hideaway has a lot of things going for it: super-easy parking on a Sunday, a flower-filled back patio handily outfitted with umbrellas or heat lamps (depending on what the weather is doing that day), and you can reserve your table ahead of time. It really is about the patio, so hope for a sunny day (the interior, outfitted with oil paintings, will be pleasing to grandma, but not to a thirtysomething). The majority of the crowd is the Coach/Jaguar/estrogen set, with many a table filled with baby showers, mother-daughter brunch duos, chick birthday gatherings, and the occasional gay couple or parents with children who know how to sit up straight. Well-executed brunch dishes, especially the eggs Benedict with house-made hollandaise.

Universal Cafe $$–$$$ *2814 19th St. at Florida St., 415-821-4608, universalcafe.net*

I have adored this restaurant for years, and the brunch is just tits, especially if you score one of the coveted seats out front. Even on a chillier day, this patch of the Mission manages to be warmer than most other places in the city. Start with a fresh-squeezed juice (let's hear it for blood orange season), and you'll get all googly-eyed over the eggs (spot-on scrambles, so tender and fluffy), French toast, delectable coffee cake, and fritters (or sometimes donuts). It's all homemade, fresh, and seasonal. Dinner also rates high on the charm meter—read more on p. 26.

TIP: While waiting for your table, you can order a brunchy drink, like a Bellini, and they'll just add it to your bill when it's time to pay at the end (no drink and dash, you troublemaker). Totally perf destination for a sexy midweek lunch (served Wed.–Fri. 11:30 a.m.–2:15 p.m.).

SEE "OTHER IDEAS," PAGE 220.

Ironwood BBQ $–$$ *Golden Gate Park Golf Course, 47th Ave. at Fulton St., 415-751-8987, ironwoodbbq.com*
One of the city's hidden gems, this Outer Richmond café is part of the Golden Gate Park Golf Course. It's nothing fancy, but a number of outdoor tables on the patio overlook the green and some trees, so the view is a pretty one. The fun part is the kitchen has a badass wood-fired barbecue (the John Willingham Wham Turbo BBQ Pit, if you must know), so you can get a hearty and inexpensive plate of barbecue, like baby back ribs, pulled pork, chicken, or beef brisket, all of which come with barbecue sauce made with Anchor Steam beer; or just go for a meat-filled sandwich. (It's not the city's best 'cue, but the picturesque setting makes up for a lot.) Freshly made sides, ice-cold beer, and a friendly staff. This place is the kind of secret you want to keep to yourself, but you know you shouldn't.

Thorough Bread and Pastry $ *248 Church St. at 15th St., 415-558-0690, thoroughbreadandpastry.com*
What's unique about this bakery/café is that the baked goods are made by students of the San Francisco Baking Institute in South San Francisco—everything is baked and brought in fresh each morning. It's inexpensive, too, and no toity bakery attitude. There's a spacious courtyard in the back where you can wolf down one of their delicious scones or muffins in the morning (the sticky buns are also champs), or a tasty turkey sandwich or ham and cheese on fresh-baked bread in the afternoon. The breads and bakery treats are more classic and artisanal than cutting-edge, so no salt-and-chocolate items here. As your sugar pusher, I heartily recommend some chouquets and macaroons to go.

SEE "OTHER IDEAS," PAGE 220.

AFTERNOON BEER/WINE/HAPPY HOUR

Park Chalet $$ *1000 Great Hwy. at Lincoln Way, 415-386-8439, parkchalet.com*
After a day at the beach, or a bike ride through the park, this place is fresh-air HQ. The spacious lawn facing Golden Gate Park is outfitted with Adirondack chairs (quite the coveted seats), and there's even a pleasant indoor-outdoor vibe in the main bar area and dining room. The food is, er, passable (it's sadly more about the atmosphere here), so stick with classic items, like a burger, pizza, or onion strings. The Monday evening special includes bratwurst and a pint for $6, and Taco Tuesdays mean $3 pints and tacos for $2.50. Service can be spotty, eh. The outdoor barbecue on the weekends is when it really goes off, with live music, too (sometimes a little "jammy"—I think the jazz is better). The outdoor barbecue is on hiatus during the winter. And dogs *and* kids are welcome. How novel!

SEE "OTHER IDEAS," PAGE 221.

La Mar Cebicheria Peruana $$$ *Pier 1 1/2, The Embarcadero at Washington St., 415-397-8880, lamarcebicheria.com*
An import from Peru, this place could hardly have a better location: it's right on the water in a historical building, with stunning bay views and a spacious back patio to enjoy it from. The restaurant is quite ginormous—there's a bar in the front where you can get lit on pisco sours, a lounge and ceviche bar area, and a mega dining room. The room is filled with light and punches of cerulean blue. The food is equally colorful, like the bright purple potatoes in the *causas* (my favorite dish here—get the tasting plate of these whipped potatoes topped with crab, or tuna and avocado) and bright chile sauces and dips. The seafood is sushi-fresh, from the seven different ceviches to the tender medley in the *arroz jugoso*, almost a juicy seafood risotto. The food is best shared, so get your group together and have at it—there's a big group table in the back. One flaw is the service; it can be erratic. Hey, it's not *siesta* time yet. I need my check!

TIP: Here on a date? There's a small seating area on the back patio reserved for walk-ins—it's the couch with the best view in the city (shhhhh).

Pizza Nostra $$ *300 De Haro St. at 16th St., 415-558-9493, pizzanostrasf.com*
Tucked into a random little minimall with one other restaurant and a nail salon is this neighborhood pizza place, serving authentic Neapolitan pizzas with a bit of French *je ne sais quoi.* (Try a glass of the lightly chilled Bonarda with your pizza.) During the next heat wave, while people are waiting two hours for their two-top on the sidewalk in the Mission, you'll already be well into your second glass of nero d'avola on the patio here (so savvy, you). There are something like forty-five seats outside, and while your view is basically of the parking lot, it'll still be a treat to be outside (it's a good spot for lunch, too). The menu has a variety of small plates (plenty are vegetarian-friendly), plus pastas and a burger for those who don't want to embark on an Italian path. There's also a *tronchetto* on the menu, kind of like a Neapolitan Hot Pocket. The look is industrial and simple—it's casual, fine for kids and sporty types who just finished their workout at the gym across the way and are ready for some carbo-loading.

SEE "OTHER IDEAS," PAGE 222.

SAN FRANCISCO STYLE

Farmers' Market Freshy Fresh

If you're craving the freshest local ingredients you can find, these places will remind you of the pleasure of a perfect carrot. Got someone visiting from a flyover, excuse me, landlocked state? Here's where you can show off the seasonal voodoo that we do.

Coi $$$$ *373 Broadway at Montgomery St., 415-393-9000, coirestaurant.com*
Are you a food geek? Then welcome to your new church. Chef-owner Daniel Patterson is doing some of the city's most innovative Northern California cuisine, with a modern European sensibility, using the finest ingredients available. This tiny restaurant is tucked in just across the street from Déjà Vu Showgirls and other seedy Broadway joints, so don't be alarmed. Inside is an oasis of calm (the name, pronounced *kwah*, is an archaic French word for tranquil). You can hear your dining partner; heck, you can hear yourself think. Eleven courses of exquisite bite after bite. Luxurious linens, thoughtful flatware and plates, well-timed service, excellent wine pairings—jeez, the whole thing is quite the culinary showstopper. A must-do for anyone who wants to experience ingredients on an entirely different level.

TIP: The front lounge is decidedly more casual, with natural-modern décor (like burl wood tables) and a less expensive à la carte menu. It's a perfect back-pocket last-minute dinner date location—you'll sink right into the flokati pillows.

OTHER IDEAS: A16 (p. 58), Absinthe (p. 7), The Alembic (p. 16), Americano (8 Mission St., 415-278-3777), Aziza (p. 79), Bar Crudo (p. 121), Bar Jules (p. 31), Bar Tartine (p. 33), BIX (p. 20), Boulettes Larder (p. 123), Boulevard (p. 80), Cane Rosso (1 Ferry Bldg., 415-391-7599), Citizen Cake (p. 86), COCO500 (p. 90), Conduit (p. 67), Contigo (p. 49), Delfina (p. 137), Fifth Floor (p. 101), Fish & Farm (339 Taylor St., 415-474-3474), Foreign Cinema (p. 32), Gialina (p. 62), Greens (p. 112), Hayes Street Grill (p. 62), Incanto (p. 92), Jardinière (p. 13), Kokkari (p. 103), Laïola (p. 30), Luce (888 Howard St., 415-616-6566), Magnolia (p. 30), Maverick (3316 17th St.,

415-863-3061), Millennium (580 Geary St., 415-345-3900), Mission Beach Café (p. 125), Moss Room (p. 68), nopa (p. 17), Nopalito (p. 130), Olea (p. 85), One Market (p. 99), Orson (p. 15), Pauline's Pizza (p. 72), Perbacco (p. 102), Piccino (p. 52), Quince (p. 137), Range (p. 59), Serpentine (p. 59), Slanted Door (p. 98), Slow Club (p. 30), SPQR (p. 51), Spruce (p. 100), Terzo (p. 5), Universal Cafe (p. 26), Zuni Café (p. 52)

Big City Dining

Nope, you're not in Kansas anymore. Here's a lineup of some of San Francisco's finer destinations, whether they're splashy, fancy, luxe, edgy, urban, or all of the above, in the hizzouse.

Masa's $$$$ *648 Bush St. at Powell St., 415-989-7154, masasrestaurant.com*
You like the idea of a *mignardise* cart, loaded with candy and bonbons? As Grace Jones would say, pull up to the bumper, baby. Masa's is a San Francisco fine dining tradition (twenty-five years and counting), and while the cuisine occasionally feels a bit less than cutting edge, it always remains a genteel experience, dahling. Three courses, six courses, nine courses, the vegetarian menu . . . take your pick. Chef Grergory Short's contemporary Cal-French menu features Japanese influences, so don't be surprised if you get a sake pairing with a dish *(kanpai!).* The modern room is comfortable and visually interesting—tables are well spaced, your heinie can last in the padded toile chairs for the necessary three-plus hours, linens are top drawer, there are lovely fresh roses on each table, the wine pairings are notable, and service is attentive without being annoying. Oh yeah, and there's that cart o' temptation at the end.

OTHER IDEAS: Ame (p. 88), BIX (p. 20), Boulevard (p. 80), Campton Place Restaurant (340 Stockton St., 415-955-5555), Coi (p. 135), Dining Room at the Ritz-Carlton (p. 38), EPIC Roasthouse (p. 91), Farallon (p. 82), Fifth Floor (p. 101), Fleur de Lys (777 Sutter St., 415-673-7779), Gary Danko (p. 37), Jardinière (p. 13), Kokkari (p. 103), La Folie (p. 38), Michael Mina (p. 53), Perbacco (p. 102), Quince (p. 137), RN74 (p. 128), Slanted Door (p. 98), Spruce (p. 100), Waterbar (p. 105), Zuni Café (p. 52)

RN74

There's nothing like scrambling to figure out where to take your Chelsea art gallery–owning urban warrior cousin and his fashionista wife with a penchant for pastis. Now, if they are even slightly gourmand-ish, you can assuredly impress them with stellar California ingredients (just look at the "Farmers' Market Freshy Fresh" section, p. 135). But if you're in need of a location with chic or stylish design, here are some places that can help you look like you know the difference between Peretti and Prada.

Delfina $$–$$$ *3621 18th St. at Guerrero St., 415-552-4055, delfinasf.com*
This ten-year-old Mission mainstay is always packed, so you'll immediately look like you chose a happening place (you did). Don't fret over how long it's been around—the rustic-industrial interior is quite timeless, with stainless-steel tabletops, wood-slat banquettes, warm lighting, fresh flowers, and a busy adjoining wine bar area. Delfina is often on the must-do list of any visitor—just make your reservation well in advance. Craig Stoll's Cal-Northern Italian menu is full of fresh and seasonal produce, so be sure to order a salad or some of the unique greens they source, like puntarelle. And some pastas, of course. Do the tripe *alla fiorentina* if you're even remotely into delicious things. And for those seeking something a little safe, the steak here is a benchmark . . . the same with the roast chicken. Panna cotta for dessert, oh, you better. Your tattooed server will be able to steer you to some spot-on Italian wine choices, trust.

TIP: Keep in mind there is always room for walk-ins, so if you desperately want to dine here, just show up.

Quince $$$–$$$$ *470 Pacific Ave. at Montgomery St., 415-775-8500, quincerestaurant.com*
Opening in the former Myth space in Jackson Square, this is the new and much larger location for Quince, which moved from its intimate space in Pacific Heights. Michael and Lindsay Tusk's restaurant was newly opened at press time, but their commitment to making remarkable house-made pastas, their impeccable service style, and refined taste will assuredly continue at the new location. Plus there's a new bar area (and cocktail list). Shaping up to be one of the hottest tickets in town.

OTHER IDEAS: A16 (p. 58), Ame (p. 88), Bar Tartine (p. 33), BIX (p. 20), Chez Spencer (p. 9), Coi (p. 135), Conduit (p. 67), Farina (p. 127), Fifth Floor (p. 101), Gitane (p. 24), Kokkari (p. 103), nopa (p. 17), Orson (p. 15), Perbacco (p. 102), RN74 (p. 128), sebo (p. 53), Slanted Door (p. 98), Spruce (p. 100), Town Hall (p. 103), Zuni Café (p. 52)

Under the Radar

Ten, no, eleven places that people who really love food and wine know about—and you should too. Many are restaurant industry faves.

La Ciccia $$–$$$ *291 30th St. at Church St., 415-550-8114, laciccia.com*
I so adore this neighborhood place, which is run by the nicest husband-and-wife team (Massimiliano Conti and Lorella Degan). San Francisco's only Sardinian restaurant, it's a little off the beaten path but really should be on everyone's GPS. Don't be intimidated by the strange-looking words on the menu—it's just funky Sardinian. You'll want to share a platter of the house-made salumi and a thin-crust pizza for sure. Order a couple of pastas (that's all you need—the portions are hefty), like the *fregola* or the *malloreddus* (semolina gnochetti), both traditional shapes. Main dishes include seafood and slow-braised meats. I know, I know, you're full, but the house-made gelato must make its way to the table. The wine list, although you need a microscope to read it, is full of well-chosen Italian gems (the chef was a former sommelier), so be sure to indulge in a bottle or two.

OTHER IDEAS: Aziza (p. 79), Canteen (p. 67), Coi (the lounge; p. 135), Gialina (p. 62), Kiss Seafood (p. 33), Namu (p. 65), Piccino (p. 52), The Ritz-Carlton Bar (600 Stockton St., 415-773-6198), Spices! and Spices II (p. 42)

Food that Rates as Good as the View

It's often a shame: the nicer the view, the lousier the vittles. Fortunately, there are a few restaurants in San Francisco where what's on your plate is as good as what you're looking at out the window.

butterfly $$$ *Pier 33 at Bay St., 415-864-8999, butterflysf.com*
This waterfront restaurant is literally perched right on the water, with massive floor-to-ceiling windows. There's also an outdoor deck with rows of tables along a walkway, ideal for lunch and brunch. The loungey look is white tablecloth-meets-modern, featuring concrete floors, woven chrome chairs, and dramatic light fixtures. Chef Rob Lam's menu is rooted in Asian flavors and ingredients, while highlighting excellent meats, from Berkshire pork to five spice–braised Angus short rib, while the kalua pig with butter lettuce cups is a signature dish. It's food that's big on personality and easy to share, so large groups are a natural fit (request the corner booth of table 23, great for six or seven diners). There's a full bar so it gets clubby on Friday and Saturday evenings after 9 p.m., when a late-night happy hour kicks off (it runs until midnight).

TIP: On a date? Request table 22: the two seats are side by side so you can both look upon the water together; it's one of the city's most romantic tables with a view.

Scoma's Restaurant $$$$ *Pier 47, Al Scoma Way at Jefferson St.,*
415-771-4383, scomas.com

I'm the first to admit it: I thought everything at Fisherman's Wharf was just a tourist trap. Boy, was I wrong. This seafood restaurant charmed the hell out of me: the majority of the staff has been there for years, like, you're a newbie if you've only worked at Scoma's for twelve years. The walls are packed with memorabilia from when the restaurant opened in 1965 (it was originally just a coffeeshop)—it really is a slice of San Francisco wharf history. The seafood is super-fresh (they have their own boats and fish-receiving station). The tender calamari (get the spicier Calabrese style), halibut, petrale sole, and, of course, the Dungeness crab will all impress. A fave on the menu is the lazy man's cioppino—you get a bowl full of prawns, shrimp, clams, and scallops, and the best part: the crab is already picked, so you don't have to get your hands dirty (and for only $3 more than the regular cioppino—but it's still $35).

TIP: They offer complimentary valet parking. Classy!

Sutro's at the Cliff House $$$–$$$$ *1090 Point Lobos Ave. at Great Hwy.,*
415-386-3330, cliffhouse.com

It really is one of the best views in San Francisco, no joke. The American menu features seasonal soups like a delicious corn soup, asparagus salad, and a rather outstanding filet of beef with an herb potato cake; other dishes aren't exactly thrilling, but still pretty decent. The crowd is a total hodgepodge of tourists and romantic dates, all slack-jawed over the sweeping view of the ocean and Seal Rocks.

TIP: Since you can't reserve a spot by the window in advance, make your reservation for when they open so you can request a window seat upon arrival.

OTHER IDEAS: Americano (8 Mission St., 415-278-3777), Boulevard (p. 80), EPIC Roasthouse (p. 91), Greens (p. 112), La Mar (p. 134), One Market (p. 99), Ozumo (p. 150), The Rotunda (view of Union Square; p. 10), Slanted Door (p. 98), Venticello (1257 Taylor St., 415-922-2545), Waterbar (p. 105)

Less-Expensive Food with a View: Cane Rosso (1 Ferry Bldg., 415-391-7599), Crown & Crumpet (p. 12), Ferry Plaza Seafood (1 Ferry Bldg., 415-274-2561), Hog Island Oyster Co. (p. 151), Mijita (1 Ferry Bldg., 415-399-0814), The Plant Café Organic (Embarcadero; p. 144), Red's Java House (p. 212)

This is definitely a city where you can eat well on the cheap. Whether you're a local or just passing through, here are ten flavor-packed bites under $10. (Be sure to check out "These Are a Few of My Favorite Things," p. 143, for additional discoveries.)

Barbecue Pork Buns at Wing Lee Bakery $ *503 Clement St. at 6th Ave., 415-668-9481*

There's mighty cheap dim sum at this little Richmond dive—the *siu mai* is decent, and I recommend the sticky rice with peanuts. But it's the baked barbecue pork buns that keep me coming back. Get a bag of these warm pork-filled buns (they're only 90¢ each) and sneak them into a movie. (I usually visit Green Apple Books across the street before or after eating here.)

Crispy/Dorado Tacos at La Taqueria $

2889 Mission St. at 25th St., 415-285-7117

The prices seem to keep climbing here, but as long as the food quality continues to rock *la casa*, I'll keep paying. There are tacos, and then there are the off-the-menu *dorado*/crispy tacos, which will get you one fried taco folded inside a soft one with melted cheese in the middle, and wrapped around meat (I am a slave to the carnitas), frijoles, avocado, sour cream, and salsa. The best $5 taco ever.

Donuts from Dynamo $ *2760 24th St. at*

Hampshire St., 415-920-1978, dynamosf.com

You'll find these artisan donuts at a variety of cafes around the city (Coffee Bar [p. 109], Four Barrel Coffee [p. 148], The Corner [2199 Mission St., 415-875-9258]), but you might as well go to the mother ship in the heart of the Mission and enjoy one with a Four Barrel coffee (there are tables where you can sit, and a patio is due to open in the back). Flavors include the much-discussed maple-bacon-apple number, but the chocolate spice one is my little troublemaker. There's also lemon pistachio, banana *dulce de leche*, salted caramel, a Monte Cristo version, and all kinds of rotating flavors that make you say, "I'd like that one, and that one, oh, and that one, please and thanks."

Egg Custard Tart from Golden Gate Bakery $ *1029 Grant Ave. at Pacific Ave., 415-781-2627*

These wickedly wonderful egg custard tarts are usually served up a little warm. The line can be long, but don't fret. Buy more than you think you'll eat because you'll find yourself craving another one two hours later. The coconut buns, macaroons, and barbecue pork buns should also be investigated. And call before heading over, since they sometimes close for a random day, or even an entire month. (Sob.)

Focaccia from Liguria Bakery $ *1700 Stockton St. at Filbert St., 415-421-3786*

A San Francisco tradition, this cash-only joint specializes in focaccia, from a pizza style to a transcendental one with rosemary and garlic to even a sweet one with raisins (get it for breakfast!). The bread is so moist, fresh, oily, and squishy . . . *perfetto!* You can have them cut up an entire sheet for you into eight pieces or just get a slice. Either way, it will get wrapped up in butcher paper and string before you head out to Washington Square Park to scarf it. Try to get here before noon since it often sells out, and when the focaccia is gone, the place closes shop. And don't mind the gruff lady who works here; it's not you, it's just her way.

Gourmet Sandwiches from The Sentinel $ *37 New Montgomery St. at Stevenson St., 415-284-9960, thesentinelsf.com*

Dennis Leary of Canteen (p. 67) does a sublime corned beef, smoked trout, or roast beef sandwich at his little sandwich shop during the week. There's nowhere to sit, so you'll need to find a spot nearby to enjoy your sando. (Check the website for daily listings.) The line moves quickly, so don't let that deter you.

Hash Brown Sandwich from Art's Cafe $ *747 Irving St. at 9th Ave., 415-665-7440, artscafesf.com*

I can't believe the hash brown sandwich doesn't exist anywhere else. It's a straight-up brilliant addition to the usual lineup of breakfast suspects. Imagine a stuffed half-moon omelette, but instead of eggs, the exterior is made of extra-crispy hash browns with a stuffing of your choice (I like the ham and onions). Plus there's melted cheddar cheese in there, and it comes with two eggs on the side, and two pieces of toast. All for $6.55! It's a borderline BLD (breakfast, lunch, dinner), all in one handy meal. This old-school diner has been around for more than sixty years, and the hard-working Korean husband and wife who own it have been working at Art's for twenty years straight. Take a seat at one of the fourteen or so stools at the counter, and yay, breakfast is served all day, you little hooligan. Let's hear it for diners!

Ice Cream 2.0 in the Mission $

Head to **Humphry Slocombe** (2790 Harrison St. at 24th St., 415-550-6971, humphryslocombe.com) for inventive flavors like foie gras, prosciutto, Thai chile lime sorbet, and Secret Breakfast (think vanilla with bourbon and cornflakes). And there's a reason the salted caramel ice cream from **Bi-Rite Creamery** (3692 18th St. at Guerrero St., 415-626-5600, biritecreamery.com) is San Francisco's cult artisanal ice cream. (Pssst, it's magic with a scoop of roasted banana or coffee in a banana split.)

Mosakhan from Goood Frikin' Chicken $ *10 29th St. at Mission St.,*
415-970-2428, gfcsf.com

What is this, you ask, this mysterious *mosakhan*? It's like the grandmaster Mediterranean mother ship: a juicy pile of chicken that's been cooked with soft golden onions, sumac, olive oil, and pine nuts, all wrapped up in lavash like a burrito and grilled to crispy perfection. Mother of god, it's a total goldmine of goodness: the mack, the man, the *mosakhan*. It's frikin' delicious. The open-flame chicken here is great, too (order it extra crispy, with garlic sauce and spicy sauce on the side).

Roast Pork Heaven at Gourmet Delight $

1045 Stockton St. at Jackson St., 415-392-3288

Feel like chowing down on pieces of the most delicious roast pork? Oh, yes you do. Just walk up to the counter and tell them how much you want (a pound is plenty for two people to pig out on). The pork meisters behind the counter will chop it up into delectable bite-size pieces for you so you can eat it out of a Chinese takeout box like it's pig popcorn or something (there are no tables). It's so good you're gonna freak out. Really.

THESE ARE A FEW OF MY FAVORITE THINGS

When people ask me for my favorite restaurant, I always ask, "For what?".
But when it comes down to favorite food items, well, that's a bit easier to answer.
Below are lists, short and sweet, with up to three (often four—hey, it's hard to choose!) of my favorite spots for food in several different categories. (By the way, I didn't forget about barbecue—the goods just aren't found in this city.

Burger (Cloth Napkin)

Absinthe Brasserie & Bar (p. 7) *The Decadent Burger*
You ready for a burger made of pure evil? Here it goes: a grass-fed beef patty on an Acme brioche bun, topped with gruyère, spicy caramelized onions, and the additional option of a fried egg (just say *oui*). Plus devilishly good frites that come with Dijon, thyme-infused malt vinegar, and rouille. Is it me, or is it getting hot in here?

BIX (p. 20) *My Favorite*
This was the winner in my 2009 Best Cloth-Napkin Burger in SF competition—juicy, beefy, and perfectly ground. It even utilizes special technology developed by chef Bruce Hill, the Plancha Press. This beauteous burger comes with well-melted cheese, house-made aioli, and spectacular fries.

Spruce (p. 100) *The Posh Burger*
I love perching at the bar here, scarfing down the beautifully formed patty inside a house-baked bun (nice buns!), with pickled onions, thinly sliced zucchini, and rémoulade. And you can get it with a glass of faboo Burgundy.

More Burger Love: Balboa Cafe (p. 21), Fish & Farm (339 Taylor St., 415-474-3474), Hayes Street Grill (p. 62), Namu (p. 65), nopa (p. 17)

Bill's Place $–$$ *2315 Clement St. at 24th Ave., 415-221-5262, billsplace.qpg.com*
Good burgers are about the details: here the bun is griddled, the bacon is crisp, the fresh-cut fries are hot, and the pickles? Tasty. (Shame about the meh tomato.) It's not the finest beef in the world, but it is hand-cut and ground here daily and comes cooked exactly to order. And this burger is super-affordable. The extras include friendly and great service, a long counter, huge milkshakes, and did I mention the chandeliers? There's a patio out back, too. Very kid friendly.

Chez Maman $–$$ (p. 50)
J'adore this burger so much: it's a juicy patty that fast-tracks it to bliss, with Brie and caramelized onions on top and sandwiched inside a soft roll from Crepe & Brioche that is the bomb (it's almost like a squishy ciabatta loaf). Good herb-dusted frites are served on the side, too.

Taylor's Automatic Refresher $–$$ *1 Ferry Bldg., 415-318-3423,*
taylorsautomaticrefresher.com
San Francisco was lucky to get this import from St. Helena (p. 185). It's made from good beef, I love the eggy bun, and yeah, there's a secret sauce. Be sure to get a side of the sweet potato fries and a milkshake. There's great outdoor seating (pssst, a wonderful sunny day location for happy hour), so don't let the long line freak you out.

Other Strong Contenders: In-N-Out (333 Jefferson St., 800-786-1000), Mo's (1322 Grant Ave., 415-788-3779), Pearl's Deluxe Burgers (708 Post St., 415-409-6120), Prather Ranch burger at the Tuesday and Saturday Ferry Plaza Farmers' Market (get an egg on it), the Tuesday burger at Rosamunde Sausage Grill (545 Haight St., 415-437-6851), Zeitgeist (p. 116)

Burger (Vegetarian)

The Plant Café Organic $–$$ *3352 Steiner St. at Chestnut St., 415-931-2777;*
The Embarcadero, Pier 3, 415-984-1973, theplantcafe.com
I actually get cravings for this non-beef burger—it's a house-made patty of lentils, mushrooms, beets, cashews, and bulgur wheat, topped with grilled onions, garlic aioli, and the usual suspects, plus a side of pickles and mixed greens. I like the Cali version topped with avo and white cheddar on grilled sourdough. It's one hell of a nonburger. And very filling.

Castillito Taqueria $ *136 Church St. at Duboce Ave., 415-621-3428*

The "Upper Safeway" location is my fave. They do burrito assembly *correctomundo* from the get-go, placing the tortilla on the griddle and melting the slew of cheese they always seem to pile on. I order mine with fatty carnitas, pinto beans, salsa, fresh avocado, sour cream, and I like to hold the rice and the onions. Now ask them to put that puppy back on the grill for a second and make it *dorado* (golden). Hells yeah.

Papalote $ *3409 24th St. at Valencia St., 415-970-8815; 1777 Fulton St. at Masonic Ave., 415-776-0106, papalote-sf.com*

Who knew a healthy burrito could taste so good? Whether you're going for meat (grilled organic chicken or carne asada), or one of their vegetarian options (so good with Soyrizo or marinated tofu—I know, I just said that), the food here is consistently tasty. I think they put gold in their black refried beans—they're that special. I'm a big fan of the "secret-recipe" salsa, although I wish it were hotter.

Taqueria Can-cún $ (p. 116)

I have eaten more burritos at this treasured standby than I care to count. It got me through my underfunded twenties, that's for sure. I am an *amiga* of their *al pastor* (tender marinated pork cooked on a vertical rotisserie), and they do a vegetarian burrito that I also order fairly often. The chips have always sucked, but the atomic green tomatillo salsa is a star on my spice-lovin' meter.

Tip o' the Sombrero: The Little Chihuahua (p. 63) has burritos that are all kinds of awesome (ditto on their salsas).

Chilaquiles

Los Jarritos $ *901 S. Van Ness Ave. at 20th St., 415-648-8383, losjarritos.com*

These chilaquiles don't feature my favorite salsa (see Pastores, below), but I still enjoy the execution here (the eggs are scrambled and come with good beans on the side). Try the Remo with chicken, cheese, and sour cream. Major points for serving breakfast all day, *gracias*. And the décor and staff are super-cheerful.

Pastores $$ *3486 Mission St. at Cortland St., 415-642-5385*

It's like your mom cooking for you (with major *amor*). Get ready for the champ of chilaquiles: a plate of crispy freshly fried tortilla strips slathered in a bright and spicy tomatillo salsa, with cheese and over-easy eggs, plus beans and rice on the side. I equally love the red salsa that comes with the chips. Cool off with a refreshing *agua fresca.* This place totally takes me back to Mexico—all the way down to the nondescript interior. The hours can be funky, so call ahead.

Primavera $–$$ *Stand at the Saturday Ferry Plaza Farmers' Market at the Ferry Building Marketplace*
One of those rare things in life that is worth the long line. I almost want to burst into tears when the chilaquiles run out (and they do). Expect an awesome medley of flavors, from the rotating salsas, chorizo, *crema, cotija,* avocado, onion, and soft-scrambled eggs and black beans on the side.

Couscous

Aziza (p. 79) No one in the city can touch the hand-rolled couscous here. (Well, besides the chef.) Embrace the butter.

Dessert

There are so many ways to rot your teeth in San Francisco; don't miss "Just Dessert" on p. 125.

Mission Beach Café (p. 125) Take one bite of the superlative butterscotch banana cream pie here and you will agree: Alan Carter makes one of the best piecrusts in the city. And the lemon velvet cream pie is so good it makes me want to order that, too. Your brain will start to tell you, "Yup, two pieces in one sitting. That's totally normal." Tread carefully here, it's dangerous.

Range (p. 59) Pastry chef Michelle Polzine does magnificent things with seasonal produce, creating desserts that balance homespun authenticity with a flair for flavor and elegant ingredient pairings. Another easy spot to swing by just for dessert at the bar (aw heck, you might as well get a nightcap since you're there).

More Sweet Treats: Citizen Cake (p. 86), Dianda's (it's all about the St. Honoré cake, a Gagliardi family favorite; 2883 Mission St. at 24th St., 415-647-5469)

S&T Hong Kong Seafood Restaurant $$ *2578 Noriega St. at 33rd Ave., 415-665-8338*

I am so grateful for being introduced to this place. It's crazy affordable, and I heart the shrimp noodle roll. My hands-down fave for dim sum feasting, and it will only put you back $20 for a total tour. Amazing but true.

Yank Sing (p. 97) I had to mention this one because they serve delicious *xiao long bao* (Shanghai soup dumplings). Yes, it's spendy here, but these dumplings alone are worth the outlay.

Honorable Dumplings: Dol Ho (cheap; 808 Pacific Ave., 415-392-2828), Gold Mountain (644 Broadway, 415-296-7733), Great Eastern (649 Jackson St., 415-986-2500), South Sea Seafood Village (1420 Irving St., 415-665-8210)

Eggs Benedict

Canteen (p. 67) No one does fresh hollandaise like Canteen, poured over perfectly poached eggs, a purposefully squashed and grilled buttery English muffin, and slightly seared ham. Order a side of the house-baked brioche, a total butter and carb overload, but hey, you're ordering eggs Benedict to begin with, right? Right.

Espresso

Espresso is the the nude beach of coffee making—there is just no hiding. You can tell with one look whether that shot is tight or flabby. These are places whose shots can proudly walk along the shore in the unforgiving light of day.

Blue Bottle Coffee Co. $ *Various locations; bluebottlecoffee.net*

Happiness is . . . a Gibraltar (p. 148) in the alley where I first fell in love with Blue Bottle's coffee. There are numerous locations around the city, but the kiosk at 315 Linden Street is where I consistently have their best pulls. I also swoon over the New Orleans iced coffee on a (rare) hot day.

Gibraltar An off-the-menu coffee drink that was started at Blue Bottle Coffee, named after the little glass it's always served in. It's like a very milky macchiato, and is a barista fave because it's quick to drink.

Four Barrel Coffee $ *375 Valencia St. at 14th St., 415-252-0800*

I commend their commitment to doing things right here, from their sourcing to pulls to their in-house roasting to the über-cool interior. The supply of Dynamo donuts and music from vinyl records equals a high score that should be on a Donkey Kong video game screen.

More Hotshots: It's not espresso, but I'm crazy for the stellar iced coffee from Philz (various locations; philzcoffee.com) that comes with heavy cream, sugar (I ask for light sugar), a touch of cardamom, and their trademark sprig of mint. Hauntingly delicious and refreshing . . . and quite vroom! Coffee Bar (p. 109) and Ritual Coffee (various locations; ritualroasters .com) also do great macchiatos.

Falafel Wrap

Ali Baba's Cave $ *531 Haight St. at Fillmore St., 415-255-7820*

I don't think I've ever had a more lovingly crafted falafel sandwich, from the perfect ingredient dispersion (it even comes with spears of fried potato) to the way they smush the falafel before wrapping it all up—sheer genius. The hot sauce means business (don't order it extra spicy—it's just too much), and ask them to grill it a tiny bit more than usual. This wrap is a beast; plan to share with a pal. The best in show, and the best deal.

Old Jerusalem $ *2976 Mission St. at 25th St., 415-642-5958, oldjerusalemsf.com*

What a deal, this place. Order the stuffed falafel in lavash, which brings onion and pine nuts to the mix and comes with potato spears. They also get high marks for the incredible spread that accompanies a simple order of their dips, like *ful* (a fava bean dip) or baba ghanoush. This joint rules.

Sunrise Deli & Café $ *2115 Irving St. at 23rd Ave., 415-664-8210, sunrisedeli.net*

A clean and friendly little spot in the Outer Sunset with some of the city's fluffiest and most tender falafel. I wish the hot sauce was truly hot, but otherwise it's a pretty good sandwich. Get the super with eggplant and potato, all wrapped up in lavash.

Truly Mediterranean $ *3109 16th St. at Valencia St., 415-252-7482, trulymedsf.com*
The benchmark for lavash wraps in the city. The falafel are smaller and crispier here, joined by a savory harissa-laden sauce, well-seasoned onion, and tahini, and the wrap is grilled to perfection. (I also have quite a thing for their shwarma, especially the chicken version, which is available only on Tuesdays and Fridays.)

Fried Chicken

The Front Porch (p. 65) All I want in my popcorn bucket from now on is fried chicken (how it's served here). The juicy bird has a great exterior, and is chopped into manageable pieces. Plus collard greens and mashed potatoes on the side.

farmerbrown's little skillet $–$$ *330 Ritch St. at Brannan St., 415-777-2777, littleskilletsf.com*
Who knew you'd fall in love with chicken served from an alley window? And backed up with a waffle on the side? Uh-huh. Good chicken, too (they use Rocky The Range Chicken, an antibiotic-free, free-range bird). The Cobb salad with fried chicken is also delish. The mother hen of this takeout window, the restaurant farmerbrown (p. 64), can also knock some fried chicken out of the park, but it's not always consistent.

Town Hall (p. 103) They do really, really dark things to the buttermilk-fried bird here (like inject it with some secret ratio of butter and hot sauce). It's kind of how you'll feel after eating it. It comes with a side of collard greens, Yukon gold potatoes, and country bacon gravy—and you are aces.

Honorable Bwok: The five-spice or Madras curry fried chicken at Foreign Cinema (p. 32).

Hot (Diggity) Dogs

Absinthe Brasserie & Bar (p. 7)
I know, $12 for a dog is ridiculous, but chef Jamie Lauren makes this deluxe tube steak with pork shoulder, American Kobe beef, house-made bacon, and some fatback. Plus, the Guinness mustard and chile ketchup are made in house. Freaking perfection, and wait until you try the yogurt-dill chips.

Da Beef $ *300 7th St. at Folsom St., dabeef.com*
Yup, from a cart, just as it should be. It's a true Chicago Vienna Beef dog, made with love and served with a smile. Plus, a pickle spear, celery salt, and a pile of sport peppers (medium-hot green peppers that are fundamental to an authentic Chicago dog). No ketchup. Don't even ask.

Showdogs $ *1020 Market St. at 6th St., 415-558-9560, showdogssf.com*
You can try all kinds of local artisanal dogs here, from Fatted Calf's to 4505's top-notch dawgs, with a melee of gourmet toppings and buns and sauces. Fantastic corn dog, and some of the best onion rings in town. Woof. Plus a good list of suds.

Underdog $ *1634 Irving St. at 17th Ave., 415-665-8881*
At this quirky little hippie enclave in the Sunset, your dog comes with a great soundtrack, and they even sell local honey. Mad props: they lightly toast your bun (you can get an organic wheat bun); they have all kinds of organic (and vegan!) dogs and sausages to choose from, as well as at least three kinds of mustard; and the staff has the nicest attitude. And an eco-friendly/jah love philosophy. Plus tater tots. Dude.

Absinthe

One More Woof: Moishe's Pippic (425-A Hayes St., 415-431-2440) has a Wrigley Field dog, another super-authentic Chicago-style dog.

KFC (Korean Fried Chicken)

San Tung $$ *1031 Irving St. at 12th Ave., 415-242-0828*
The dry-fried chicken wings here are so damned addictive, glazed in a sticky-sweet sauce that's garlicky, gingery, a touch constarchy, and pure culinary crack. Looking at the line of people, I can't even imagine how many wings the kitchen blazes through in a night. It's mind-boggling. (Note that it's closed Wednesdays.)

Shin Toe Bul Yi $$ *2001 Taraval St. at 30th Ave., 415-566-9221*
This off-the-beaten-path Korean joint kicks butt with wings: order up the "chicken small pieces—little spicy." But you get the exact opposite: it's more like "chicken big pieces—not spicy." The chicken is covered in a crispy and golden batter that isn't too greasy—let's hear it for super-hot oil. And the hefty portion rules.

Toyose $$ *3814 Noriega St. at 45th Ave., 415-731-0232*
Big props to the "chicken garage" (the restaurant is located in what was once a residential garage). There's a raucous scene, and the super-late hours can be a lifesaver. The wings here are juicy, crispy, and feature a little hit o' spice. The batter has a nice dark hue, too. The kimchi pancake is also quality.

Honorable Mention: The brothers at Namu (p. 65) have a killer version of KFC made with local chicken on their menu. But that bird ain't cheap.

Noodles/Ramen

Katana-ya $–$$ *430 Geary St. at Mason St., 415-771-1280*
Get the *chashu* (barbecued) pork ramen or fried chicken on top. The rich *shoyu* (soy) broth is the one to order. Open until 1:15 a.m.

Miki Restaurant $$ *3639 Balboa St. at 37th Ave., 415-387-0874*
Wow, what a gem, and it's a bit stealth. Right by the Balboa Theater (great before a show). Get the *tonkotsu* (pork) broth or *tonkotsu shoyu* (soy); seriously excellent *dashi* (broth) here. But be forewarned that there's often a long wait before showtime.

Honorable Slurps: Sapporo-ya (p. 63) and Tanpopo (1740 Buchanan St., 415-346-7132) for ramen; Mifune (1737 Post St., 415-922-0337), On the Bridge (1581 Webster St., 415-922-7765), and Takara (22 Peace Plaza, Suite 202, 415-921-2000) for udon.

Oysters

Foreign Cinema (p. 32) There's always an excellent selection here—and they often carry the rare Olympia oyster. Bring on the bubbles.

Hog Island Oyster Co. $$ *1 Ferry Bldg., 415-391-7117, hogislandoysters.com*
It's dangerously easy to put down a dozen of their Sweetwaters and Kumamotos in the blink of an eye. I don't understand why they do the happy hour with dollar oysters on Mondays *and* Thursdays (5 p.m.–7 p.m.), but am thankful they do; it's downright kind.

Swan Oyster Depot (p. 123) About as authentic as you can get as far as seafood counters go. Too legit to quit since 1912. Aw shucks.

Zuni Café (p. 52)

There's always great oyster service here; it's my favorite in town, actually. A super-extensive list, and they're served at the perfect temperature with thinly sliced Acme bread. Oh yeah, and there are all kinds of nice liquidy things to pair with them.

Philly Cheesesteak

Phat Philly (p. 21) There are others places around the city that do good cheesesteaks, but for me it's all about the taste of the beef. After a few bites of the American Kobe they use here, others just can't compare. Amoroso bun, check. Pepper bar, thanks. And while you can be a traditionalist and order it "Whiz with," the house-made Newcastle Ale cheddar sauce gets my vote.

Pho

Beef pho at Bodega Bistro (p. 40)

No one's beef pho in town tastes like chef Jimmie Kwok's does: the broth has been simmering for hours, the filet is tenderized à la minute (which you can dip into the bowl of accompanying sriracha and hoisin), the rice noodles are perfection. Go for the *pho bodega dac biet*, which comes with the hand-cut rare filet, well-done brisket, and meatballs.

Beef pho at Pot de Pho $–$$ *3300 Geary Blvd. at Parker Ave., 415-668-0826, potdepho.com*

The rich and deep broth is made with American Wagyu bones and is full of the flavors of herbs and spices, with a definite note of star anise. I also like the thick texture of the handmade noodles, and the lightly pickled onions on the side. The nicer-than-usual interior makes it a good place to bring pho virgins.

Satay beef pho at Pho Phu Quoc (a.k.a. PPQ) $ *1816 Irving St. at 19th Ave., 415-661-8869, ppqsf.com*

When I'm not ordering the five-spice chicken with vermicelli and imperial rolls, I like the nasal-clearing spicy satay beef pho—perfect during July in SF.

A bowl of the Northern-style *pho ga* (chicken soup) here is one of the city's finest executions. Get ready to sweat as you start inhaling the wonderful broth, loaded with free-range chicken (I usually ask for dark meat) and silky handmade rice noodles. I can't even finish a large bowl. It will clear up any cold, help you recover from a rotten hangover, and will warm you up on a chilly day. Don't worry about the line of people; it moves fast.

TIP: A friend (and regular) also turned me on to the #6 with beef and braised leeks.

Honorable Mentions: Pho Tan Hoa (beef tendon; 431 Jones St., 415-673-3163), Tu Kim Café (609 Ellis St., 415-567-1685), Yummy Yummy (1015 Irving St. at 11th Ave., 415-566-4722)

Pizza (Deep Dish)

Little Star Pizza (p. 115) I'm a big fan of their cornmeal crust. It's worth the twenty-five minutes it takes to make it, let alone score a table. And it's one of my favorite things to warm up and eat the next day. Mmm, leftovers.

Pizza (Neapolitan/Thin Crust)

A16 (p. 58) The oven gets crankin' here, and I always hope for a ringside seat to watch them make the pies. For me, it's all about the simplicity of the Margherita, or a Romana, with bright tomato, the punch of garlic and olive oil, salty anchovies, black olives, and the final rat-a-tat of Calabrian chiles.

Gialina (p. 62) There is something about the unique crust here, with its big crispy lip and a certain tang and texture that conspire to one big meow for me. I find it hard to decide between the Atomica and Puttanesca—both pack some spice—but the seasonal toppings also rock.

Pizzeria Delfina (p. 66) Some days are better than others, but when it's on, I have had some transcendental pizzas here, like the Gricia, with onion, guanciale, and cream; and the Purgatorio, with spicy tomato sauce and egg. I also have an ongoing affair with the clam version—it's a spendy pizza, but one I keep paying for.

More Pizza Perfection: Arinell Pizza (509 Valencia St., 415-255-1303), flour + water (p. 61), Pizzetta 211 (p. 49), Tony's Pizza Napoletana (p. 96).

Pizza (Old School)

Gaspare's Pizza House & Italian Restaurant $$ *5546 Geary Blvd. at 19th Ave., 415-387-5025, gasparespizza.com*
This pizzeria saves me when Pizzetta 211 (p. 49) runs out of dough, or when the desire for a dinner over checkered tablecloths strikes. The quality of the toppings isn't *fantastico* (for example, the olives taste canned), but the crust is really good, and hey, sometimes you just want an old-school pizza. Props for the family-run history, Chianti bottles hanging from the ceiling, and the individual jukeboxes.

Tommaso's $$ *1042 Kearny St. at Pacific Ave., 415-398-9696, tommasosnorthbeach.com*
Having a pizza here makes me smile: there's a warm family atmosphere, they make an excellent crust, and damn, it's home to the city's oldest wood-fired pizza oven (much respect). The pizzas can be a bit overloaded with ingredients, so come hungry, and expect lots of kids in the early hours, too.

Tony's Pizza Napoletana (p. 96) Yes, the Margherita here is notable (and a world champion), but the one that flipped my rig and my wig was the tomato pie, a garlicky roasted tomato number with one of the tastiest crusts I've ever sunk my choppers into. The flat-top brick oven here really does magical things. This place may be new, but it's like Tony has been making pizza here for years.

Pupusas

My favorite import from El Salvador: imagine thick and fluffy patties handmade with corn masa stuffed with fillings like beans, cheese, or the traditional loroco flower and then griddled. (There is also a version made with rice flour.) Pupusas are traditionally served with a side of curtido, a spicy pickled coleslaw.

Balompie Cafe $ *3349 18th St. at Capp St., 415-648-9199; 3801 Mission St. at Richland Ave., 415-647-4000*
Sometimes you just want to kick back, drink a cold one, eat some cheap pupusas, and listen to sports in the background. Here's your spot. (This place is like being in El Salvador.) They have a rice-flour version, FYI, and the plantains are sick, *hombre*. Great combo plate specials as well, so go *loco*.

El Zocalo $ *3230 Mission St. at 29th St., 415-282-2572*
You'll hear the telltale *slap slap slap* of pupusa making as soon as you walk in. It's open crazy late (3 a.m.), and I love their chips. I usually get one with *loroco* flower, and another with pork and cheese, or bean and cheese. I also request a side of sour cream, and pile some *curtido* and Tapatio on top. Wash it all back with a Pacifico or a Regia from El Salvador. Yay.

The New Spot $ *632 20th St. at 3rd St., 415-558-0556*
I can't believe how good these pupusas are. *El primero*, in my opinion. So tender, and not heavy or greasy. The pupusa of the day can yield wonderful results. It's a bit of a trek to Dogpatch, but so destination-worthy. Minimum of two, you say? *No problema*.

Salad

Bar Crudo: Lobster Salad (p. 121) What. The. Hell. Who knew the combination of burrata cheese and lobster would prove to be so singularly fascinating? Holy cow. There are either tomatoes or beets in the mix; plus mâche, pistachio oil, and a Banyuls vinaigrette bring it all home.

Green Chile Kitchen: Heartland Taco Salad $$ (p. 93)
I don't know what it is about this salad. I think it reminds me of childhood or something. I eat it way too much. It comes with ground beef, pinto beans, cheddar cheese, fresh avocado, tomato, and their green chile buttermilk dressing—and the nice part is that it's all organic. I also crunch up some blue corn tortilla chips for extra texture. Chomp.

nopa: Little Gem Salad (p. 17) The creamy herb dressing has something like fifteen ingredients in it, and it haunts me. The perfectly crisp and cool little gems live up to their name, and the additional crunch from the bread crumbs makes it all sing. What song? I dunno, it's just really good.

South Park Cafe: Pig Salad $$ *108 South Park Ave. at Jack London Alley, 415-495-7275, southparkcafe.com*
The first time I tried this salad, I was like, whoa, where have you been all my life? You get a jumble of fresh greens perfectly coated with a tangy mustard dressing, plus slices of tart green apple, shallots, and glorious hunks of slow-cooked pork confit mixed in, almost like a French version of carnitas! Le oink.

See You in the Green Room: Blue Barn Gourmet (2105 Chestnut St., 415-441-3232), and of course the Caesar at Zuni Café (p. 52).

Perbacco (p. 102) There are a lot of people making salumi around town, perhaps too many, but no one consistently wows me the way chef Staffan Terje does. Some people have the Midas touch; well, he has the touch o' pork. It must be all those Sundays (his day off) that he spends making salumi—he's dedicated to delicious.

Sandwiches

I'm the daughter of a deli owner, so you know I love me some sandwiches.
I could write a book just on sandwiches, but that's for another day.
Here are a few of my faves (of which there are too many to count).

BAHN MI

Irving Cafe & Deli $ *2146 Irving St. at 23rd Ave., 415-681-2326*
There are incredible *bahn mi* (a "Saigon sub" on a French roll) to be found all over town, but I have a sweet spot for the ladies at this shop. The roll is nicely warmed up, the mystery meat quotient clocks in (pig ear, anyone? Hmm, what is in that pate?), and everything is sliced up just right. And for the paltry fee of $4, are you kidding?

Other Bahn Mi Favorites: Little Paris Coffee Shop (939 Stockton St., 415-982-6111), Sing Sing Sandwich Shop (309 Hyde St., 415-885-5159), Tu Kim Café (609 Ellis St., 415-567-1685), Wrap Delight (426 Larkin St., 415-771-3388). Why no Saigon Sandwiches on Larkin? That's a story for another day.

DELI

Arguello Super Market $ *782 Arguello Blvd. at Cabrillo St., 415-751-5121*
God damn, the turkey sandwich here is a thing of bird beauty: the juicy and well-seasoned meat is hand carved when you order it (request 50/50 for a dark and white combo!), and I recommend getting that bad boy on Dutch crunch with avocado. Gobble gobble.

Ike's Place $ *3506 16th St. at Sanchez St., 415-553-6888, ilikeikesplace.com*
Day-am, this sandwich shop turns it out. Mmmm, dirty sauce. I like Ike. I've never had a lame one here, and there are lots of veggie/vegan options (get the Meatless Mike meatball sub, for those of you who roll that way). Don't miss a peek at the binder,

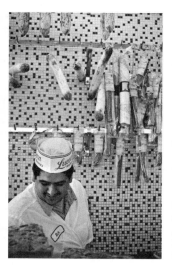

where you'll find more sandwiches than you ever imagined. There's also a long wait (usually—and on the weekends, it's sheer insanity), and limited seating (always), so have a plan B for where you're gonna scarf that mutha.

Morty's Delicatessan: Reuben (p. 21)
Ahhh, the Reuben. Now, this is what I'm talking about. Meaty, messy, and mine, all mine. Nom nom nom.

More Tasty Deli Sandwiches: Kitchenette
(958 Illinois St., kitchenettesf.com), La Spiaggia Delicatessen (1556 Stockton St., 415-362-3354), Lucca Ravioli Co. (1100 Valencia St., 415-647-5581), Moishe's Pippic (pastrami perfection; 425-A Hayes St., 415-431-2440), Molinari Delicatessen (373 Columbus Ave., 415-421-2337), Pal's Takeaway (in Tony's Market, 2751 24th St., 415-203-4911)

TORTA
....

La Torta Gorda $ *2833 24th St. at Bryant St., 415-642-9600*
This place is a one-way ticket to a fat ass. They serve a mother lode of mega-delicious meaty Mexican sandwiches. I'm a fan of the *tinga,* a flavorful stewed chicken with onion and chipotle, and the *pierna enchilada,* a pork-o-rama, both of which are tucked into a squishy roll and slathered with avo, refried beans, mayo, jalapeño, and cheese. It's ridonkadonk. As if that's not enough, wait until that puppy gets panino pressed. Don't even try to finish half; attempting to do so will have you hanging up your *cerrado* sign. (Maybe just order a small.) Oh, and it's a totally cute former diner; just wait until you see it. Plus there's a patio out back (shhh).

Another Fave for Tortas: Tortas Los Picudos (2969 24th St., 415-824-4199)

Steak

Bobo's $$$ *1450 Lombard St. at Franklin St., 415-441-8880, boboquivaris.com*
The décor kind of creeps me out (clowns, stripes, etc.), and I'm not much inspired by the other items on the menu (well, except the burrata). But my attention is usually rapt with the bone-in filet mignon steak they serve—and I don't even eat filet mignon

(I'm a rib eye or New York girl). It's juicy, beefy, and has a texture unlike any other. Plus, it comes with free valet, yo.

Harris' Restaurant (p. 18) Hey, if you're going to do a steak, this is your high church. They serve some of the best steaks I've ever eaten, in all of their guilt-inducing corn-fed glory. The Harris' Steak (a bone-in New York) and the porterhouse are dry aged, and even though the rib eye isn't aged, it's quite stellar. I also find the prime rib to be irresistible. The old-school steakhouse style is one-of-a-kind. Beeftastic.

House of Prime Rib $$$$ *1906 Van Ness Ave. at Washington St., 415-885-4605, houseofprimerib.net*
Beef headquarters, with huge slabs of prime beef served from stainless steel carts (you can actually request a second helping if you're not full), and spinning bowls of salad served tableside (chilled fork = classy). Total old fogey scene, but it's an integral part of the charm.

Lark Creek Steak (p. 11) This place grills up great steaks, and anyone who depends on different purveyors for different cuts definitely says something to me, like, "We know exactly what is going to taste good on your fork."

Sushi

Ino (p. 42) There are some things they do extremely well here, like serve up attitude. And excellent sushi (with too much wasabi, but it's still great).

sebo (p. 53) When people ask me where to get sushi, this is my one-word answer. The quality of the fish and the thoughtful preparations always impress me, and Danny and Michael really care about the sustainability of the fish they use. I wish I could eat here every week. Gotta get rich first.

More Sushi Samurais: Kappa (1700 Post St., 415-673-6004), Kiss Seafood (p. 33), and Zushi Puzzle (amazing live scallop, live uni, and live octopus; 1910 Lombard St., 415-931-9319).

El Tonayense Taco Trucks $ *Parked at Harrison St. at 14th St.; Harrison St. at 19th St.; Harrison St. at 22nd St.; Shotwell St. at 16th St.; 415-550-9192*
Look, when it's taco time, I head to the trucks. These guys always rock my preferred trio o' tacos: *al pastor,* carnitas, and *cabeza* (yeah, it means head, but you actually get tender cheek). Squirt some lime over the top of these onion- and salsa-studded beauties and your palate says *hola*. Oh, and did you see that health department score of 100? Sho' enough. Cheap eats at their finest.

La Taqueria (p. 140) Life is good when La Taqueria's off-the-menu *dorado* (crispy) tacos are in it.

La Palma Mexicatessan $ *2884 24th St. at Florida St., 415-647-1500*
I love everything they do here, from the handmade tortillas (look for "a mano") to the chicharrón tacos to the salsas to the carnitas to . . . you get the picture.

The Taco Shop at Underdog's Sports Bar & Grill $ *1824 Irving St. at 19th Ave., 415-566-8700, tacoshopsf.com*
What the heck is this delicious taco shop doing in the Outer Sunset? Fortunately Nick Fasanella, previously of Nick's Crispy Tacos, decided to move west into the fogbank. Order a taco "Nick's Way" (one soft; one hard; plus pinto beans, cheese, guac, and salsa) and you'll soon be back for more. Excellent battered "Baja" fish tacos. And all the ingredients are quality, *mang*.

Más Tacos: El Cachanilla (2948 21st St., 415-550-9410) Taco window. Fish taco. *Al pastor. Barbacoa, barbacoa*. Salsa bar. Cheap tacos. Tasty tacos.

SPECIFIC LOCATIONS

Sometimes you just want to know where to eat in a specific neighborhood around town. Here are a few picks (by no means exhaustive) for ya.

By Cuisine

CHINESE IN CHINATOWN

Bow Hon (great claypots; 850 Grant Ave., 415-362-0601), Bund Shanghai (640 Jackson St., 415-982-0618), Gourmet Delight (takeout; p. 142), Great Eastern (Peking duck; 649 Jackson St.. 415-986-2500), Hing Lung (congee; 674 Broadway, 415-398-8838), Jai Yun (p. 126), Lichee Garden (p. 71), R & G Lounge (deep-fried crab; 631 Kearny St., 415-982-7877), Utopia Café (clay pots and salt-and-pepper wings; 139 Waverly Pl., 415-956-2902), Yuet Lee (late night; 1300 Stockton St., 415-982-6020). (For dim sum, see p. 121.)

ITALIAN IN NORTH BEACH

Da Flora (p. 25), L'Osteria del Forno (519 Columbus Ave., 415-982-1124), North Beach Restaurant (love the cannelloni; 1512 Stockton St., 415-392-1700), Ristorante Ideale (p. 50), Tommaso's (p. 154).

JAPANESE IN JAPANTOWN

Ino (p. 42), Kappa (1700 Post St., 415-673-6004), Kiss Seafood (p. 33), Maki Restaurant (p. 68), Takara (22 Peace Plaza, Suite 202, 415-921-2000). (See also "Noodles/Ramen," p. 151.)

MEXICAN IN THE MISSION

El Farolito (p. 116), El Tonayense Taco Trucks (p. 159), La Palma Mexicatessan (p. 159),

La Taqueria (p. 140), Los Jarritos (p. 145), Los Rosales (birria; 301 S. Van Ness Ave., 415-552-2326), Mi Lindo Yucatan (401 Valencia St., 415-861-4935), Papalote (p. 145), Taqueria Can-cún (p. 116). (See also "Torta," p. 116.)

RUSSIAN IN THE RICHMOND

Katia's Russian Tea Room (p. 12)

SEAFOOD ON FISHERMAN'S WHARF

Scoma's (p. 139)—or just pick a stand, get some crab, find a bench, voilà.

By Location

CIVIC CENTER (JURY DUTY LUNCH)

Here's where to grab something delicious for lunch when you're fulfilling your civic duty.

Ananda Fuara (vegetarian; 1298 Market St., 415-621-1994), Bodega Bistro (Vietnamese; p. 40), Brenda's French Soul Food (p. 34), Burmese Kitchen (452 Larkin St., 415-474-5569), El Castillito (taqueria; 370 Golden Gate Ave., 415-292-7233), Gyro King (Middle Eastern; 25 Grove St., 415-621-8313), Lers Ros (Thai; p. 75), Thai House Express (901 Larkin St., 415-441-2248), Turtle Tower (pho; p. 153), Wrap Delight (*bahn mi;* 426 Larkin St., 415-771-3388)

TIP: The Wednesday Heart of the City Farmers' Market has all kinds of good options, from falafel to tamales.

GOLDEN GATE PARK

There are some good spots for dining in the park (Academy Café, Moss Room, p. 68), but here are a few places that are close enough to the park entrances so you can grab a bite before or after a bike ride in the park, or a trip to the de Young or The Academy of Sciences.

Art's Cafe (p. 141), Katia's Russian Tea Room (p. 12), Koo (408 Irving St., 415-731-7077), Magnolia (p. 30), Marnee Thai (1243 9th Ave., 415-731-9999), Namu (p. 65), Park Chow (1240 9th Ave., 415-665-9912), The Richmond (615 Balboa St., 415-379-8988), Zazie (p. 35)

HAYES VALLEY

Where to eat before or after a performance at the symphony, opera, or ballet.

Absinthe (p. 7), Bar Jules (p. 31), Bistro Clovis (1596 Market St., 415-864-0231), CAV Wine Bar & Kitchen (p. 14), Citizen Cake (p. 86), Hayes Street Grill (p. 62), Jardinière (p. 13)/J Lounge (p. 15), sebo (p. 53), Suppenküche (p. 72), Zuni Café (p. 52)

MOSCONE CONVENTION CENTER

Good options for chow within a few blocks from the convention floor.

54 Mint (p. 61), Ame (p. 88), Anchor & Hope (p. 94), Chez Papa Resto (4 Mint Plaza, 415-546-4134), COCO500 (p. 90), Fifth Floor (p. 101), Fringale (570 4th St., 415-543-0573), Lark Creek Steak (p. 11), Le Charm French Bistro (315 5th St., 415-546-6128), Luce (888 Howard St., 415-616-6566), LuLu (816 Folsom St., 415-495-5775), Oola (p. 55), Orson (p. 15), Out the Door (865 Market St., Westfield San Francisco Centre, 415-541-9913), Salt House (545 Mission St., 415-543-8900), Samovar Tea Lounge (p. 8), XYZ (181 3rd St., 415-817-7836), Zaré at Fly Trap (p. 112)

THEATER DISTRICT

Off to see a show? Here's where to eat within walking distance.

Canteen (p. 67), Colibrí Mexican Bistro (438 Geary St., 415-440-2737), farmerbrown (p. 64), Fish & Farm (339 Taylor St., 415-474-3474), Grand Cafe (501 Geary St., 415-292-0101), Heaven's Dog (p. 74), Masa's (p. 136), Scala's Bistro (open late; p. 92)

THEATER DISTRICT: ON THE CHEAP

Hope you don't mind smelling smoky.

Lahore Karahi (p. 41), Shalimar (532 Jones St., 415-928-0333), Sultan (340 O'Farrell St., 415-775-1709)—or hot dogs at Showdogs (p. 150).

ONE-, TWO-, AND THREE-DAY ITINERARIES

Is your favorite part of planning a trip deciding where you're going to eat? Here are three itineraries for you in San Francisco, totally based on pleasing your taste buds, and whether you planned ahead or are visiting at the last minute. (Since it doesn't really matter whether you plan breakfast ahead, it's treated separately.) Try to have lunch on the early side and dinner later so you have time to digest and get hungry again. As for your stomach, well, you better pack your Tums.

One Day in San Francisco

So you have only twenty-four hours? And it's your first time here? You've got your work cut out for you. Let's eat.

BREAKFAST

Grab a coffee from **Blue Bottle Coffee Co.** (act like an insider and ask for a Gibraltar, see p. 147–148) at the Ferry Building Marketplace, then walk over to **Boulettes Larder** (p. 123) to start the day with perfect poached eggs or house-made yogurt *(lebne)* with rose petal jam. Bonus: there's a view of the water. Or you could go to the Mission for an expertly drawn espresso or cappuccino at the industrial-cool **Four Barrel Coffee** (p. 148) and a donut from their stash of **Dynamo** donuts (p. 140), like the chocolate spice. Or get the city's best croissant (or a morning bun) at **Tartine Bakery** (p. 131) and try to snag a ringside seat at one of San Francisco's most popular bakeries. If it's the weekend, run, don't walk, to **Canteen** (p. 67) for brunch.

It's not like it needs more customers, but **Slanted Door** (p. 98) at lunch is quite a special Vietnamese feast (I'm a fan of the daikon rice cakes, shaking beef, and pho). And, since the view is marvy, daytime is really the time to hit it. On a budget? **Bodega Bistro** (p. 40) is your answer for excellent and affordable Vietnamese. I also recommend **Zuni Café** (p. 52) for a true California lunch. The light is lovely, and so are their pizzas and the famed Tuscan chicken for two. Neapolitan-inspired **A16** (p. 58) serves lunch Wednesdays through Sundays, so that's another way to visit this popular restaurant; the burrata and pizzas will conspire to deliver you *pranzo* perfection. You want seafood and a view, don't you? Okay: **Scoma's** (p. 139) is an unexpectedly delicious old-school seafood restaurant in the middle of touristy Fisherman's Wharf, with super-fresh seafood like calamari and the "lazy man's cioppino." Or there's the less-retro **Waterbar** (p. 105). You get a stunning view of the water, tasty seafood (quite the memorable presentation of fish-and-chips), and you can stroll along the waterfront when you're done. Or there's the Peruvian **La Mar** (p. 134), another location with fresh seafood and a view (also on The Embarcadero).

LAST-MINUTE LUNCH

You should get yourself on down to the **Ferry Building Marketplace** (at The Embarcadero and Market St.), where you can taste exquisite local oysters at **Hog Island Oyster Co.** (p. 151). Get the grilled cheese sandwich, a decadent way to enjoy Acme bread and cheese from Cowgirl Creamery all at once (plus there's a great view). If you have kids in tow, a cheeseburger and a milkshake at **Taylor's Automatic Refresher** (p. 144) is a good call. **Cane Rosso** (1 Ferry Bldg., 415-391-7599) is HQ for delicious rotisserie meats, like a savory *porchetta* (slow-roasted pork) sandwich, and a smashing egg salad. You could also have a Euro-gourmand lunch at **Boulettes Larder** (p. 123), which strikes the right balance of being fit for a culinary aesthete but still manages to feel casual and homey. Here's an idea: pack your own picnic lunch of sourdough bread from **Acme**, cheese from **Cowgirl Creamery**, salumi from **Boccalone**, and sit yourself down at the **Ferry Plaza Wine Merchant** for a glass of California wine, or sit out back at the tables outside and enjoy the view of the water (but no wine is allowed with this option). Be aware the Ferry Plaza Farmers' Market is on Saturdays, making the place a total zoo—but it's worth navigating the crowds. There is also an outdoor Thursday market at lunch, full of artisan street food vendors, from tacos to sandwiches.

If you really want to experience seasonal San Francisco produce at its prime, book a table at Cal-Moroccan **Aziza** (p. 79). It's a little off the beaten path, but your meal will be worth any cab ride you had to endure to get there. If you want refined California fare with a view to match, hopefully you will have planned far enough in advance to get a table at **Boulevard** (p. 80). If you didn't make it for lunch, **Zuni Café** (p. 52) is another California classic—and the urban crowd offers great people watching. A cocktail and high-end American dinner at **BIX** (p. 20) will ensure your evening is a swank one. (I never tire of the supperclub atmosphere there.) And if you want to do an avant-garde tasting menu highlighting some of the area's finest ingredients, the intimate and modern-elegant **Coi** (p. 135) is the way to go.

LAST-MINUTE DINNER

Let's begin your evening with a cocktail—get one of the city's best at **Beretta** (p. 4) in the Mission—and then walk on over for a casual thin-crust pizza dinner at **Pizzeria Delfina** (p. 66). You might even be able to dine at the bar or counter overlooking the dining room at the Cal-Ital **Delfina** (p. 137)—ask if there's an open spot. Finish the evening with salted caramel ice cream (if you have room, try it in a half-size banana split) from **Bi-Rite Creamery** (p. 142) across the street. Since you're without reservations, you could also try to score a coveted seat at the counter overlooking the kitchen at **Boulevard** (p. 80) or **A16** (p. 58); the bar at **Spruce** (p. 100) is luxe (like the hamburger and boudin blanc). If you're a sushi fanatic, go to the inimitable **sebo** (p. 53) and pray that you snag a seat at their intimate counter for an *omakase* (chef's choice) experience (the doors open at 6 p.m.). Even if you end up at one of the regular tables, it'll still be a spectacular meal.

COCKTAIL

My first choice for a well-crafted cocktail is **The Alembic** (p. 16) in the Haight—and since the kitchen is open until 1 a.m., you can enjoy a delicious midnight snack if you're up late and peckish. You can also get a nightcap at the "speakeasy" **Bourbon & Branch** (p. 56); just be aware the neighborhood is a bit gritty. When you ring the buzzer, say "books" for access to their back room with open seating (but it's always worth inquiring if there are any seats available at the main bar or in a booth). Their sister bar, **Rickhouse** (p. 211), is a less-sketchy location, but can be really busy. **Absinthe** (p. 7) in Hayes Valley is a fave for top-shelf cocktails (wait until you see the list of boozy options), with an always-busy bar. The **J Lounge at Jardinière** (p. 15) across the street is a sexy cocktail spot, and a memorable way to end the night.

Two Days in San Francisco

So now you're ready to advance to day two: deeper San Francisco.

BREAKFAST

Want to explore more of San Francisco's delicious coffee? Start with one at cult Mission coffeehouse **Ritual Coffee** (1026 Valencia St., 415-641-1024), or go to the chic **Blue Bottle Coffee Co.** café (p. 147) on Mint Plaza for waffles or their version of toad in the hole ("Popeyes"), and quite the coffee experience (wait until you see the Japanese siphon bar). If you're staying downtown, **farm:table** (754 Post St., 415-292-7089) is tiny but full of neighborhood charm, with excellent coffee and treats for breakfast, like fruit bread pudding. Are you a tea drinker? Check out **Samovar Tea Lounge** (p. 8)—it handily has a couple of locations, depending on where you're staying. If you're up for a hearty breakfast, I am a sucker for **Brenda's French Soul Food** (p. 34). But you better plan on a light lunch, if you even get hungry for it at all—this is the kind of breakfast that will stay with you all day (blame it on the savory beignets and superlative biscuits). For the record, yes, I love **Dottie's True Blue Café** (p. 110), but you have limited time in San Francisco, and the lines there will take all day. If you're going to Golden Gate Park, breakfast on the garden patio at the quaint **Zazie** (p. 35) in Cole Valley is a *très jolie* launch pad. If you need to walk some of those calories off, visit the **Warming Hut** (Marine Dr. at Long Ave., 415-561-3040) for coffee and breakfast after your stroll along the Golden Gate Promenade. If you plan on going to SFMOMA, be aware there is a **Blue Bottle** coffee bar on the rooftop (p. 28).

PLANNED-AHEAD LUNCH

Adore dim sum? There are many places in SF (see my favorites on page 147), but it's worth going to the easy-to-reach **Yank Sing** (p. 97) at Rincon Center to be able to chomp on their excellent *xiao long bao* (Shanghai soup dumplings). **Perbacco** (p. 102) is a spiff spot to take in the Financial District scene over delicious house-made salumi, Piemontese pastas, and anything with pork. **Rose's Café** (p. 10) in Cow Hollow has a fun ladies-who-lunch vibe and plenty of nearby boutiques to complete the picture (or there's **Café Claude** [p. 31], near Union Square).

LAST-MINUTE LUNCH

If it's a Friday, lunch at the diminutive **Canteen** (p. 67) is an under-the-tourist-radar treasure. Since **Tadich Grill** (p. 101) doesn't take reservations, you can try to snag a seat at the counter of San Francisco's oldest restaurant for a classic seafood lunch of sand dabs and a martini served by white-jacketed old-school waiters. Another fun one for seafood is the family-run **Swan Oyster Depot** (p. 123); go early, like at 11 a.m., or very late, around 2 p.m., because there are only eighteen seats for chowdah, oysters, crab cocktail, and smoked trout (cash only). Are you sightseeing (er, hippie hunting?) around the Haight? You'll find a good lunch at **Magnolia** (p. 30). Love pizza? Head to either of the **Pizzeria Delfina** (p. 66) locations for a stellar thin-crust pie.

PLANNED-AHEAD DINNER

Town Hall (p. 103) always has an energetic and welcoming feeling, the bar does a killer Sazerac, and the American-Southern menu has one of my guiltiest indulgences: Faith's Cheese Toast (poached egg, ham, and jalapeño cream). The Basque restaurant **Piperade** (p. 87) is a local favorite: chef Hirigoyen's dishes are so flavorful, and the atmosphere is comfortably elegant. I also love the warm interior of **Kokkari** (p. 103), with a menu of refined yet rustic Greek cuisine that always has me clearing my plate (it's also nice for lunch). Enjoy a view of the water and a steak at **EPIC Roasthouse** (p. 91) or seafood at **Waterbar** (p. 105). If you want to go high end, head to the Franco-Japanese **Dining Room at the Ritz-Carlton** (p. 38), the Frenchie-French **La Folie** (p. 38), or New American **Gary Danko** (p. 37).

LAST-MINUTE DINNER

You can probably snag a seat at the counter at **Farina** (p. 127) in the Mission, where you can order one of my must-try San Francisco dishes: the *mandilli al pesto* (handmade handkerchief pasta napped in a best-in-class pesto that will make you think you're in Genova). Another one of my favorite SF dishes is "Lissa's staff meal" (cuttlefish "noodles," salmon eggs, vegetables, sea urchin, a quail egg, and wasabi) at the elegant Franco-Japanese **Ame** (p. 88). (There's also a sushi bar where you might be able to land a couple seats if the dining room is all booked.) **R & G Lounge** (631 Kearny St., 415-982-7877) is a good pick for those craving a Cantonese/Chinatown experience—the salt-and-pepper crab, Peking duck, and geoduck clam should definitely be on your table. (Try to score a table upstairs if you want a nicer vibe. The downstairs is more low-end, but it's also where the locals hang out.) It's a bit of a trek, but I adore the Korean-Japanese fare from **Namu** (p. 65)—cool vibe, and the kind of food I just crave. More hip dining: Californian restaurant **Range** (p. 59) in the Mission has a fantastic bar to hang out at while waiting for your table, and the chic **Bar Tartine** (p. 33) is another Cali-Mission outpost. And if you want fancy, there's the bar at **Gary Danko** (p. 37), where walk-ins can often find success.

COCKTAIL

Okay, let's forget craft cocktails for a second. It's time for a San Francisco view at its finest: it comes with a martini at the **Top of the Mark** (p. 212); even if it's not the best cocktail, it'll be a spectacular view. The quirky **Grandviews** (345 Stockton St., 36th Floor, 415-398-1234) at the Grand Hyatt is another option, although it definitely has a 1970s vibe. The **Empress of China** (838 Grant Ave., 415-434-1345) in Chinatown is also stuck in a 1970s time warp (very *Blade Runner*). It has a dingy, er, shabby lounge with an awesome view, but only come for a drink (the tourists losing money on dinner there obviously don't have this book).

Three Days in San Francisco

Okay, day three means you're ready to start acting like a local. Here are places where you can eat accordingly.

BREAKFAST

Hopefully, one of your days in the city is a Saturday, because you need to head to the **Ferry Plaza Farmers' Market** (101 The Embarcadero, ferrybuildingmarketplace.com) and witness the madness. Wake up with a Gibraltar (p. 148) from **Blue Bottle Coffee Co.** and then get in line for breakfast at the **Primavera** (p. 148) stand (you've never had chilaquiles like these—killer tamales, too), or something from the **Hayes Street Grill** or **Rose Pistola** stands. Afterward, you'll have to join the other hungry market shoppers trying to find a spot to sit down outside. Chilaquiles or huevos rancheros and an agua fresca from **Mijita** (1 Ferry Bldg., 415-399-0814) are also delish, and you can sit at a table there. Or there's the ingredient-driven **Cane Rosso** (1 Ferry Bldg., 415-391-7599), which has a decadent egg sandwich with pancetta in the morning. Be sure to try some fruit samples from the market vendors, and finish the morning with a container of **Saint Benoît** honey yogurt that you can buy at their stand. Another location for breakfast is the stylish (but welcoming) **Mission Beach Café** (p. 125), also open for weekend brunch. Soufflé pancakes, brioche French toast, house-made English muffins, and the huevos with beans are all winners. You'll find some of the very best baked goods in the city, including a spectacular cannelé (a little cake that hails from Bordeaux) and cream pies (it's okay, you can have banana cream pie for breakfast). **Bar Tartine** (p. 33) and **Foreign Cinema** (p. 32) are other popular weekend brunch spots in the sunny Mission, and for good reason—the food and atmosphere of both are totally unique. Or go hunt down some chilaquiles in the Mission (see p. 145 for more on those).

Piccino

Craving some captivating flavors? **Dosa** (Fillmore; p. 4) offers a memorable lunch—I'm obsessed with the *pani puri* (bite-size puffs that you fill with potato, chickpeas, spicy tamarind-mint water, and mung beans, and pop into your mouth). Or if you have time for a leisurely lunch, go for a fresh Cal-Italian meal sitting outside the charming **Piccino** (p. 52), a much-adored local destination (and do not pass up a coffee from their café next door). But to get there, you'll probably need a car, or have the time to figure out how to catch the 3rd Street rail to get out to Dogpatch (it's a bit of a schlep, but worth it, which is why I am mentioning it). Lunch at the posh **Rotunda** (p. 10) in Neiman Marcus overlooking Union Square is quite breathtaking—and so are their popovers and the lobster club.

LAST-MINUTE LUNCH

COCO500 (p. 90) is a cute little corner spot in SoMa, featuring seasonal and fresh Cali ingredients—you'll feel like you're part of the working class on their lunch break—but ha, you're on vacation. Hit the Mission for a burrito (see p. 145 for my faves) or tacos (p. 159). If you want something cuter than a taqueria, **Nopalito** (p. 130) is a casual place, serving Mexican fare made with choice ingredients, from a soul-satisfying pozole to my favorite carnitas. For a million-dollar view but inexpensive burger and a beer, head to the divey **Red's Java House** (p. 212). Chilly? Warm up with a bowl of superlative pho at **Bodega Bistro** (p. 40) or **Turtle Tower** (p. 153)—also divey spots, FYI.

PLANNED-AHEAD DINNER

Taste some of the city's most refined pastas at the chic and atmospheric **Quince** (p. 137)—and experience some of the finest service. If you want something a little more down home, **Da Flora** (p. 25) in North Beach is quaint and romantic, and feels like an insider's secret. **Frascati** (1901 Hyde St., 415-928-1406) is another Italian restaurant with charming San Francisco ambience; I also adore the cozy, welcoming, and unpretentious **La Ciccia** (p. 138). Or there's the quirky **Canteen** (p. 67)—you won't believe how good the food is considering it just looks like an updated diner. Cal-Med **Foreign Cinema** (p. 32) overdelivers on dramatic atmosphere (it plays movies on the back wall of the outdoor patio), and the pork chop is a champ. Are you a wino? Then head to the sleek **RN74** (p. 128) in SoMa; the wine list is so good you'll match your food to your wines instead of the other way around.

Over in the Western Addition/Nopa neighborhood, hope you get lucky and nab a spot at the raw bar at **Bar Crudo** (p. 121) for fantastic seafood in unique presentations and pairings (love the uni and avocado on toast), or head down the street to **nopa** (p. 17) for hyper-seasonal food and faboo cocktails (note: both of these places are a bit hip and fairly raucous). The long counters at **Heaven's Dog** (Chinese; p. 74) and **Laïola** (Cal-Spanish; p. 30) make them good for walk-ins (and cocktails!) For more California fare, the industrial-chic **Universal Cafe** (p. 26) is a charmer on the outskirts of the Mission (the casual **Slow Club** [p. 30] is also out there: it always has seats reserved for walk-ins, and there's a bar in the back). Flying solo? The Hayes Valley German restaurant **Suppenküche** (p. 72) is social, rustic, and fun (*ja*, there's a lot of beer). **Contigo** (p. 49) is all about Spanish dishes made with love (and seasonal ingredients), and since they don't take reservations, you can walk in and wait like everyone else—it's hard not to fall in love with this place.

COCKTAIL

Foggy nights call for a boozy "house cappuccino" (which is steamed milk, brandy, and chocolate) at the fabulously retro **Tosca Cafe** (p. 56) in North Beach. Or act like a local and get a White Nun (Kahlua, brandy, and steamed milk), which was reportedly Carol Doda's (the world's first entertainer to perform topless at the neighboring Condor Club) drink of choice. Here you can play Puccini on the opera-heavy jukebox. Maybe Francis Ford Coppola or Sean Penn will swing by (it happens). Or not. It's still swell. Just around the corner, there is the hidden-away bar, **15 Romolo** (p. 209), which shakes and stirs some remarkable concoctions. For more classic atmosphere, I think a cocktail at the **Pied Piper Bar** (p. 210) at the Palace Hotel is another must-do so you can admire the Maxfield Parrish mural, or a cocktail made by Ty at the lounge in the **Big 4** (p. 89) at the top of Nob Hill is a San Francisco treat I will never tire of.

THE 510:

TWENTY-FIVE THINGS WORTH THE DRIVE ACROSS THE BAY BRIDGE

I'm the first to admit I have issues with crossing the bridge. The trip is usually plagued with a nightmare traffic jam, or if I take BART, it's a pain to even get to a station. But for the twenty-five things I've listed below, I won't even think twice about how to get to the 510—just how quickly I can get these items on my fork.

Cornmeal waffle at Brown Sugar Kitchen $–$$
Be sure to upgrade to the apple cider maple syrup, and get fried chicken on the side.
2534 Mandela Pkwy. at 26th St., Oakland, 510-839-7685, brownsugarkitchen.com

California breakfast and soufflé pancakes at the counter at Bette's Oceanview Diner $
1807 4th St. at Hearst Ave., Berkeley, 510-644-3230, bettesdiner.com

Café au lait and Irish oatmeal with maple syrup at Café Fanny $
(Followed by a visit to neighbors **Kermit Lynch** and **Acme Bread Company,** natch.) The oatmeal is only available until 10:30 a.m., and often sells out before then. When that happens, get the poached eggs on toast.
1603 San Pablo Ave. at Cedar St., Berkeley, 510-524-5447, cafefanny.com

Breakfast pizza (topped with farm eggs and pancetta) at Oliveto Café $$
(Plus the special dinners upstairs at Oliveto, like the Tomato Dinners, Truffle Dinners, the Whole Hog Dinners, and Oceanic Dinners.)
5655 College Ave. at Shafter Ave., Oakland, 510-547-5356, oliveto.com

Fried chicken sandwich and lemon ice from Bakesale Betty $
(The brisket and egg salad are also tasty.)
5098 Telegraph Ave. at 51st St., 510-985-1213, bakesalebetty.com

A deli sandwich (and shopping for Italian groceries) at Genova Delicatessen $

Call your sandwich order in if you're in a rush—the line can be *pazzo*.
5095 Telegraph Ave. at 51st St., Oakland, 510-652-7401

Lunch at Wood Tavern $$–$$$

I heart the crispy pork belly, hot pastrami sandwich, juicy burger, and delicious fries.
6317 College Ave. at 63rd St., Oakland, 510-654-6607, woodtavern.net

A huarache and weekend barbacoa (lamb) at El Huarache Azteca $–$$

3842 International Blvd. at 39th Ave., Oakland, 510-533-2395

Pizza of the day at The Cheeseboard Pizza Collective $

Oh yeah, and some cheese. Duh.
1512 Shattuck Ave. at Vine St., Berkeley, 510-549-3055, cheeseboardcollective.coop

A three-way plate of links, ribs, and brisket from Everett and Jones Barbeque $$

With medium sauce (plus hot sauce on the side, beans, and a Coke).
*Various locations (I prefer the one with outside tables at 1955 San Pablo Ave.),
EandJBBQ.com*

A macrobiotic (and incredibly affordable) lunch or dinner at Manzanita $–$$

Super-filling, too. *4001 Linden St. at 40th St., Oakland, 510-985-8386,
manzanitarestaurant.com*

Carb-fest at dopo $$

Arancini, pasta (lasagne), and pizza!
4293 Piedmont Ave. at Echo Ave., Oakland, 510-652-3676

The lamb sandwich for Friday-only lunch at Zatar $$

Request feta on it. *1981 Shattuck Ave. at University Ave., Berkeley, 510-841-1981,
zatarrestaurant.com*

The long-ass list of house-made salumi and Italian wines at Adesso $$

(But let the meats sit for five minutes—they're served too cold.) They also have
a generous happy hour/"aperitivo"—actually, two: one in the early evening, and
another around 10:30 p.m.—call for details.
4395 Piedmont Ave. at Pleasant Valley Ave., Oakland, 510-601-0305

A wood-fired pizza at Pizzaiolo $$

(Yup, it's my favorite pizza in the Bay Area.)
5008 Telegraph Ave. at 51st St., Oakland, 510-652-4888, pizzaiolooakland.com

A handcrafted cocktail at Flora $–$$

Oh, how to choose just one?
1900 Telegraph Ave. at 19th St., Oakland, 510-286-0100, floraoakland.com

Peking duck and the "I can't stop my fork from scooping this up" double-skin dish at Great China Restaurant $–$$$

The crab with house-made buns is also delicious, and decadent.
2115 Kittredge St. at Shattuck Ave., Berkeley, 510-843-7996, greatchinaberkeley.com

Weekend *chaat* (savory Indian street snacks) at Vik's Chaat Corner $–$$

2390 4th St. at Channing Way, Berkeley, 510-644-4432, vikschaatcorner.com

A feast of a dinner at Ohgane Korean Restaurant $$–$$$

3915 Broadway at 38th St., Oakland, 510-594-8300, ohgane.com

Dinner at Chez Panisse Café $$$

(Including a bottle of Domaine Tempier Bandol Rosé, but of course, and seasonal fruit for dessert.)
1517 Shattuck Ave. at Cedar St., Berkeley, 510-548-5049, chezpanisse.com

Dinner at the counter at Commis $$$$

3859 Piedmont Ave. at Montell St., Oakland, 510-653-3902, commisrestaurant.com

Potato showdown: is it the puffs at Grégoire, or the patatas bravas at Barlata or César? All of 'em!

Grégoire $: *4001 B Piedmont Ave. at Glen Ave., Oakland, 510-547-3444; 2109 Cedar St. at Shattuck Ave., Berkeley, 510-883-1893, gregoirerestaurant.com*
Barlata $$: *4901 Telegraph Ave. at 49th St., Oakland, 510-450-0678, barlata.com*
César $$: *4039 Piedmont Ave. at Glen Ave., Oakland, 510-985-1202; 1515 Shattuck Ave. at Vine St., Berkeley, 510-883-0222, barcesar.com*

Meyer lemon ice cream and gingerbread sandwich at Ici $

2948 College Ave. at Ashby Ave., Berkeley, 510-665-6054, ici-icecream.com

A black and tan at Fentons Creamery & Restaurant $

A perfect sundae: creamy toasted almond and vanilla ice cream, caramel, chocolate fudge, whipped cream, almonds, and a cherry on top.
4226 Piedmont Ave. at Entrada Ave., Oakland, 510-658-7000, fentonscreamery.com

A trio of the remarkable gelato from Almare Gelato Italiano $

(The caffè and gianduia flavors are particularly notable.)
2170 Shattuck Ave. at Allston Way, Berkeley, 510-649-1888, almaregelato.com

THERE'S GOLD IN THEM THERE SUBURBS:

FIFTEEN GEMS IN THE 650 (AND 408)

Whether you live south of the 415, work there, have a meeting there, or perhaps need a place to meet up with your Peninsula-dwelling friends, here are fifteen places I'd totally drive to from San Francisco. And yes, some are totally destination-worthy just for the sake of an amazing meal, or even the perfect deli sandwich. Note: I didn't take on San Jose or Mountain View. I could write a separate book on those cities' ethnic eats alone.

BELMONT

Divino $$–$$$ *968 Ralston Ave. at 6th Ave., 650-620-9102, divinobelmont.com*
Chef-owner Vincenzo Cucco's little Italian *ristorante* is tucked away in a nondescript area of Belmont, but is worth the quest. His *mamma's* meatballs are on the menu, plus homemade pastas, like tender gnocchi and ravioli. And just like the good Sicilian he is, his *cannoli* are tops.

DALY CITY/MILLBRAE

The Kitchen $$ *279 El Camino Real at La Cruz Ave., 650-692-9688*
I was brought here for dim sum and had already started plotting my return after the first few dumplings. Such sweet shrimp in the *har gow* and rice noodle roll, plus delectable chicken feet (if you're into that kind of thing), not to mention one of the best baked barbecue pork buns I've ever chomped. There are definitely some more outré dishes available (like snails!), and you'll still only spend $25 a head if you try really hard. Finish with the coconut custard bun. Accommodating and attentive staff.

TIP: If you have time to kill at the SFO airport, hop in a cab and come here!

Hong Kong Flower Lounge (dim sum; 51 Millbrae Ave., Millbrae,
650-692-6666), Koi Palace (Cantonese seafood and dim sum; 365 Gellert Blvd., Daly
City, 650-992-9000)

HALF MOON BAY AREA

Mezzaluna $$–$$$ *459 Prospect Way at Capistrano Rd., Princeton by the Sea,*
650-728-8108, mezzalunabythesea.com
I get extra-special treatment at this cozy Italian restaurant because they're close
family friends (hey, it's the Calabrese connection), but here are the dishes to order:
the prosciutto, fried calamari (one of the few places I order it), baccalà croquettes,
and tender gnocchi . . . and wait until you try the house-made bread—you're gonna
snarf a loaf of it. The seafood is freshly caught, so I often go with specials for my main
course, and I like to get a pizza at the bar after a day at the beach. Friendly staff, too.

OTHER IDEAS: Cetrella (upscale Med; 845 Main St., 650-726-4090), Navio (brunch
and a view; Ritz-Carlton Half Moon Bay, 1 Miramontes Point Rd., 650-712-7000), Pasta
Moon (incredible lasagne; 315 Main St., #C, 650-726-5125), Sam's Chowder House (love
the lobster roll; 4210 N. Cabrillo Hwy., 650-712-0245)

LOS ALTOS

Sumika $$ *236 Central Plaza at 3rd St., 650-917-1822, sumikagrill.com*
I can't believe what a gem this place is; it's a *kushiyaki* joint (which means meat
and vegetables are grilled on skewers over charcoal) that's hidden off a parking lot
(so random). You can order organic chicken thighs on skewers, but the tastier ones
include chicken skin, fatty pork, and other meaty parts. Lunch means *oyako-don*
(chicken and barely cooked egg over rice—so homey). Charming all-Japanese staff,
pleasant décor, and jazz music over the speakers, awww.

OTHER IDEAS: Zitune (modern Moroccan; 325 Main St., 650-947-0247)

LOS GATOS

Dio Deka $$$–$$$$ *210 E. Main St. at Jackson St., 408-354-7700, diodeka.com*
This upscale Greek restaurant tucked away in the Hotel Los Gatos has a warm and
well-appointed atmosphere (ditto on the well-off crowd), a gracious staff, and plenty
of wines to choose from. The cuisine is modern Greek fare, with some unique dishes,
like *loukaniko*, a pork and orange peel sausage, or the *taramas* spread made with
lobster. I can't imagine how many lamb chops they blow through in a week here.
Absolutely do not pass up the Greek yogurt for dessert.

Manresa $$$$ *320 Village Lane at Almendra Ave., 408-354-4330, manresarestaurant.com*

One bite of David Kinch's "Into the Vegetable Garden" dish stopped me in my tracks. The produce (much of it from the restaurant's biodynamic garden) is some of the finest you'll taste—the pinnacle of fresh and seasonal—and all the ingredients are shown great respect. A variety of tasting menus are available, showcasing Kinch's decidedly European style. The comfortable room (with Oriental rugs) is pleasantly devoid of pretension. Worth every mile to get here.

MENLO PARK

Kaygetsu $$$$ *325 Sharon Park Dr. at Monte Rosa Dr., 650-234-1084, kaygetsu.com*
I know, another amazing restaurant hidden away in a strip mall. The refined *kaiseki* menu here is quite the stellar tasting experience, with contemporary presentations and exquisite flavors; the seasonal menu changes monthly. The room is understated and elegant, a calm setting for a memorable three-hour taste journey. Swoon.

OTHER IDEAS: The Dutch Goose (burgers and beer; 3567 Alameda de las Pulgas, 650-854-3245)

PALO ALTO

Evvia Estiatorio $$–$$$ *420 Emerson St. at University Ave., 650-326-0983, evvia.net*
It's pretty much Kokkari (p. 103) South, but smaller, and with a super-petite bar in the back. Delicious Greek food, from the fried smelts to decadent moussaka to lamb chops that will convert the most dedicated lamb hater with one tender bite. The upscale environment is well-suited for the Shallow Alto crowd, whether it's business or a midweek date or dinner with the parents (though the tables are close and it can get noisy, FYI).

Tootsie's $$ *Stanford Barn, 700 Welch Rd. at Quarry Rd., 650-566-8445, tootsiesbarn.com*
Hmmm, I'm not crazy in love with the name, but the impressive salads and sandwiches at this Italian café in the Stanford Barn are crazy delicious. The breads like focaccia and rarely seen *tigelle* (a small and thin flatbread from Modena) are homemade, and wait until you try the potato chips. Heavier items include the fried chicken sandwich with endive slaw, and a rich veal and pork burger with caramelized onions that sometimes sells out (it's major). There's also breakfast with pancakes, an egg panino, and frittata, all to be enjoyed on the outdoor terrace overlooking a field of lavender.

OTHER IDEAS: Junnoon (contemporary Indian; 150 University Ave., 650-329-9644), Madera (VC lunch, nice bar; 2825 Sand Hill Rd., 650-561-1540); Mayfield Bakery & Café (Cali breakfast, lunch, or dinner; Town & Country Village, 855 El Camino Real,

(spendy Italian; Four Seasons, 2050 University Ave., 650-566-1200), Tamarine (upscale
Vietnamese, don't miss the shrimp cupcakes; 546 University Ave., 650-325-8500)

REDWOOD CITY

Woodside Delicatessen $ *1453 Woodside Rd. at Rutherford Ave.,*
650-369-4235, woodsidedeli.net

I've been eating Woodside Deli sandwiches for years, and I mean years. I get mad
hankerings for the Godfather sandwich, the best damned deli sandwich ever. EVER!
It's a sourdough roll dressed with olive oil, vinegar, and oregano and stuffed with
Toscano salame, coppa, prosciutto, mortadella, lettuce, onions, artichoke hearts,
pepperoncini, and provolone. Hold. The. Phone.

OTHER IDEAS: Donato Enoteca (Italian; 1041 Middlefield Rd., 650-701-1000), Old
Port Lobster Shack (lobster rolls; 851 Veterans Blvd., 650-366-2400, oplobster.com)

SAN MATEO

Romolo's Cannoli & Spumoni Factory $ *81 W. 37th Ave. at Colegrove St.,*
650-574-0625, romolosfactory.com

Who knows how to make better cannoli than a Sicilian? Exactly. I've been coming
here since I was a tyke. Great old-school atmosphere with red-and-white-checkered
floors. You get crisp cannoli shells with a rich ricotta filling, and they're made to order.
(There's also an ice cream cannolo, which is tasty, but I'm a purist.) Good spumoni, too.
Total family joint (since 1968!). They take a long vacation in the summer, so call first.

Santa Ramen $–$$ *1944 S. El Camino Real at W. 20th Ave., 650-344-5918*
One of the best ramen places in the area, and certainly better than most in San
Francisco. Some say it's overrated, but whatever, I like it—and judging by the long
lines, so do a lot of other people. Extra toppings can add up, but I get the *tonkotsu*
(pork) ramen with stewed pork and hard-boiled egg. Or sometimes I get kimchi, or
fried chicken *karaage* on top instead. Slurp.

Sushi Sam's Edomata $$$ *218 E. 3rd Ave. at S. Ellsworth Ave., 650-344-0888,*
sushisams.com

I always find quality sushi here, from traditional nigiri to more inventive dishes. Faves
include the *chawan mushi* (custard), the Arctic char, and the baby lobster tail, and
I usually dig what's on the specials board, too. It can be super-busy, especially during
lunch. If you snag a seat at the friendly bar, be sure to do *omakase* (p. 33).

OTHER IDEAS: Wakuriya (incredible *kaiseki* tasting menu in a shopping mall
location; 115 De Anza Blvd., 650-286-0410)

Plumed Horse $$$$ *14555 Big Basin Way at 4th St., 408-867-4711,*
plumedhorse.com

Whoa, who knew Vegas existed in Saratoga? I want to transport this place to the 415,
stat. It's got a jaw-dropping wine cellar and a contemporary look that is quite swish.
In fact, it's even flashy, and there's quite the chic lounge as well. Chef Peter Armellino
is such a talent. His Cali-luxe tasting menus overflow with elegant presentations and
seductive flavors, from a black pepper and Parmesan soufflé with uni to infinitely
tender antelope.

TIP: This restaurant has one of the coolest chef's tables I've seen: it's actually a private
room that looks upon the kitchen through a floor-to-ceiling window. Marvy.

OTHER IDEAS: Sent Sovi (French; 14583 Big Basin Way, 408-867-3110)

WOODSIDE

The Village Pub $$$$ *2967 Woodside Rd. at Mountain Home Rd., 650-851-9888,*
thevillagepub.net

I know it has pub in the name, but it's the furthest thing from one, as you can tell
once you see all the detailed cars in the parking lot. The Village Pub is an ideal
location to celebrate a special occasion, while the bar is where you'll want to pull over
for cocktails, the duck liver mousse, and a burger. Great charcuterie, a tasty trio of
lamb, a fat wine list, and professional service that blows my mind.

OTHER IDEAS: Alpine Inn (burgers al fresco; 3915 Alpine Rd., Portola Valley,
650-854-4004), Buck's (breakfast; 3062 Woodside Rd., 650-851-8010)

TOP PICKS NORTH OF SAN FRANCISCO

(THE WINE COUNTRY AND MORE)

Look, there is simply no way I can cover every single restaurant in Wine Country, in Marin, and beyond, but here are some of my favorites when I'm north of the city, whether it's for a Wine Country visit, or I'm hungry for pizza on my way back from the car races. Or when I'm on a mission for an Indian burrito, yesiree.

NORTH BAY

LARKSPUR

Picco Restaurant $$$ *320 Magnolia Ave. at King St., 415-924-0300, restaurantpicco.com*
So delicious—and yay, the plates are designed for sharing, so you can taste more than just a couple. The inventive California fare is seriously market-fresh, seasonal . . . the whole shebang, thanks to chef-owner Bruce Hill. A total Marin crowd tucks into booths or at the bar, all heeding their craving for the avocado bruschetta, tuna tartare, and risotto available every half hour. Get a trio of milkshakes to finish, natch.

Pizzeria Picco $$ *320 Magnolia Ave. at King St., 415-945-8900, pizzeriapicco.com*
Always packed, with people spilling out all over the street waiting for their table. This spot serves wonderfully blistered thin-crust pizzas, piled with ingredients in an American fashion (I prefer the lighter and simpler Margherita). Straus soft-serve ice cream with DaVero olive oil and sea salt is a cult classic for dessert.

OTHER IDEAS: Table Café (breakfast/lunch; 1167 Magnolia Ave., 415-461-6787), Tavern at Lark Creek (fun for cocktails and brunch; 234 Magnolia Ave., 415-924-7766)

Fish. $$–$$$ *350 Harbor Dr. at Gate 5 Rd., Sausalito, 415-331-3474, 331fish.com*
This seafood shack of sorts is located on a pier with only a smattering of seats inside, so don't come here on a rainy day or after 8 p.m. (open until 9 p.m. in the summer). Faboo view, casual picnic table setup, wine in bistro glasses—you get the drift. The crab roll is painfully expensive but delicious (actually, most things are as spendy as they are sustainable), and who knew coleslaw could be so memorable? Cash only.

Murray Circle $$$–$$$$ *601 Murray Circle, Sausalito, 415-339-4750, murraycircle.com*
Stunning setting on Fort Baker, with a porch and view of the city unlike any other. Kick it over a burger or cocktail in the casual Farley Bar, or there's the more formal restaurant serving a California menu, either à la carte or as a tasting menu. (Downright affordable considering the quality and talent of chef Joseph Humphrey.) Neat historic setting, and a smart choice for wining and dining the parents (the dining room isn't noisy).

Poggio $$$ *777 Bridgeway at Bay St., Sausalito, 415-332-7771, poggiotrattoria.com*
This Northern Italian restaurant keeps getting better, and chef Peter McNee's menu is stocked with wood-fired pizzas, house-made pastas, rotisserie meats, and special seasonal menus (if you're down with animal meatses partses, try dishes like the tripe or terrine). Impress out-of-towners here, and the outdoor terrace is molto Mediterranean. Ciao!

Sushi Ran $$$–$$$$ *107 Caledonia St. at Pine St., Sausalito, 415-332-3620, sushiran.com*
A sushi benchmark, adored by many in the area for its fresh fish (try to snag a seat at the bar). It's quite inventive, so if you're game for exploring, you'll be well rewarded. (It's worth noting that the overall dining experience can sometimes be quite transcendent, but other times just fine. Hope for the former.)

OTHER IDEAS: Avatar's Punjabi Burritos (15 Madrona St., Mill Valley, 415-381-8293), Buckeye Roadhouse (cocktail and burger HQ; 15 Shoreline Hwy., Mill Valley, 415-331-2600), Cottage Eatery (cozy spot for Cal-Ital; 114 Main St., Tiburon, 415-789-5636), Marinitas (late-night Latin; 218 Sir Franciso Drake Blvd., San Anselmo, 415-454-8900).

POINT REYES STATION

Osteria Stellina $$ *11285 Hwy. 1 at Sir Francis Drake Blvd., 415-663-9988, osteriastellina.com*
If you're doing the Point Reyes/Cowgirl Creamery tour, schedule your lunch or dinner at this casual Italian charmer. The menu highlights a bounty of homegrown ingredients, and includes a few raw selections, seasonal salads, a unique oyster pizza, house-made

pastas, and rustic meats. It's all served on local Heath ceramic dishes—and all made
with *amore*.

OTHER IDEAS: I'm a fan of breakfast (awesome corned beef hash) at the Pine Cone
Diner (60 4th St., 415-663-1536), but don't be offended with the notoriously "prickly"
service, and bring your cash. Up the coast in Marshall, a cold beer and oysters at Nick's
Cove (23240 Highway 1, Marshall, 415-663-1033) while overlooking Tomales Bay is a
fitting way to end the day.

SAN RAFAEL

Sol Food $–$$ *732 4th St. at Lincoln Ave., 415-451-4765; 901 Lincoln Ave. at
3rd St., 415-256-8900; solfoodrestaurant.com*
Super-casual and popular for its juicy free-range chicken plate *(pollo al horno)*, a
pressed grass-fed steak sandwich, scrumptious side dishes of *maduros* (sweet fried
plantains), *tostones* (savory mashed and fried plantains), and black beans, and the
can't-miss limeade and orange-mango iced tea. Finish with the coconut pudding–
meets–panna cotta *tembleque*. You're gonna be full.

TIP: The 4th Street location has a late-night window open until 2 a.m. Fridays and
Saturdays.

WINE COUNTRY

*A small disclaimer before we dive in: this section does not contain every
restaurant that exists in the Wine Country—so if your favorite has been
left out, well, sorry about that. These are places I have visited over the
years, many of them favorites of mine, or simply where I've had good
meals (and I hope you do, too). Note: many Wine Country restaurants
close on Mondays and/or Tuesdays, so plan accordingly.*

NAPA VALLEY

CALISTOGA

JoLe $$$ *1457 Lincoln Ave. at Washington St., 707-942-5938, jolerestaurant.com*
A fresh addition to the sleepy Calistoga scene, run by a husband-and-wife team. It
serves contemporary American small plates with a farm-to-table organic approach,
and great wines (many boutique-y) available by the glass and *pichet* (small carafe), plus
microbrews. The bill can rack up quickly, but the flavors are bright and well composed.

Solbar $$$ *755 Silverado Trail at Brannan St., 707-226-0850, solagecalistoga.com*
It's all about dining on the patio, overlooking the pool at the sleek Solage resort. The menu is local California cuisine meets soul food (you got that?). Lighter dishes like a chilled corn soup and shrimp lettuce wraps share menu real estate with sliders and baby back ribs, so it simply depends on what kind of spa eater you are (all are hearty portions). There's a busy weekend brunch, and a bar scene in the evenings.

Vallarta Market $ *1009 Foothill Blvd. at Pine St., 707-942-8664*
I get crazy cravings for these tacos. It's super low-key: you order up your tacos in the market and scarf them down in the parking lot (I've been known to brown bag a cerveza from time to time, ahem). Single ladies, you'll get too much attention in the parking lot if you're flying solo, and trust me, you don't want to use the bathroom.

OTHER IDEAS: Locals and tourists alike enjoy grabbing breakfast at Cafe Sarafornia (1413 Lincoln Ave., 707-942-0555), and a glass of wine over some small plates at Bar Vino (1457 Lincoln Ave., 707-942-9900) in the evening. The Calistoga Roastery (1426 Lincoln Ave., 707-942-5757) roasts some mighty fine espresso, and you can hang with wine-making locals in the morning. Don't leave town without a Big 'n Tasty fried chicken sandwich and homemade Ding Dong from Palisades Deli Cafe (1458 Lincoln Ave., 707-942-0145), and hot wings at Calistoga Inn (1250 Lincoln Ave., 707-942-4101).

CARNEROS

Boon Fly Café $$ *The Carneros Inn, 4048 Sonoma Hwy. 121 at Cuttings Wharf Rd., 707-299-4870, thecarnerosinn.com*
Here's what you do: leave the city *early* with your coffee and skedaddle on up to this tiny spot for a foundation-laying breakfast one hour later of warm cinnamon sugar donuts, breakfast flatbread, and eggs Benedict with jalapeño hollandaise before starting your day of purple teeth. (The American Kobe burger with onion rings on the side is also a champ—but that's what to have for lunch.)

NAPA

Alexis Baking Company (ABC) $$ *1517 3rd St. at School St., 707-258-1827, alexisbakingcompany.com*
A retail bakery that serves breakfast daily and weekend brunch. It's a local hangout, with hearty huevos rancheros, lemon ricotta pancakes, and a Mexican egg sandwich on their delicious potato bun. It's all freshly made, but a touch on the spendy side for a place where you order at the counter. Anyway. Extra points for the slight undercurrent of naughtiness (check out the bathroom signs) and carrot cake.

Bistro Don Giovanni $$$ *4110 Howard Lane. at St. Helena Hwy., 707-224-3300,*
bistrodongiovanni.com
The atmosphere here makes this one of the more captivating destinations in Napa and
it's one of the closest stops if you're coming from the city. The terrace is lovely during
the day and early evening, while I prefer the festive main dining room at night (get
a booth). The robust food isn't my first choice for Italian per se (hey, we Italians are
notoriously picky), but it's still pretty *buono*. Faves include the carpaccio and Sonoma
duck bolognese. (Pssst, request the off-the-menu pizza with pancetta and an egg.)

Oxbow Public Market $–$$$ *610 1st St. at McKinstry St., 707-226-6529,*
oxbowpublicmarket.com
It's like a Napa Ferry Building Marketplace! Many culinary delights lie within; my
favorites are the *arepas* (stuffed corn patties) with *pernil* (pulled pork) from Pica Pica,
oysters from Hog Island, and a Gibraltar (p. 148) from Ritual. Pick up some seasonal
produce at the market, fresh eggs from Soul Food Farm and meat-tastic charcuterie at
Fatted Calf, and spices from the engaging Shuli at Whole Spice Company.

ubuntu $$–$$$ *1140 Main St. at Pearl St., 707-251-5656, ubuntunapa.com*
I'd drive from San Francisco for a dinner here in a heartbeat. Yes, it's vegetarian, but
hippie food this is not. You'll taste extraordinary vegetables, spices, herbs—inspiring
flavors and food that everyone should experience (yes, I am talking to you, my fellow
omnivores!). Kudos to chef Jeremy Fox and his wife/pastry chef Deanie Fox for their
innovative vision. Pleasing atmosphere, with stone walls, vaulted ceilings, and artsy
touches, plus there's a patio, and—how Cali—a yoga studio upstairs.

ZuZu $$–$$$ *829 Main St. at 2nd St., 707-224-8555, zuzunapa.com*
Tasty tapas made with heart (and organic ingredients), happily feeding late-night
diners until 11 p.m. Fridays and Saturdays. Go with a group and graze on ceviche,
grilled bread with egg and anchovy, a flatiron steak with chimichurri, and other
savory plates that are priced quite fairly. The eclectic atmosphere, a number of wines
by the glass, and Latin music keep the vibe relaxed and sociable. No reservations.

OTHER IDEAS: Angèle (country French; 540 Main St., 707-252-8115) is quaint, or get
steaks at Cole's Chop House (1122 Main St., 707-224-6328). Neela's (975 Clinton St.,
707-226-9988) offers contemporary Indian. Just want a nibble? Get spicy *al pastor* or
hefty fish tacos (for only $2!) at the notably delicious La Esperanza taco truck (parked
at Soscol Ave. at Napa St.). If it's the weekend, nab some *birria* (goat stew) tacos at Mi
Favorita Market (3385 Old California Way, 707-255-7796)—there are a few tables in
the parking lot.

Auberge du Soleil $$$$ *180 Rutherford Hill Rd. at Auberge Rd., 707-963-1211, aubergedusoleil.com*

Does it get any prettier? Jeez. The terrace is the dreamiest location for lunch; or at least come by for wine and apps at the bistro and bar at sunset, with a peerless view of the valley and the vineyards and olive trees below. Impeccable service across the board. Honeymoon HQ. Come for breakfast if dinner is out of your league.

La Luna Taqueria $ *1153 Rutherford Rd. at St. Helena Hwy., 707-963-3211, lalunamarket.com*

It's not much—just a market with a taqueria inside and a few picnic tables in the back—but it's a good taco and burrito filling station if you need a bite, or want to go cheap for lunch so you can save your *dinero* for dinner. The carnitas are rawr.

Rutherford Grill $$$ *1180 Rutherford Rd. at St. Helena Hwy., 707-963-1792, hillstone.com*

Grab yer bottle of Cab you bought today, and here's all you need to know: skillet cornbread, barbecue ribs, rotisserie chicken, blue cheese potato chips (yeah, it's all good dude food), no corkage, and there's a patio. Make a reso.

OTHER IDEAS: Blow $20 at Oakville Grocery Co. (7856 St. Helena Hwy., 707-944-8802), there since 1881.

ST. HELENA

Cook $$–$$$ *1310 Main St. at Hunt Ave., 707-963-7088, cooksthelena.com*

It's where many locals like to chow, with simple dishes done well, like a BLT or burger for lunch, plus house-made pastas, crispy Brussels sprouts, and seasonal selections. It's a tiny spot, more like a lunch counter with some tables along the wall. A welcome break from all the spendy Napa places—sometimes you just wanna eat, dammit.

Gillwoods Cafe $–$$ *1313 Main St. at Hunt Ave., 707-963-1788, gillwoodscafe.com*

Weirdly, there are very few places to get breakfast in St. Helena, let alone breakfast served all day, but this unpretentious spot will get your motor running with hearty scrambles, French toast, and the like. The staff is lickety split.

Martini House $$$–$$$$ *1245 Spring St. at Oak Ave., 707-963-2233, martinihouse.com*

During the winter, I prefer eating indoors in this cozy (and oh-so-romantic) converted Craftsman bungalow with fireplaces galore. Meanwhile, the patio with the gurgling fountain is perfect on a warm summer evening or during the weekend lunch. Chef-owner Todd Humphries has a way with 'shrooms, so if you're into them, get the mushroom tasting menu—or at least the cream of mushroom soup (it's deserving of all its fame). Oh, and the carpaccio with crispy potatoes, hubba.

TIP: The downstairs cellar/bar is a great place to hang out for a cocktail or two in the evening. In fact, it's *the* place. Good bar bites and a killer burger, too.

Pizzeria Tra Vigne $$ *1016 Main St. at Charter Oak Ave., 707-967-9999, travignerestaurant.com/pizzeria*

For those seeking something affordable, the Neapolitan thin-crust wood-oven pizzas are the draw, and they serve good salads, too. It's where you should go if you have kids in tow. Meanwhile, adults are happy with the no-corkage policy, and the cold beers are a welcome change after a full day of wine (hic).

The Restaurant at Meadowood $$$$ *900 Meadowood Lane at Silverado Trail, 707-967-1205, meadowood.com*

Spectacular grounds, with a quietly elegant dining room that's the picture of class, with stellar service and wine pairings. Chef Christopher Kostow's creative and modern-luxe tasting menu pops with fresh ingredients, many from the on-premise garden, and wow on the foie gras done four ways. It's quite the experience. At the end of dinner, retire by the fireplace and break out the snifters.

Taylor's Automatic Refresher $–$$ *933 Main St. at Charter Oak Ave., 707-963-3486, taylorsrefresher.com*

Yeah, that line is nuts. But it moves quickly, so get in it already. Picnic tables under umbrellas in the back grassy area fill up with folks wolfing down burgers and sweet potato fries. The ahi burger or Miss Kentucky (a slutty chicken breast sandwich) satisfies those who aren't into beef. Enjoy a cold beer or wine, because hey, this sure ain't McDonalds. Great milkshakes, as well. In business since 1949; I tip my cap.

Terra Restaurant $$$$ *1345 Railroad Ave. at Adams St., 707-963-8931, terrarestaurant.com*

Romantic in all the right ways, this lovely Wine Country establishment is also historic (it even has stone walls). The atmosphere is intimate without being stuffy, so it works equally well for couples celebrating a special occasion or groups of friends out for a nice dinner. Japanese-inflected dishes offer a changeup from the usual Cal-Med style of the 707; standouts include sweetbreads with crayfish, Alaskan black cod in a shiso broth, and the spaghettini with tripe. The chef's tasting menu is another smart choice. Owners Hiro Sone and Lissa Doumani also have Ame in SF (p. 88).

TIP: Request the South room if you're on a date. And no, you're not wasted (well, maybe you are)—there isn't an exterior sign to the restaurant.

OTHER IDEAS: In case you're having a picnic at a winery, be sure to visit Giugni W F & Son Grocery Co. (1227 Main St., 707-963-3421) for a well-constructed sandwich, complete with "Giugni juice." Want some munchies in your hotel room? Find all kinds of gourmet goodies at Sunshine Foods (1115 Main St., 707-963-7070). Want a spendy steak to go with that Cabernet? Go on Kobe patrol at Press (587 St. Helena Hwy., 707-967-0550). Do lunch on the patio at Cindy's Backstreet Kitchen (1327 Railroad Ave., 707-963-1200) or seafood and sake at Go Fish (641 Main St., 707-963-0700)—good patio scene in the evening. And swing by upscale Woodhouse Chocolate (1367 Main St., 800-966-3468) for handmade chocolates, like the Champagne truffle (ignore the frosty service).

YOUNTVILLE

Ad Hoc $$$ *6476 Washington St. at Oak Circle, 707-944-2487, adhocrestaurant.com*
At the casual cousin in the Keller clan of restaurants, the prix-fixe menu is served family-style and changes nightly. Four faboo courses for $49—check out the menu online. Monday is the famed fried chicken night, and Sundays there's a prix-fixe brunch. The room is rustic, simple, and comfortable, so leave the heels at home. Note that they're closed Tuesdays and Wednesdays.

Bardessono Dining $$$–$$$$ *6526 Yount St. at Finnell Rd., 707-204-6030, bardessono.com/wine_dine*
There's a bit of a hotel restaurant sensibility here, but then again, there aren't many hotels like this one (quite eco-fabulous). The ingredients are as fresh as your language, and the cuisine features a variety of seasonings and spices that take it beyond the usual Cali lineup. The patio is perfect for brunch/brekkie. Popular lounge scene, and wait until you take a trip to the facilities—full service, that's all I'm sayin'.

Bottega Ristorante $$$ *6525 Washington St. at Yount St., 707-945-1050, botteganapavalley.com*
Michael Chiarello's Italian cuisine is a delightful *giro dell'Italia,* from the decadent burrata to some of the tenderest octopus ever to ancient grain polenta. Lots of innovative touches and presentations as well. Yup, this TV personality has chops (and it's not just lamb). The rustic space is a pleasure to dine in—a Napa dining experience that delivers on all fronts, from service to wine to atmosphere. The heated outdoor patio with a fireplace is a sexy spot to lounge over a cocktail or glass of something-something.

Bouchon $$–$$$$ *6534 Washington St. at Yount St., 707-944-8037, bouchonbistro.com*
This atmospheric restaurant is a brasserie done Thomas Keller style (read: every detail is considered). The classic menu includes delicious salmon rillettes, and the croque madame and a platter of oysters are often spotted at the bar. Actually, the bar is the preferred hangout, with excellent cocktails and plenty of industry folks spending their tips, since the kitchen is the only place in town serving until 12:30 a.m. nightly. Continuous hours make the patio a coveted seat for an end-of-day bite and bubbles.

TIP: There's a boudin blanc on the menu, but there's an off-the-menu boudin noir for those who aren't afraid of such things.

The French Laundry $$$$ *6640 Washington St. at Creek St., 707-944-2380,*
frenchlaundry.com

So, you ready to do this? Make sure there's room on the credit card and in your clothes. You're about to experience a barrage of flavors and tastes, a culinary tour that can put some people over the edge, but every gourmand has to check this one off the list (now, whether you return is what remains to be seen). Expectations run high when the tariff is this stratospheric—but then again, the gracious staff and sublime produce from the restaurant's garden help tip the scales favorably. Pure class, all the way down to how they present the bill. Dress sharp, mmmkay?

TIP: Service is included. You can request a tour of the kitchen. Be sure to ask for donuts and coffee when your server takes your order. And at the end of the meal, you can request a signed menu to be sent to your house. Sorry, I can't help you with a reservation, but here are some ideas: be sure to call ahead (lines open at 10 a.m.) two months *to the day* for a table, and keep your finger above the redial button. Recruit your friends to call for you, too. Some folks also have luck with cancellations on OpenTable, but you have to be a table of four. Google for more tips!

Mustards Grill $$$ *7399 St. Helena Hwy. at Yount Mill Rd., 707-944-2424,*
mustardsgrill.com

Located in the middle of a bunch of wineries, this mainstay definitely wins the popularity contest for lunch, so I hope you have a reservation. Cindy Pawlcyn's hearty menu doesn't miss a beat, so all you have to do is go with what sounds appealing (good luck deciding), but faves include the rabbit tostada, the quail, and the burger. Delivering a quality Napa Valley experience for twenty-five years and counting.

Redd $$$$ *6480 Washington St. at Oak Circle, 707-944-2222, reddnapavalley.com*

A study in postmodern minimalism, this restaurant shows its style in every detail, from the stemware to the bentwood chairs. Richard Reddington's cuisine is, quite simply, gorgeous: full of color, flavor, and artful presentations, occasionally with Asian elements. The wine list is also impressive (too bad the same can't be said of the service). There's a spacious outdoor patio—but then you miss out on the sleek dining room. The bar draws quite the scene (good bar bites).

OTHER IDEAS: When it's caffeination time in the morning, head over to the Yountville Coffee Caboose (6523 Washington St.) for a Ritual coffee, and then snag a croissant from Bouchon Bakery (6528 Washington St., 707-944-2253) and park it on their patio. Do lunch over bubbles at étoile (1 California Dr., 707-204-7529). Lunch at Brix (7377 St. Helena Hwy., 707-944-2749) overlooking the gardens is good for out-of-town guests (or grandma). J'adore the steak tartare with fries (genius) and tomato soup *en croute* at Bistro Jeanty (6510 Washington St., 707-944-0103). Meanwhile, the spot for late-night drinks is Pancha's (6764 Washington St., 707-944-2125), quite the mix of locals, Benz drivers in town for dinner at The French Laundry, and the people who served them. (Note: it's smoky inside.) Ma(i)sonry (6711 Washington St., 707-944-0889) is a cool spot for a taste of wine and choice art and furnishings (open until 10 p.m.)

FORESTVILLE

Farmhouse Inn & Restaurant $$$$ *7871 River Rd. at Wohler Rd.,*
707-887-3300, farmhouseinn.com
A special family-run place tucked away in the Russian River Valley, with turn-of-the-
century charm. Rustic Wine Country style, with a local wine list to match. The market-
fresh menu includes the favorite "Rabbit Rabbit Rabbit" (a trio of preparations) and
Sonoma lamb, and who could not love finishing with do-your-own totally homemade
s'mores at the fire pit outside?

FREESTONE

Wild Flour Bread $ *140 Bohemian Hwy. at Bodega Hwy., 707-874-2938,*
wildflourbread.com
Just five miles west of Sebastopol is this must-visit organic bakery on the way to
Bodega Bay (there is often a long line). They open at 8:30 a.m. Friday to Monday
only, offering a variety of breads from the wood-fired brick oven, including a cheese
fougasse, sticky buns, and wickedly good cream scones. Viva carbs! You can grab a
spot at the communal table or the bench seats outside, plus there's a garden, and a
pony and goats to please the kiddies. (Cash only.)

GEYSERVILLE

Diavola Pizzeria & Salumeria $$ *21021 Geyserville Ave. at Hamilton Lane,*
707-814-0111, diavolapizzeria.com
Chef-owner Dino Bugica's pizzas from the wood-burning oven here kick ass; I just wish
it wasn't so far away. I'm also a big fan of his stellar house-made salumi, and there's
even a house wine on tap. In sum: I'd drive miles for this place. Oh wait, I do.

Santi $$–$$$ *21047 Geyserville Ave. at Hamilton Lane, 707-857-1790,*
tavernasanti.com
A total gem in Geyserville (look it up), with Italian food that is unexpectedly *fantastico*.
The savory *spaghettini al sugo calabrese* (with beef and pork rib ragu), spicy braised
tripe with an egg, and chicken under a brick are standouts. The restaurant has a simple
look, with tile floors and a nonfussy interior, and is located in a historic space, dating
back to 1902. The back patio is heaven on a warm day or evening. Full bar.

NOTE: Santi is due to move to a new location in spring 2010: 2097 Stagecoach Blvd.
at Fountaingrove Pkwy., Santa Rosa, phone number TBD.

Willow Wood Market Cafe $$ *9020 Graton Rd. at Edison St., 707-823-0233,*
willowwoodgraton.com

This café does such honor to breakfast (mmm, French folded eggs with Fontina) and brunch (a killer Monte Cristo), plus there are big latte bowls. Lunch has a variety of sandwiches and polenta specials, and dinner has more of the same. Considering the charming vintage vibe and interior, and pleasant outdoor seating, it's worth the wait for a table (kill time shopping at the little shop that's attached).

OTHER IDEAS: Underwood Bar & Bistro (9113 Graton Rd., 707-823-7028) for harissa fries or an ice-cold beer or great wines by the glass—and bocce in the back!

HEALDSBURG

Bovolo $–$$ *106 Matheson St. at Healdsburg Ave., 707-431-2962,*
bovolorestaurant.com

This casual café-like space (behind Copperfield's Books) makes me wish I had four stomachs. Get the COO-COO frites (fried dough with mozzarella and salumi), but order the off-the-menu version with house-cured black pig bacon. Pizzas are *delicioso*—and the pork cheek sandwich with roasted peppers and salsa verde is soooo good. Yay for the hand-crafted gelato. Weather permitting, eat on the back patio.

Cyrus $$$$ *29 North St. at West St., 707-433-3311, cyrusrestaurant.com*

This is one of my favorite fine-dining establishments, hands down. The superlative service is about being personable rather than stuffy, and chef Douglas Keane's elegant, inspired tasting menus feature the freshest ingredients (order the live spot prawns, if you see them). The entire experience is beautiful. If you can swing it, the tableside Champagne and caviar service is totally memorable. Go, go, go.

Madrona Manor $$$$ *1001 Westside Rd. at W. Dry Creek Rd., 707-433-4231,*
madronamanor.com

Yet another destination-worthy restaurant in Healdsburg—and it's located in a grand Victorian mansion. In contrast to the historic setting, chef Jesse Mallgren's innovative "New California" fare is full of surprises (do it up and order the chef's choice "Grande Dame" tasting menu). Expect excellent wine pairings, cheeses . . . and wait until you see the tableside ice cream presentation (and coffee cart). There's soft candlelit ambience (although decór is a little worn), a lush garden, and a porch that is the stuff of proposals—or at least after-dinner drinks.

Scopa $$ *109A Plaza St. at Healdsburg Ave., 707-433-5282, scopahealdsburg.com*

Casual Italian in a shotgun space (it gets really packed, and tables are close). The menu is rustic and hearty, with spicy Calabrese meatballs that are notably delicious, and the tomato-braised chicken is another "mamma-is-cookin'" kind of dish. Try to score a seat at the tiny but fun bar for wine and antipasti.

Willi's Seafood & Raw Bar $$–$$$ *403 Healdsburg Ave. at North St., 707-433-9191, willisseafood.net*

A good destination for a spinach salad for lunch, oysters and bubbles before dinner on the outdoor patio, or a night of casual eating (it's about small plates here) and cocktails with friends. The barely fried calamari with a kicky gremolata, baby back ribs, and lamb skewers aren't shy on flavor, either. Full bar = fun scene.

OTHER IDEAS: When I'm in town, I drink as many macchiatos as I can at Flying Goat Coffee (324 Center St., 707-433-3599). Try Snowbunny Yogurt (312 Center St., 707-431-7669), made with Straus Family Creamery yogurt (get the original tart flavor). Swing by Jimtown Store (6706 Hwy. 128, 707-433-1212) for a breakfast or lunch (like the grilled cheese of the week, or the famed Brie and olive sandwich) before winery hopping. And the Ravenous Café (420 Center St., 707-431-1302) does one hell of a burger.

PETALUMA

Della Fattoria Downtown Café $ *141 Petaluma Blvd. N. at Western Ave., 707-763-0161, dellafattoria.com/cafe*

If there is any remote reason for me to come by this bakery's retail store, I'll find it. Their breads are sublime, so it's a good spot for breakfast items like eggs on toast and the baker's breakfast sandwich with prosciutto. High marks for the éclair. Cozy and rustic café environment, and open for dinner on Fridays.

OTHER IDEAS: Central Market (seasonal eats; 42 Petaluma Blvd. N., 707-778-9900)

ROHNERT PARK

(It's between Petaluma and Santa Rosa, in case you were wondering. I was.)

Hana Japanese Restaurant $$$–$$$$ *101 Golf Course Dr., in Double Tree Plaza, 707-586-0270, hanajapanese.com*

A sushi beacon for those who live in the North Bay, and is even visited by folks in outlying areas (it's that good). Yup, yet another gem in a strip mall. Do *omakase* (p. 33) at the sushi bar for just-flown-in-from-Tsukiji fish. You really are in good hands here with chef-owner Ken Tominaga and his crew. Star dishes include the smoked salmon (try it as nigiri), the "W" maki with uni and toro, and the *ikura* (salmon roe). Great sake list, plus off-the-menu hot shochu, chef's preferred beverage (hint hint).

TIP: You will also find Ken doing his seafood magic at Go Fish in St. Helena.

zazu $$–$$$ *3535 Guerneville Rd. at Willowside Rd., 707-523-4814,*
zazurestaurant.com
This off-the-beaten-path roadhouse-restaurant is operated by the wonder duo of
Duskie Estes and John Stewart of Bovolo (p. 189). The menu features seasonal and
garden-fresh Cal-Med–New American small plates (many are vegetarian), plus some
bigger meaty plates, too. Funky and a fun local winemaker scene.

TIP: The Pinot and Pizza Nights on Wednesdays, Thursdays, and Sundays are popular.

OTHER IDEAS: Willi's Wine Bar (tapas; Orchard Inn, 4404 Old Redwood Hwy.,
707-526-3096)

SONOMA

Cafe La Haye $$$ *140 E. Napa St. at 1st St. E., 707-935-5994, cafelahaye.com*
It's a small space (come with a reso) that's warm and welcoming, with a clean, modern
look. The New American seasonal menu wasn't necessarily groundbreaking, but the
new chef may be making some changes in that department. It's a long-standing local
favorite just off Sonoma's main square, and is wino approved.

Estate $$–$$$ *400 W. Spain St. at 4th St. W., 707-933-3663, estate-sonoma.com*
This one covers all the bases, from weekend brunch on the outdoor patio to dining
with the kids to a nice dinner to cocktails with friends. If you choose the great "pizza
and pinot" deal at the bar ($10), get a Sonoma egg on top of your wood-fired pie. The
affordable Cal-Ital fare features fresh herbs from the garden in the back—ditto with
your cocktail, which could be made with citrus right off the tree.

Harvest Moon Cafe $$–$$$ *487 1st St. W. at W. Napa St., 707-933-8160,*
harvestmooncafesonoma.com
What a fab little Frenchie patio out back at this husband-and-wife outfit; try to come
for a glass of wine and appetizers or an early supper to enjoy the dusky light. Sunday
brunch is another good idea. The seasonal Cali menu changes daily, but it always
features local ingredients, flavorful salads, and good homemade desserts, too.

LaSalette Restaurant $$$ *452-H 1st St. E. at E. Spain St., 707-938-1927,*
lasaletterestaurant.com
This delicious Portuguese restaurant is conveniently open for lunch and dinner—but
it's rather casual, so I wouldn't come here for a special occasion. Start with a trio of
charcuterie, like the warm linguiça or the smoky *lomo* (pork), and then share rustic
dishes like the rich tripe *a porto* with white beans, or the baked *bacalhau* with potato.
Note: service can be a little absent-minded.

OTHER IDEAS: You'll love your lunch or dinner on the great patio at the girl & the fig (110 W. Spain St., 707-938-3634). The back patio at Juanita Juanita (19114 Arnold Dr., 707-935-3981) is fun for chips and salsa, chicken mole or verde, and cervezas. Carneros Bistro & Wine Bar (1325 Broadway, 707-931-2042) has a unique surf-and-turf tartare, as well as good wines by the glass. Swing by the sleek El Dorado Kitchen/EDK (405 1st St. W., 707-996-3030) for cocktails—and margies by the pool! Hang out at the Swiss Hotel (18 W. Spain St., 707-938-2884) and get a Glarifee, a chilled Irish coffee of sorts, especially delicious at the end of the night. And I like to perk up in the morning with an espresso at Sunflower Caffè (421 1st St. W., 707-996-6645).

DRINK YOUR DINNER

This town has no shortage of fantastic bars . . . and no, I am not about to list all of them. Below are some of my handpicked faves. A caveat: I'm in my late thirties and a little bit more into cocktails and (much) less into places slinging vodka sodas or with bottle service (blergh).

Blind Date or First Date

Meeting someone for the first time is always nerve-wracking. The question is, wine or booze? I'll leave it up to you. Check out "Let's Meet Up: Online Dating ;)," p. 27, for more ideas.

WINE

Hôtel Biron *45 Rose St. at Market St., 415-703-0403, hotelbiron.com*
This tucked-away Hayes Valley place is date central, just atmospheric enough without being overly romantic. And you look "in the know" for suggesting it. (Although wine temps can be a bit off.) If things go well, you can hit Zuni Café (p. 52) afterward for a late-night burger in the bar area. And if they don't, well, it's dark enough so that you don't have to be embarrassed for being seen with your lame date.

Nectar Wine Lounge *3330 Steiner St. at Chestnut St., 415-345-1377,*
nectarwinelounge.com

An obvious spot for those on the Marina (a.k.a. "Campus") side of town, this lounge
features approachable wines with saucy descriptions. It looks chic, but still has an
easygoing vibe. There's a menu of snacky items (like truffle popcorn), and you can go
to A16 (p. 58) if the date feels promising and needs to continue over some vittles and
more vino. Oh, and you can make reservations!

OTHER IDEAS: Bar 821 (821 Divisadero St., no phone, bar821.com), Café Royale
(800 Post St., 415-441-4099), CAV Wine Bar & Kitchen (p. 14), The Corner
(2199 Mission St., 415-875-9258), The Liberty Café (wine bar; Thurs.–Sat. only; p. 78),
Uva Enoteca (p. 28), Yield Wine Bar (2490 3rd St., 415-401-8984)

BOOZE

The Alembic *1725 Haight St. at Cole St.,*
415-666-0822, alembicbar.com

This place is in the pocket for the first meeting. How
do I know? Let's just say I know. The lighting is warm,
the choice bar blows my mind (I hope you're "down
with brown"), the bartenders know how to shake it
don't break it, and there are some excellent bites you
can share so you don't fall off your barstool. For extra
glamour, ladies, order the Gilded Lily and end up with
gold leaf on your lips. Hott.

TIP: This place gets crazy busy Thurs.–Sat., with a
waiting list to get seats, FYI.

Lone Palm *3394 22nd St. at Guerrero St.,*
415-648-0109, lonepalmbar.com

This bar (more of a lounge, really) totally hits the sweet
spot between dive and vintage gem: the drinks are solid,
the attitude is delightfully unpretentious, the lighting is
low, and it's on a quieter street in the Mission, so it's not one of those rowdy Valencia
spots. Pull up a chair at one of the cocktail tables (set with white tablecloths), order up
strong and classic drinks like an old-fashioned or Manhattan, and let the night unfold.

OTHER IDEAS: Bourbon & Branch (p. 56), Cantina (p. 211), Club Deluxe (p. 206),
Dalva (3121 16th St., 415-252-7740), Heaven's Dog (p. 74), Laszlo (2526 Mission St.,
415-401-0810), Latin American Club (p. 206), The Orbit Room (1900 Market St.,
415-252-9525), Pisco (p. 196), Rye (p. 203), Slow Club (p. 30)

Date Night

Time to cozy up and make eyes over some cocktails. Be sure to read "Blind Date or First Date," p. 192, for more ideas.

Bourbon & Branch *501 Jones St. at O'Farrell St., 415-931-7292, bourbonandbranch.com*
This place has it all: dark lighting, a quiet speakeasy vibe, and fab cocktails, and you can even reserve your table, which is great on Friday and Saturday nights (I like the ones in the back for an intimate tête-à-tête). I know, what a brilliant feature. The sketchy atmosphere outside is a bit of a buzzkill, but the inside is truly an oasis.

Jardinière *300 Grove St. at Franklin St., 415-861-5555, jardiniere.com*
The bar here is so dang special. So are the prices ($14, cough cough), but if you're looking for a swish place to drink a handcrafted lovely, here's your spot. I prefer the horseshoe bar, but the J Lounge is also really comfy, with low-slung tables and chairs. The fried olives and Wagyu beef sliders on the lounge menu are tops.

Minx *827 Sutter St. at Jones St., 415-346-7666, minxdrinx.com*
I loved the space back when it was the Red Room, and am happy the new owners have kept the retro vibe alive (complete with a taxidermied mink with a rhinestone collar above the bar). There are decent cocktail options and a nice staff, and it feels personal and cute, and is a comfy hideaway.

OTHER IDEAS: 1300 on Fillmore (p. 128), 15 Romolo (p. 209), Betelnut (p. 82), Big 4 Lounge (p. 89), BIX (p. 20), Bliss Bar (4026 24th St., 415-826-6200), Clock Bar (p. 203), Fifth Floor Lounge/café (12 4th St., 415-348-1555), Gitane (p. 24), Hidden Vine (wine bar; 620 Post St., 415-674-3567), La Folie Lounge (p. 197), Laszlo (2526 Mission St., 415-401-0810), Lingba Lounge (1469 18th St., 415-355-0001), The Bar at the Ritz-Carlton (600 Stockton St., 415-773-6198), Lobby Lounge at the St. Regis Hotel (125 3rd St., 415-284-4000), Make-Out Room (p. 206), Masa's (this bar is a secret gem; p. 136), Michael Mina (bar; p. 53), Oola (p. 55), The Rite Spot Cafe (p. 207), RN74 (p. 128), Seasons Bar (757 Market St., 5th Floor, 415-633-3737), Swank (488 Presidio Ave., 415-346-7431), Tosca Cafe (p. 56), Waterbar (p. 105)

Birthday Drinks

So you've got the posse together, and it's time to tie one on. Here are some good scenes for your imminent partying crimes.

Olive *743 Larkin St. at O'Farrell St., 415-776-9814, olive-sf.com*
This Tenderloin standby is known for its friendly attitude. I have been to too many birthday parties here to count. Cheap pizzas your group can share, and an insane

happy hour (daily 5 p.m.–7 p.m.) with $5 cocktails and $7 pizzas (yeah, it gets packed).
The décor is a bit dated (ditto on some of the froufrou cocktails and quirky music), but
I still love dig it. (Be sure to notify them ahead of time if your group is larger than ten.)

Tunnel Top *601 Bush St. at Stockton St, 415-722-6620*
This bar fits the bill for a lot of things: meeting up with friends, having a drink on a
date (there are candlelit tables on the mezzanine), flirting with menz, and yes, tying
one on. The DJ lineup can sometimes be a little off, but it's usually good *musique*.

Vertigo Bar *1160 Polk St. at Sutter St., 415-674-1278*
This aptly named bar is gonna wreck you. Some of my favorite bar owners in the city
are here, and they make a mean Manhattan. Strong drinks, a mini-dance floor, and
smokers dig the front patio. It's a total shitshow on the weekend (bouncers, lines,
loud music, etc.), so be prepared for mayhem. Which I think you are.

OTHER IDEAS: 15 Romolo (p. 209), Argus (3187 Mission St., 415-824-1447),
Bloodhound (1145 Folsom St., 415-863-2840), Blur (p. 206), Cantina (p. 211), Casanova
Lounge (p. 200), Cha Cha Cha (Mission location; 2327 Mission St., 415-648-0504),
El Rio (3158 Mission St., 415-282-3325), Hemlock Tavern (1131 Polk St., 415-923-0923),
Hobson's Choice (1601 Haight St., 415-621-5859), Homestead (p. 196), Koko Cocktails
(p. 206), Laszlo (2526 Mission St., 415-401-0810), Latin American Club (p. 206), Madrone
Art Bar (500 Divisadero St., 415-241-0202), R Bar (1176 Sutter St., 415-567-7441),
Rosewood (732 Broadway, 415-951-4886), Rye (p. 203), Solstice (p. 78), Swig
(561 Geary St., 415-931-7292), Tonic (2360 Polk St., 415-771-5535), Velvet Cantina (p. 6),
WISH (1539 Folsom St., 415-431-1661)

Private Party Rooms

*Sometimes it's not worth trying to cram a big group into a bar, so here
are some private rooms you can turn into your own personal rumpus
room. See "Just Drinks and Bites (Private Rooms/Areas)," p. 78,
for more party location ideas.*

Cantina (p. 211)
Near Union Square is the always-bumping Cantina (blame it on the drinks by the
pitcher). There's a downstairs party room with a DJ setup and space for up to sixty-
five. There's no food on the premises, but ask about having La Cocina cater it (the
bar has a relationship with them). See more on Cantina on p. 211.

Church Key (p. 205)
Well, if you're looking for a low-budget option, just get here when the bar opens and
take over the upstairs mezzanine, which could fit about thirty folks or so. (You can't
reserve it in advance.) See more on Church Key on p. 205.

Fly *1085 Sutter St. at Larkin St., 415-441-4232, flybarandrestaurant.com*
Pssst, want to know a secret? Fly on Sutter has a party room that doesn't require
a minimum! Which means more booze for you. The living room-esque back room has
room for twenty. Share some passed apps (dips, nachos, pizzas), order cocktails, have
fun; just be sure to call ahead to reserve it. (The original location at 762 Divisadero St.
serves only beer and wine, with no private room.)

Homestead *2301 Folsom St. at 19th St., 415-282-4663*
One of the city's best private room deals: reserving the back room is only $25, and
they even donate the fee to charity. It's an old-timey saloon (brocade wallpaper,
stamped tin ceiling) with a comfy vibe, big dogs, a good jukebox, and peanuts for
$1—which will explain all the shells on the ground.

Pisco *1817 Market St. at Octavia St., 415-874-9951, piscosf.com*
This mid–Market Street bar claims to have found Duncan Nicol's secret (and exact)
recipe for a Pisco Punch. Just know this refreshing drink will eventually take you down
without blinking. Party posses will want to book the pagoda in the back.

Rosewood *732 Broadway at Stockton St., 415-951-4886, rosewoodbar.com*
This North Beach bar has a secluded back bar and patio that can be all yours, and you
can bring in your own food. Load up an iPod so you have your own beats.

OTHER IDEAS: 83 Proof (mezzanine; 83 1st St., 415-296-8383), The Ambassador
(673 Geary St., 415-563-8192), Andalu (mezzanine; 3198 16th St., 415-621-2211),
Beretta (downstairs; p. 4), Bliss Bar (4026 24th St., 415-826-6200), Bourbon & Branch
(p. 56), Bruno's (2389 Mission St., 415-643-5200), Butter (354 11th St., 415-863-5964),
District (216 Townsend St., 415-896-2120), Element Lounge (1028 Geary Blvd.,
415-440-1125), Laszlo (mezzanine; 2526 Mission St., 415-401-0810), La Trappe (p. 205),
Lava Lounge (527 Bryant St., 415-777-1333), Le Colonial (p. 84), Li-Po (p. 204), Mini Bar
(p. 207), Nihon Whisky Lounge (1779 Folsom St., 415-552-4400), Rickhouse (p. 211),
Shanghai 1930 (133 Steuart St., 415-896-5600), Slide (430 Mason St., 415-421-1916),
Sugar Cafe (679 Sutter St., 415-441-5678), Supperclub (657 Harrison St., 415-348-0900),
Swank (488 Presidio Ave., 415-346-7431), Swig (561 Geary St., 415-931-7292), Taverna
Aventine (582 Washington St., 415-981-1500), Tommy's Mexican Restaurant (p. 60),
Tosca Cafe (p. 56), Tres Agaves (130 Townsend St., 415-227-0500)

Girls' Night Out

*So, the ladies are out. Here are classy and sassy spots where you won't find
peanuts on the floor (but maybe something that sounds like peanuts).*

Eve *575 Howard St. at 2nd St., 415-806-0075, eveloungesf.com*
This bar is in a historic building and has been designed to appeal to female tastes,

with a jazzy lounge-meets-boudoir feel. Handcrafted cocktails and wines by the glass, rotating DJs, and a good happy hour.

La Folie Lounge *2316 Polk St. at Green St., 415-776-5577, lafolie.com*
Could this bar be any prettier? *C'est impossible!* And you haven't even had one of the warm gougères yet, one of the city's finest bar snacks. Great wine selections by the glass, too. If you have a group of ladies getting together for a birthday, this place is pure class—it's like a Tiffany box. (It would also be a purr-fect spot to buy out.)

OTHER IDEAS: 15 Romolo (p. 209), Beretta (p. 4), Bliss Bar (4026 24th St., 415-826-6200), Bossa Nova (139 8th St., 415-558-8004), Bubble Lounge (714 Montgomery St., 415-434-4204), Candybar (just beer and wine; p. 85), Clock Bar (p. 203), District (216 Townsend St., 415-896-2120), Koko Cocktails (p. 206), Laszlo (2526 Mission St., 415-401-0810), Lobby Lounge at the St. Regis Hotel (125 3rd St., 415-284-4000), Minx (p. 194), nopa (p. 17), Oola (p. 55), Ottimista Enoteca-Café (1838 Union St., 415-674-8400), Owl Tree (601 Post St., 415-359-1600), Redwood Room (495 Geary St., 415-929-2372), RN74 (p. 128), Sugar Lounge (377 Hayes St., 415-255-7144), Swank (488 Presidio Ave., 415-346-7431), Vertigo Bar (p. 195)

Bromance

Absolutely no drinks with straws tonight. Here are spots where guys can hang out over some drinks. See "Suds," p. 205, for more listings.

The Alembic

Broken Record *1166 Geneva Ave. at Edinburgh St., 415-963-1713, brokenrecordsf.com*
Yeah, this Excelsior bar requires a schlep, but it's worth every mile. There is an unexpectedly extensive whiskey selection, plus darts, a pool table, sausages served late, and a back patio. High-five, bro.

Elixir *3200 16th St. at Guerrero St., 415-552-1633, elixirsf.com*
With a serious saloon pedigree (since 1858), this is a total favorite for straight dudes for the following reasons: quality cocktails, you can watch the game on the TVs, there are occasional barbecue cookouts, and there's a killer Bloody Mary bar (with bacon) on Sundays. Signed, sealed, delivered.

OTHER IDEAS: The 500 Club (500 Guerrero St., 415-861-2500), 83 Proof (83 1st St., 415-296-8383), The Alembic (p. 16), Bloodhound (1145 Folsom St.,

415-863-2840), Blue Light Café (taco Tuesdays; 1979 Union St., 415-922-5510), Fly (p. 196), Grant and Green Saloon (1371 Grant Ave., 415-693-9565), Hemlock Tavern (1131 Polk St., 415-923-0923), Horseshoe (older crowd; 2024 Chestnut St., 415-346-1430), Lucky 13 (2140 Market St., 415-487-1313), MoMo's (760 2nd St., 415-227-8660), Nickie's (466 Haight St., 415-255-0300), The Phoenix Bar & Irish Gathering House (p. 116), R Bar (1176 Sutter St., 415-567-7441), The Red Jack Saloon (131 Bay St., 415-989-0700), Rickhouse (p. 211), Tommy's Mexican Restaurant (p. 60), Tony Nik's (1534 Stockton St., 415-693-0990)

Get Lucky (by Neighborhood)

Straight? On the prowl? Here's a list of places by neighborhood that are complete and total meat markets. Unless you're a cougar or silver badger (the older male equivalent—think about it), most of these places are all about a horny twenty- and early thirtysomething scene, so don't say I didn't warn you. Now, does the tablehopper consider these places personal favorites? Quite the opposite. But we're just talking about fulfilling a need here, and I'm here to help. Get those beer goggles on: it's hunting season.

DOWNTOWN/FINANCIAL DISTRICT

Americano *8 Mission St. at The Embarcadero, 415-278-3777, americanorestaurant.com*

Chaya *132 The Embarcadero at Mission St., 415-777-8688, thechaya.com*

The Cosmopolitan *121 Spear St. at Mission St., 415-543-4001, thecosmopolitancafe.com*

MR. Barbershop and Urban Lounge *560 Sacramento St. at Montgomery St., 415-291-8800, mrthebarbershop.com*

Ozumo (p. 105)

FILLMORE (UPPER/LOWER)/PAC HEIGHTS

Harry's Bar *2020 Fillmore St. at California St., 415-921-1000, harrysbarsf.com*

Lion Pub *2062 Divisadero St. at Sacramento St., 415-567-6565*

Solstice (p. 78)

Hemlock Tavern *1131 Polk St. at Hemlock St., 415-923-0923, hemlocktavern.com*

Lush Lounge *1221 Polk St. at Sutter St., 415-771-2022, thelushlounge.com*
(mixed crowd—good if you're bisexual)

McTeague's Saloon *1237 Polk St. at Bush St., 415-776-1237, mcteagues.com*

Olive Bar & Lounge (p. 199)

R Bar *1176 Sutter St. at Polk St., 415-567-7441. therbar.com*

Vertigo Bar (p. 195)

POLK (UPPER)

Royal Oak *2201 Polk St. at Vallejo St., 415-928-2303*

Shanghai Kelly's *2064 Polk St. at Broadway, 415-771-3300, shanghaikellys.com*

Tonic *2360 Polk St. at Union St., 415-771-5535, tonic-bar.com*

LOWER NOB HILL/TENDERNOB/UNION SQUARE

The Ambassador *673 Geary St. at Leavenworth St., 415-563-8192, ambassador415.com*

Cantina (p. 211)

Le Colonial (p. 84)

Owl Tree *601 Post St. at Taylor St., 415-359-1600*

Redwood Room *495 Geary St. at Taylor St., 415-929-2372, clifthotel.com*

Rye (p. 203)

Slide *430 Mason St. at Post St., 415-421-1916, slidesf.com*

Swig *561 Geary St. at Jones St., 415-931-7292, swigbar.com*

Balboa Cafe (p. 21)

Bar None *1980 Union St. at Buchanan St., 415-409-4469*

CIRCA *2001 Chestnut St. at Fillmore St., 415-351-0175, circasf.com*

Eastside West *3154 Fillmore St. at Greenwich St., 415-885-4000, eastsidewestsf.com*

Mauna Loa *3009 Fillmore St. at Union St., 415-563-5137*

Umami (p. 57)

MISSION (16TH ST. AREA)

Blondie's *540 Valencia St. at 16th St., 415-864-2419, blondiesbar.com*

Casanova Lounge *527 Valencia St. at 16th St., 415-863-9328, casanovasf.com*

Dalva *3121 16th St. at Valencia St., 415-252-7740*

Double Dutch *3192 16th St. at Guerrero St., 415-503-1670, thedoubledutch.com*

Elbo Room *647 Valencia St. at Sycamore St., 415-552-7788, elbo.com*

MISSION (FURTHER OUT)

Beauty Bar *2299 Mission St. at 19th St., 415-285-0323, beautybar.com*

Beretta (p. 4)

Doc's Clock *2575 Mission St. at 22nd St., 415-824-3627, docsclock.com*

El Rio *3158 Mission St. at Cesar Chavez St., 415-282-3325, elriosf.com*

Homestead (p. 196)

Make-Out Room (p. 206)

Medjool *2522 Mission St. at 21st St., 415-550-9055, medjoolsf.com*

Velvet Cantina (p. 6)

NORTH BEACH/JACKSON SQUARE

Amante *570 Green St. at Columbus St., 415-362-4400, amantesf.com*

Bubble Lounge *714 Montgomery St. at Columbus St., 415-434-4204, bubblelounge.com*

Cigar Bar & Grill *850 Montgomery St. at Pacific Ave., 415-398-0850, cigarbarandgrill.com*

Rosewood (p. 196)

Savoy Tivoli *1434 Grant Ave. at Union St., 415-362-7023, savoy-tivoli.netfirms.com*

HAIGHT (LOWER)/NOPA

Fly *762 Divisadero St. at Fulton St., 415-931-4359, flybarandrestaurant.com*

Madrone Art Bar *500 Divisadero St. at Fell St., 415-241-0202, madronelounge.com*

HAIGHT (UPPER)/COLE VALLEY

Finnegan's Wake *937 Cole St. at Carl St., 415-731-6119, finneganswakesf.com*

Gold Cane Cocktail Lounge *1569 Haight St. at Clayton St., 415-626-1112* (because hippies need to get laid, too)

Hobson's Choice *1601 Haight St. at Clayton St., 415-621-5859, hobsonschoice.com*

Martin Mack's *1568 Haight St. at Clayton St., 415-861-2236*

The Milk Bar *1840 Haight St. at Shrader St., 415-387-6455, milksf.com*

Bloodhound *1145 Folsom St. at 7th St., 415-863-2840, bloodhoundsf.com*

Butter *354 11th St. at Folsom St., 415-863-5964, smoothasbutter.com*

Eve (p. 196)

Harlot *46 Minna St. at 1st St., 415-777-1077, harlotsf.com*

John Colins *138 Minna St. at New Montgomery St., 415-543-2277, johncolins.com*

XYZ *W Hotel, 181 3rd St. at Howard St., 415-817-7836, xyz-sf.com*

Wino Meat Markets

If you're looking to do some hunting over a glass of Gewürztraminer, here are your targets.

Amélie *1754 Polk St. at Washington St., 415-292-6916, ameliesf.com*

BIN 38 *3232 Scott St. at Chestnut St., 415-567-3838, bin38.com*

California Wine Merchant *2113 Chestnut St. at Steiner St., 415-567-0646, californiawinemerchant.com*

District *216 Townsend St. at 3rd St., 415-896-2120, districtsf.com*

Ottimista Enoteca-Café *1838 Union St. at Octavia St., 415-674-8400, ottimistasf.com*

Cougar Dens

Here's where older ladies in tight clothes "with needs" do their prowling.

Balboa Cafe *3199 Fillmore St. at Greenwich St., 415-921-3944, balboacafe.com*
See, the burgers bring the boys, and then the boys bring the cougars. At least that's how I think the food chain works here.

Clock Bar *Westin St. Francis, 335 Powell St. at Geary St., 415-397-9222, michaelmina.net/clockbar*
There are all kinds of options for trouble here: people from out of town staying in rooms upstairs in the St. Francis, strong and excellent cocktails, and a sexy atmo.

OTHER IDEAS: Americano (8 Mission St., 415-278-3777), City Tavern (3200 Fillmore St., 415-567-0918), District (216 Townsend St., 415-896-2120), Harry Denton's Starlight Room (450 Powell St., 21st Floor, 415-395-8595), Harry's Bar (p. 119), Le Colonial (p. 84), Lobby Lounge at the St. Regis Hotel (125 3rd St., 415-284-4000), Medjool (2522 Mission St., 415-550-9055), Redwood Room (495 Geary St., 415-929-2372), Rouge (1500 Broadway, 415-346-7683), Swig (561 Geary St., 415-931-7292)

Drink with Industry Folks

When restaurant and bar folks punch the clock, or have the rare night off, here are some places where they like to let the healing begin.

Beretta *1199 Valencia St. at 23rd St., 415-695-1199, berettasf.com*
The lineup of startenders here is off the hook—but be prepared to wait a while for your Rattlesnake. What seals the deal is that the kitchen serves affordable and decent Italian fare until 1 a.m.

nopa *560 Divisadero St. at Hayes St., 415-864-8643, nopasf.com*
This place put the neighborhood on the map. Where else in town can you get on-point cocktails, great beers, killer wines, and tasty California eats that get much chef respect, all the way until 1 a.m.? It's like an industry feedbag.

Rye *688 Geary St. at Leavenworth St., 415-474-4448, ryesf.com*
This bar hosts so many cocktail competitions (usually once a month on Mondays) that the drink menu is like a winner's circle of local bartenders (the menu features many winning cocktails). The enclosed smoker's patio (kind of like a nicotine cage) means you don't have to leave your drink.

OTHER IDEAS: 15 Romolo (p. 209), Gino & Carlo's (548 Green St., 415-421-0896), Heaven's Dog (p. 74), R Bar (1176 Sutter St., 415-567-7441), Range (p. 59), Tommy's Mexican Restaurant (p. 60), Zeki's (1319 California St., 415-928-0677)

Dive-o-Rama

It's a dying breed, but here are a few places keeping the salty bartender thing alive and well. Or at least have their own quirky style, and perhaps some cool vintage signage.

Ha-Ra Club *875 Geary St. at Larkin St., 415-673-3148*
Carl is gonna yell at you, fast-forward the track you chose on the jukebox, or maybe, just maybe, give you a mini Budweiser (if he likes you). But really, he hates you. (Some history behind the name: it was opened in 1947 by pro wrestler Hank Hanastead, and heavyweight boxer Ralph Figari.)

Li-Po Cocktail Lounge *916 Grant Ave. at Washington St., 415-982-0072*
Oh, the things that go on here—it's quite the den of iniquity (since 1937). Crazy dice playing, a kooky crowd, cherry red booths, and a commanding altar. You can tell how much that shot is going to cost you because the price is written on the bottle with a Sharpie, no lie. The mai tai here is gonna mess you up like a nunchuck blow to the head. Occasional live music and parties downstairs, and a super-grotty bathroom.

OTHER IDEAS: The 500 Club (500 Guerrero St., 415-861-2500), Dogpatch Saloon (2496 3rd St., 415-643-8592), Fireside Bar (603 Irving St., 415-731-6433), Geary Club (768 Geary St., 415-441-9336)

Open Early (Dawn Patrol)

So, looks like someone didn't get to bed, huh? Here's where you can hang with your local barflies when the rooster crows. Time for the liquid breakfast of champions.

Ace's *998 Sutter St. at Hyde St., 415-673-0644, acesbarsf.com*
Open at 6 a.m., my friend. And it's a decent-looking place considering it's open that early. Sporty crowd, with free Sunday barbecue, and beer coozies. Seriously.

Gold Dust Lounge *247 Powell St. at O'Farrell St., 415-397-1695*
What the hell is this bar doing in the middle of Union Square? It's like a dive bar that was teleported from the Barbary Coast era with live music and a sea of drunks (blame it on the $3.50 cheap bubbly, Irish coffees, and margies all day up to 8:30 p.m.). Open at 7 a.m. Cash only.

Vesuvio *255 Columbus Ave. at Jack Kerouac Alley, 415-362-3370, vesuvio.com*
There are many reasons to love this place, but the 6 a.m. opening time is definitely one of them. Still fanning its bohemian and beatnik flame.

OTHER IDEAS: Bar Drake (11 a.m.; 450 Powell St., 415-395-8555), Cinch (9 a.m. during the week, 6 a.m. on the weekends; 1723 Polk St., 415-776-4162), Gino & Carlo's (6 a.m.; 548 Green St., 415-421-0896)

205

drink your dinner

Cork Dorks

Are you more about vino than vodka? Here's your list of targets. Be sure to take a look at "Fit for Cork Dorks," p. 128, for restaurants with a wino focus.

Terroir *1116 Folsom St. at Langton St., 415-558-9946, terroirsf.com*
The Frenchie attitude here is almost a parody of itself. Dig the eclectic SoMa rustic vibe and there's a French taco truck (courtesy of Spencer on the Go) that parks out front Thursday through Saturday nights, and there are plenty of biodynamic (say it, beee-o-dee-nam-eeeque!) wines for you to swirl.

TIP: Thanks to the late hours, it's a back-pocket spot to pick up a bottle of something good if you're on your way to a party (or coming home with company, ahem).

OTHER IDEAS: BIN 38 (3232 Scott St., 415-567-3838), Bubble Lounge (714 Montgomery St., 415-434-4204), California Wine Merchant (2113 Chestnut St., 415-567-0646), CAV Wine Bar & Kitchen (p. 14), District (216 Townsend St., 415-896-2120), Ferry Plaza Wine Merchant (1 Ferry Bldg., 415-391-9400), Hidden Vine (620 Post St., 415-674-3567), Hôtel Biron (45 Rose St., 415-703-0403), Ottimista Enoteca-Café (1838 Union St., 415-674-8400), Press Club (20 Yerba Buena Lane, 415-744-5000), Uva Enoteca (p. 28), VinoRosso (629 Cortland Ave., 415-647-1268), Yield Wine Bar (2490 3rd St., 415-401-8984)

Suds

Hic! Here's where you can get hopped up.

Church Key *1402 Grant Ave. at Green St., 415-963-1713*
There's no sign out front; just look for the skeleton key sign, which marks your gateway into beer heaven. It's a small place with a big list of choice beers, and an upstairs mezzanine for chillaxing.

La Trappe *800 Greenwich St. at Mason St., 415-440-8727, latrappecafe.com*
One hundred bottles of beer on the wall, one hundred bottles of beer! Or something like that. It's a total Belgian beer bungalow, with both an upstairs and a busy

downstairs/beer dungeon. Large groups of beer drinkers may descend at will in this place. Rather meh Belgian fare (frites, mussels, etc.), sadly.

OTHER IDEAS: 21st Amendment Brewery (563 2nd St., 415-369-0900), The Alembic (p. 16), Bar Crudo (p. 121), City Beer Store & Tasting Bar (1168 Folsom St., 415-503-1033), Magnolia (p. 30), Monk's Kettle (p. 23), Rogue Ales Public House (673 Union St., 415-362-7880), Toronado (547 Haight St., 415-863-2276), Zeitgeist (p. 116)

Some of My Favorite Go-To Bars

Nothing fancy or really artisanal at these places—just kick-back bars where I can hang out and have a drank or two. Almost all are cash only, so bring it.

Blur *1121 Polk St. at Hemlock St., 415-567-1918, blursf.com*
I always get into trouble at this Lower Polk bar because I don't want to leave. Good tracks spin off an iPod, and there are strong dranks, comfy seating, low lights, a friendly staff, and two-for-one drinks during happy hour (4 p.m.–6 p.m.). Mysteriously, it's also rarely crowded (it's kind of magic like that). Plus, there's pizza. Where do I sign?

Club Deluxe *1511 Haight St. at Ashbury St., 415-552-6949, liveatdeluxe.com*
Call it nostalgia, but I've been going to this bar since I moved to San Francisco in 1994, back when the swing scene was blowing up. With its jazzy-deco look, wow Bloody Marys (the "spicy salad," as my ex-BF and I called them), freshly squeezed grapefruit juice for your greyhound, rather excellent thin-crust Italian pizzas, and a solid entertainment lineup with no cover, there's really nothing missing.

Koko Cocktails *1060 Geary St. at Van Ness Ave., 415-885-4788, kokococktails.com*
The formerly divey Korean bar is now such a find, with inexpensive and well-made drinks, quick (and hot) bartenders, rad retro décor (dig the '60s tilted roof above the bar), moody lighting, films projected on the wall, and swell music (plus DJs on some nights, playing soul to ska). If you're looking for a spot to just grab a drink, this is it.

Latin American Club *3286 22nd St. at Valencia St., 415-647-2732*
This is a chill joint to swing by before dinner. Their margaritas will put you on the floor, so be careful. A number of beers on tap, too. Cheerful funky décor (the power of piñatas), a few outdoor seats, and an unpretentious mixed crowd—*très* SF.

Make-Out Room *3225 22nd St. at Bartlett St., 415-647-2888, makeoutroom.com*
At this quintessential Mission bar, you'll find a great line-up of live acts and readings (though I'm not a fan of the DJ nights), groovy bedazzled deer heads, *muy* festive party decorations (it feels like prom!), vintage booths to share with your honey, and a stunner of a deco bar. I've been coming here for years and wonder if I'll ever outgrow it. No straws, so don't ask.

What can I say, it's my neighborhood art bar! Weekend nights it's usually too packed (refer to the name), so I just keep walking home to my own personal liquor cabinet. But come midweek, it's a solid spot with friendly folks.

The Rite Spot Cafe *2099 Folsom St. at 17th St., 415-552-6066, ritespotcafe.net*
Yeah, in case you haven't noticed, I totally dig retro bars. This good Mission hang on a lonely corner looks like a dump from the outside, but that's just to deter people who don't dig dives. Quirky and low-key live music (you might even catch a ukulele performance), pie on Fridays (I don't order anything else to eat here—just drinks), charming napkin art in the bathrooms, candles on the white-clothed tables—it all adds up to a funky kind of romantic atmosphere that charms.

My Favorite Gay Bars

Yeah, I have more than one. This is what happens when you're a straight woman living in San Francisco for fifteen years.

Aunt Charlie's Lounge *133 Turk St. at Taylor St., 415-441-2922,*
auntcharlieslounge.com
Gotta heart a Tenderloin gay bar with carpeting, cheap-ass drinks, nights like the Tubesteak Connection, and, on Friday and Saturday nights, the priceless drag show (well, it's actually $5) with Gina La Divina, Vicki Marlane, and the fab-u-lous Hot Boxxx Girls (be classy and bring dollar bills to tip the ladeez!).

The Stud *399 9th St. at Harrison St., 415-863-6623, studsf.com*
So many dance floor memories here, from "back in the day" to even throwing my own New Year's party here with my disco associate. Big shout out to the bar staff. Here's hoping they book some good parties and bring the magic back, because it's a great place to party late. The second oldest gay dance club in San Francisco—much respect.

Truck *1900 Folsom St. at 15th St., 415-252-0306, trucksf.com*
Without fail, this bar always gets me stupidly hammered. Overserved, yet again. I blame the wonderful staff.

OTHER IDEAS: Blackbird (and yay, the crowd is a bit mixed; 2124 Market St., 415-503-0630), The Cinch (1723 Polk St., 415-776-4162), The LookOut (good pizza; 3600 16th St., 415-431-0306), Moby Dick's (4049 18th St., no phone), Pilsner Inn (225 Church St., 415-621-7058), Twin Peaks Tavern (401 Castro St., 415-864-9470). Oh yeah, and Swirl on Castro (572 Castro St., 415-864-2262) is like the livingroom for winos in the neighborhood.

Lesbionic

All the ladies in the house, the ladies, the ladies!

Wild Side West *424 Cortland Ave. at Bennington St., 415-647-3099*
Damn, this saloony spot has it all: an awesome garden, a pool table, a jukebox, a fireplace, and a great laid-back attitude. Total Bernal lesbian HQ, but everyone is welcome. Where are the cats? (Kidding.)

OTHER IDEAS: J Lounge (p. 15), Lexington Club (3464 19th St., 415-863-2052), Orson (p. 15), Stray Bar (309 Cortland Ave., 415-821-9263)

Smoke Gets in Your Eyes

Wow, there are actually some bars where you don't have to leave your drink with a coaster on it to go smoke. (You really should quit, you know.)

INDOORS: Amber (718 14th St., no phone), Summer Place (801 Bush St., 415-441-2252)
PATIO: 540 Club (540 Clement St., 415-752-7276), Broken Record (p. 197), The Cinch (gay; 1723 Polk St., 415-776-4162), Connecticut Yankee (p. 22), Eagle Tavern (gay/mixed; 398 12th St., 415-626-0880), Finnegan's Wake (937 Cole St., 415-731-6119), Gold Cane Cocktail Lounge (1569 Haight St., 415-626-1112), Hemlock Tavern (1131 Polk St., 415-923-0923), Jay'n Bee Club (2736 20th St., 415-824-4190), Laszlo (2526 Mission St., 415-401-0810), Lucky 13 (2140 Market St., 415-487-1313), The Mix (gay; 4086 18th St., 415-431-8616), MoMo's (760 2nd St., 415-227-8660), Pilsner Inn (gay; 225 Church St., 415-621-7058), The Red Jack Saloon (131 Bay St., 415-989-0700), The Revolution Café (3248 22nd St., 415-642-0474), Rosewood (p. 196), Rye (p. 203), Vertigo Bar (p. 195), Wild Side West (gay/mixed; p. 208), Zeitgeist (p. 116)

SPECIFIC COCKTAIL QUESTS

Only in San Francisco: Classic Cocktailing Locations

This city has no shortage of places that are rich in classic ambience. Are you into retro style, fedoras, and old-fashioneds? For a true taste of San Francisco, take a seat on one of the barstools below and order whatever your little cocktail-lovin' heart desires.

15 Romolo *15 Romolo Pl. at Broadway, 415-398-1359, 15romolo.com*
Every time I come to this hidden-away oasis in North Beach, I fall in love with yet another cocktail—they're seasonal, balanced, clever, and supremely delicious. Since this historical space is on an alley off the main drag, it has a touch of speakeasy, with shadowy lighting and a clandestine vibe. Gotta love the kitchen turning out carnival-themed bites like smoked pork sliders and funnel cake until 1:30 a.m.

Big 4 *1075 California St. at Taylor St., 415-771-1140, big4restaurant.com*
This Nob Hill beauty in the Huntington Hotel is pure gentleman's club, with hunter green leather chairs, lots of wood, and live piano. Park yourself at the bar to indulge in Ty the bartender's show—he's one of a kind, full of cheeky jokes and banter. There are complimentary happy hour bites (weekdays 5 p.m.–7:30 p.m., or until they're gone), and it's worth parking in the lounge for dinner for the chicken potpie.

BIX *56 Gold St. at Montgomery St., 415-433-6300, bixrestaurant.com*
So stylish, this joint. The top shelf is simply captivating, and the white-jacketed bartenders who will shake up your cocktail know what the hell they're doing. Cue the live jazz and it's like being on a cruise ship in 1936. (I also like to order the bananas Foster for dessert at the bar.)

The Buena Vista Cafe 2765 Hyde St. at Beach St., 415-474-5044, thebuenavista.com

Turn-of-the-century vibe, with no-nonsense bartenders pouring rows of Irish coffees for tourists and locals alike, pow pow pow. Hits the spot on a chilly night, and you gotta appreciate a bar that's been pouring a drink the same way since 1952.

Fishermen's Grotto #9 2847 Taylor St. at Jefferson St., 415-673-7025, fishermensgrotto.com

The fact that the royally retro upstairs bar still exists, complete with blue tufted-back bar stools and an abandoned lounge area with roller chairs, is a wonder. If you don't mind having the bar to yourself, and I mean really to yourself, just request they bring your drink over from the back bar. (This lonely place is begging to be a film set.)

The Pied Piper Bar at Maxfield's 2 New Montgomery St. at Market St., 415-512-1111, maxfields-restaurant.com

My friend and I used to come here after work every Friday for what we affectionately called "chalice at the Palace." Legit old-school atmo, with the namesake Maxfield Parrish original mural above the bar, marble tables, and a mahogany bar. The crowd tends to just be passing through town, but it's still enjoyable nonetheless. Happy hour Thursdays and Fridays 5 p.m.–7 p.m. brings complimentary appetizers.

OTHER IDEAS: Alfred's Steakhouse (659 Merchant St., 415-781-7058), Bourbon & Branch (p. 56), Gold Dust Lounge (p. 204), Harris' (p. 18), Tony Nik's (1534 Stockton St., 415-693-0990), Top of the Mark (p. 212), Tosca Cafe (p. 56), Vesuvio (p. 204)

Culinary Cocktails, Handcrafted with Love

San Franciscans have an obsession with using fresh and seasonal ingredients for food, so why should our cocktails be any different? These are places with folks "behind the stick" who will turn it out for you.

Absinthe Brasserie & Bar 398 Hayes St. at Gough St., 415-551-1590, absinthe.com

The cocktails here are magic, some of the finest in the city. And the bartenders are quite the encyclopedias. It can get super-packed, but it's worth fighting for your spot at the bar. You will get your San Franciscan card revoked unless you've had at least one Ginger Rogers here. (Tasty bar food, like a house-made hot dog and fries.)

Aziza 5800 Geary Blvd. at 22nd Ave., 415-752-2222, aziza-sf.com

Whoa, my drink has tarragon in it! All that and then some. Super-inventive cocktails, and I dig the intimate and dark bar area, although it's impossible for me to come here and not eat dinner (see p. 79).

Cantina 580 Sutter St. at Mason St., 415-398-0195, cantinasf.com

Drinks can't be much fresher than the ones you'll find here: the juices will be squeezed right in front of you (watch your eye, har), then shaken or stirred with premium spirits, homemade bitters, and all kinds of primo ingredients. There's a cozy and artsy vibe, but it sometimes erupts into party central; and you'll find a fun little rumpus room downstairs.

Range 842 Valencia St. at 19th St., 415-282-8283, rangesf.com

This bar rules (and bonus, it's a restaurant, so you can get something delicious to eat as well, see p. 59). The creative cocktails are hyper-seasonal, which means people wait all year for the Sungold Zinger tomato drink. It's a perfect setting to start (or end) the night, especially on date night. Ordering the cocktail of the day often delivers some magic.

Rickhouse 246 Kearny St. at Sutter St., 415-398-2827, rickhousebar.com

The Bourbon & Branch crew is at it again. The look at this location is more whisky shack than speakeasy, with bourbon barrel staves supplying the primary design motif. Wait until you see the wall of booze—it inspires a downright Pavlovian response that makes you say, "Barkeep!" There's a hefty menu of cocktails (some classic, some contemporary), including bowls of punch you can order for your group.

OTHER IDEAS: 15 Romolo (p. 209), The Alembic (p. 16), Bar Drake (450 Powell St., 415-395-8555), Beretta (p. 4), Bourbon & Branch (p. 56), Clock Bar (p. 203), Club Deluxe (p. 206), COCO500 (p. 90), Conduit (p. 67), Dosa (Fillmore; p. 4), Elixir (p. 197), EPIC Roasthouse (p. 91), Fresca (3945 24th St., 415-695-0549), Heaven's Dog (p. 74), Jardinière (p. 13), La Mar (p. 134), Michael Mina (bar; p. 53), nopa (p. 17), The Orbit Room (1900 Market St., 415-252-9525), Rose Pistola (532 Columbus Ave., 415-399-0499), Rye (p. 203), Seasons Bar (757 Market St., 5th Floor, 415-633-3737), Serpentine (p. 59), Slanted Door (p. 98), Slow Club (p. 30), Town Hall (p. 103), Waterbar (p. 105), Wexler's (p. 104), Zaré at Fly Trap (p. 112)
NOTE: coming in spring 2010 is Comstock Saloon (155 Columbus Ave.), which will be serving both classic and culinary cocktails in a historical Chinatown saloon.

Drinks and a View

Yes, you can have both.

EPIC Roasthouse *369 The Embarcadero at Folsom St., 415-369-9955, epicroasthousesf.com*
The upstairs Quiver Bar truly has an, uh, epic view. Comfortable leather-loungey style, and a happening happy hour scene, replete with tasty and bad-for-you bites.

Red's Java House *Pier 30, The Embarcadero at Bryant St., 415-777-5626*
It's a shack with a million-dollar view. You can come for just a beer, but the blue-collar magic formula here is this: a double cheeseburger in a roll (don't ask for tomato—you won't get it), a beer, and the back deck. If it's a sunny day, you're gonna pinch yourself—like, is this real? And only costing me something like $9? Cash only (but you knew that).

Top of the Mark *1 Nob Hill at California St., 415-616-6916, topofthemark.com*
Breathtaking, really. Perched high on Nob Hill, it's quite the eagle's nest, with 360-degree views. The menu of one hundred $13 "martinis" is kind of nuts—stick with something simple. A cover is charged when there's music (check the website for the lineup), and sometimes there's a wait. Dress nicely—it's worth it.

OTHER IDEAS: Beach Chalet (1000 Great Hwy., 415-386-8439), Blooms Saloon (1318 18th St., 415-552-6707), Carnelian Room (555 California St., 52nd Floor, 415-433-7500), Empress of China (838 Grant Ave., 415-434-1345), Grandviews (345 Stockton St., 36th Floor, 415-398-1234), Harry Denton's Starlight Room (450 Powell St., 415-395-8595), Pier 23 (Pier 23, The Embarcadero at Broadway, 415-362-5125), The View (Marriott Hotel, 55 4th St., 39th Floor, 415-896-1600), Waterbar (p. 105)

Jazzy

Cocktails and jazz—like peanut butter and jelly. Note: For additional locales with music, see "Music, Maestro, Please," on p. 128.

Enrico's *504 Broadway at Kearny St., 415-982-6223, enricossf.com*
This North Beach bohemian classic (since 1958), with one of the best outdoor patios in the city and live music nightly, is known for its mojitos. And if a quirky little old lady approaches you to take your Polaroid, let her. Her name is Millie, and she's a neighborhood institution.

OTHER IDEAS: 1300 on Fillmore (p. 128), BIX (p. 20), Club Deluxe (p. 206), House of Shields (39 New Montgomery St., 415-975-8651), John's Grill (63 Ellis St., 415-986-0069), Shanghai 1930 (133 Steuart St., 415-896-5600), Top of the Mark (p. 212)

Tequila!

No matter how many people this spirit continues to take down, they just brush themselves off and ask for another shot. Here's where to find some local shelves stocked with quality tequila. (Be sure to read "Hungover," p. 116, the next day.)

Tommy's Mexican Restaurant *5929 Geary Blvd. at 23rd Ave., 415-387-4747, tommysmexican.com*
This Outer Richmond family restaurant is famous for its margaritas and mega collection of choice 100 percent agave tequilas. Julio Bermejo is a man on a tequila mission—and based on the seven thousand (and counting) members of Tommy's Blue Agave Club, it looks like he has plenty of disciples. For more, see p. 60.

OTHER IDEAS: Cantina (p. 211), Colibri Mexican Bistro (438 Geary St., 415-440-2737), Tres Agaves (130 Townsend St., 415-227-0500)

Other Ideas

Guys' Lunch (Dude Food) (p. 21)

21st Amendment Brewery (burger; 563 2nd St., 415-369-0900), Bill's Place (p. 144), El Metate (p. 70), Giordano Bros. (303 Columbus Ave., 415-397-2767), Hard Knox Café (2526 3rd St., 415-648-3770), Houston's (p. 23), Just for You Café (732 22nd St., 415-647-3033), Mario's Bohemian Cigar Store Café (566 Columbus Ave., 415-362-0536), Memphis Minnie's (576 Haight St., 415-864-7675), Miller's East Coast Deli (1725 Polk St., 15-563-3542), Moishe's Pippic (425-A Hayes St., 415-431-2440), Monk's Kettle (p. 23), O'Reilly's (622 Green St., 415-989-6222), Papalote (p. 145), Paragon (701 2nd St., 415-537-9020), Pearl's Deluxe Burgers (708 Post St., 415-409-6120), Pork Store Café (p. 34), The Ramp (855 Terry Francois St., 415-621-2378), Rosamunde Sausage Grill (545 Haight St., 415-437-6851), Suppenküche (lunch on Fridays only; p. 72), Tadich Grill (p. 101), Taylor's Automatic Refresher (p. 144), Thirsty Bear (661 Howard St., 415-974-0905), Tommy's Joynt (1101 Geary Blvd., 415-775-4216), Town Hall (barbecue during the week; p. 103)

Let's Meet Up: Online Dating ;) (p. 27)

Arlequin (p. 122), Armani Café (1 Grant Ave., 415-677-9010), Bar Bambino (patio and bar; p. 6), Café de la Presse (352 Grant Ave., 415-398-2680), Café Flore (2298 Market St., 415-621-8579), Café Reverie (848 Cole St., 415-242-0200), Caffè Trieste (609 Vallejo St., 415-392-6739), Candybar (p. 85), Coffee Bar (p. 109), The Corner (2199 Mission St., 415-875-9258), Dynamo Donut & Coffee (p. 140), Emporio Rulli Union Square (333 Post St., 415-433-1122), EOS (wine salon; 901 Cole St., 415-566-3063), Epicenter Café (764 Harrison St., 415-543-5436), Farley's (1315 18th St., 415-648-1545), The Grove Fillmore (2016 Fillmore St., 415-474-1419), Hôtel Biron (p. 192), Jackson Place Café (lovely patio; 633 Battery St., 415-225-4891), Jovino (2184 Union St., 415-563-1853), La Boulange (various locations; baybread.com), The Liberty Café (back wine bar; p. 78), Mario's Bohemian Cigar Store Café (566 Columbus Ave., 415-362-0536), Mission Pie (p. 125), Mojo Bicycle Café (back patio; 639-A Divisadero St., 415-440-2338), Momi Toby's Revolution Cafe & Art Bar (528 Laguna St., 415-626-1508), Nectar Wine Lounge (p. 193), Nook (1500 Hyde St., 415-447-4100), Ottimista Enoteca-Café (1838 Union St., 415-674-8400), Outerlands (p. 110), The Revolution Café (3248 22nd St., 415-642-0474), Ritual Gardens (1634 Jerrold Ave., 415-694-6458), Samovar Tea Lounge (p. 8),

Schmidt's Deli (p. 12), Stable Café (tapas served Thurs.–Fri. 4 p.m.–9 p.m.; 2128 Folsom St., 415-552-1199), Sugarlump Coffee Lounge (2862 24th St., 415-826-5867), Tartine Bakery (p. 131), The Warming Hut (Marine Dr. at Long Ave., 415-561-3040), Yield Wine Bar (2490 3rd St., 415-401-8984)

Cheap Date (p. 40)

B Star Bar (p. 19), Burma Superstar (p. 66), Charanga (p. 96), Chow (215 Church St., 415-552-2469), Dragonfly Restaurant (420 Judah St., 415-661-7755), Gialina (p. 62), Hotei (1290 9th Ave., 415-753-6045), Indian Oven (233 Fillmore St., 415-626-1628), La Méditerranée (2210 Fillmore St., 415-921-2956; 288 Noe St., 415-431-7210), Le P'tit Laurent (699 Chenery St., 415-334-3235), Lers Ros (p. 75), Limón Rotisserie (p. 49), L'Osteria del Forno (519 Columbus Ave., 415-982-1124), Los Jarritos (p. 145), Lotus Garden (3216 Mission St., 415-282-9088), Mandalay (4344 California St., 415-386-3896), Manora's Thai Cuisine (p. 8), Maykadeh Persian Restaurant (p. 71), Mochica (937 Harrison St., 415-278-0480), Nopalito (p. 130), Pagolac (655 Larkin St., 415-776-3234), Park Chow (1240 9th Ave., 415-665-9912), Piqueo's (830 Cortland Ave., 415-282-8812), Pizzeria Delfina (p. 66), Pizzetta 211 (p. 49), Ploy II (1770 Haight St., 415-387-9224), Pomelo (p. 35), Regalito Rosticeria (3481 18th St., 415-503-0650), Rotee (400 Haight St., 15-552-8309), Roti Indian Bistro (53 West Portal Ave., 415-665-7684), Saha (1075 Sutter St., 415-345-9547), Starbelly (3583 16th St., 415-252-7500), Ti Couz (1308 16th St., 415-252-7373), Zadin (p. 114)

Casual Midweek Date Spots (p. 50)

Aperto (1434 18th St., 415-252-1625), Blue Plate (p. 19), Chapeau! (126 Clement St., 415-750-9787), Chez Maman (p. 50), Dosa (p. 4), El Metate (p. 70), Fresca (3945 24th St., 415-695-0549), Gamine (p. 70), Gaspare's Pizza House and Italian Restaurant (p. 154), Gialina (p. 62), Home (2100 Market St., 415-503-0333), Hotei (1290 9th Ave., 415-753-6045), Il Pollaio (555 Columbus Ave., 415-362-7727), Inka's Restaurant (3299 Mission St., 415-648-0111), Katana-ya (p. 151), La Ciccia (p. 138), Le Charm French Bistro (315 5th St., 415-546-6128), Le P'tit Laurent (699 Chenery St., 415-334-3235), The Little Chihuahua (p. 63), Little Star Pizza (p. 115), Maverick (3316 17th St., 415-863-3061), Mifune (1737 Post St., 415-922-0337), Mi Lindo Yucatan (401 Valencia St., 415-861-4935), Mission Beach Café (p. 125), Namu (p. 65), nopa (p. 17), Olea (p. 85), Pauline's Pizza (p. 72), Pizza Nostra (p. 134), Pizzeria Delfina (p. 66), Plouf (40 Belden Pl., 415-986-6491), Poesia (4072 18th St., 415-252-9325), Pomelo (p. 35), Pot de Pho (p. 152), Roti Indian Bistro (53 West Portal Ave., 415-665-7684), Shalimar (532 Jones St., 415-928-0333), Slow Club (p. 30), South Park Cafe (great prix-fixe; p. 155), Spork (p. 20), SPQR (p. 51), Suzu (1825 Post St., 415-346-5083), Ti Couz (3108 16th St., 415-252-7373), Universal Cafe (p. 26), Weird Fish (p. 111), Woodhouse Fish Company (1914 Fillmore St., 415-437-2722; 2073 Market St., 415-437-2722)

A16 (p. 58), The Alembic (p. 16), Anchor & Hope (p. 94), Anchor Oyster Bar (p. 48), Bar Bambino (p. 6), Bar Crudo (p. 121), Bar Jules (p. 31), Bar Tartine (p. 33), Beretta (p. 4), BIX (p. 20), Bocadillos (p. 102), Boulevard (p. 80), The Brazen Head (p. 39), Canteen (p. 67), CAV Wine Bar & Kitchen (p. 14), Chapeau! (126 Clement St., 415-750-9787), Chez Spencer (p. 9), Conduit (p. 67), Contigo (p. 49), Delfina (p. 137), Farallon (oyster bar; p. 82), Farina (p. 127), Firefly (p. 9), Harris' (p. 18), Hayes Street Grill (p. 62), Heaven's Dog (p. 74), Incanto (p. 92), Jardinière (p. 13), Kokkari (p. 103), Loló (p. 32), Michael Mina (p. 53), nopa (p. 17), Oola (p. 55), Piperade (p. 87), Pizzeria Delfina (p. 66), Range (p. 59), Ristorante Ideale (p. 50), RN74 (p. 128), rnm (p. 6), Salt House (545 Mission St., 415-543-8900), Serpentine (p. 59), South Park Cafe (p. 155), Spruce (p. 100), Tadich Grill (p. 101), Terzo (p. 5), Ti Couz (3108 16th St., 415-252-7373), Town Hall (p. 103), Universal Cafe (p. 26), Waterbar (p. 105)

Good (or Hip) Spots for Solo Dining (p. 61)

2223 Restaurant (p. 91), A16 (p. 58), Absinthe (p. 7), Anchor & Hope (p. 94), Anchor Oyster Bar (p. 48), Ariake Japanese Restaurant (5041 Geary Blvd., 415-221-6210), Balboa Cafe (p. 21), Bar Bambino (bar and communal table; p. 6), Bar Crudo (p. 121), Bar Jules (p. 31), Bar Tartine (p. 33), Beretta (p. 4), Betelnut (p. 82), Big 4 (the bar is great; p. 89), BIX (p. 20), Bocadillos (bar and communal table; p. 102), Boulevard (p. 80), Canteen (p. 67), Chapeau! (126 Clement St., 415-750-9787), Conduit (p. 67), Contigo (p. 49), Delfina (p. 137), District (216 Townsend St., 415-896-2120), Dosa (p. 4), Ebisu (p. 64), Farina (p. 127), Firefly (p. 9), Florio (p. 57), Fresca (3945 24th St., 415-695-0549), The Front Porch (p. 65), Heaven's Dog (p. 74), Hog Island Oyster Co. (p. 151), Houston's (p. 23), Jardinière (p. 13), Kokkari (p. 103), Koo (408 Irving St., 415-731-7077), Lark Creek Steak (p. 11), Local (p. 29), Magnolia (p. 30), nopa (bar and communal; p. 17), Oola (p. 55), Ottimista Enoteca-Café (1838 Union St., 415-674-8400), Oyaji (p. 18), Ozumo (p. 105), Pisco (p. 196), Poleng Lounge (p. 72), Range (p. 59), Ristorante Ideale (p. 50), RN74 (p. 128), rnm (p. 6), Ryoko's (p. 40), Salt House (bar and communal table; 545 Mission St., 415-543-8900), Slanted Door (p. 98), Sociale (p. 37), South (p. 74), Spork (bar and communal table; p. 20), SPQR (p. 51), Spruce (p. 100), Starbelly (3583 16th St., 415-252-7500), Street (p. 115), Suppenküche (bar and communal table; p. 72), Swan Oyster Depot (lunch only; p. 123), Terzo (bar and communal table; p. 5), Tokyo Go Go (3174 16th St., 415-864-2288), Town Hall (bar and communal table; p. 103), Universal Cafe (p. 26), Waterbar (p. 105)

Balompie Cafe (p. 154), Bow Hon 4 (claypots!; 850 Grant Ave., 415-362-0601), Burmese Kitchen (452 Larkin St., 415-474-5569), Chutney (511 Jones St., 415-931-5541), Custom Burger/Lounge (121 7th St., 415-252-2635), Darbar (1412 Polk St., 415-359-1236), El Metate (p. 70), Goood Frikin' Chicken (p. 142), Hotei (1290 9th Ave., 415-753-6045), Jovino (2184 Union St., 415-563-1853), King of Noodles (1639 Irving St., 415-566-8318), King of Thai Noodle House (various locations; kingofthainoodlehouse.com), Lahore Karahi (p. 41), Lers Ros (p. 75), Los Jarritos (p. 145), Los Pastores (p. 145), Memphis Minnie's (576 Haight St., 415-864-7675), Mifune (1737 Post St., 415-922-0337), Mijita (1 Ferry Bldg., 415-399-0814), Mi Lindo Yucatan (401 Valencia St., 415-861-4935), The New Spot (p. 155), Out the Door (various locations; outthedoors.com), Pagan (731 Clement St., 415-221-3888), Pagolac (655 Larkin St., 415-776-3234), Pakwan (various locations; pakwanrestaurant.com), Pearl's Deluxe Burgers (708 Post St., 415-409-6120), Poc Chuc (2886 16th St., 415-558-1583), PPQ (p. 152), Rotee (400 Haight St., 415-552-8309), Sai Jai Thai (p. 117), Shalimar (532 Jones St., 415-928-0333), Spices! I and II (p. 120), Sultan (340 O'Farrell St., 415-775-1709), Sunflower (3111 16th St., 415-626-5022), Suzu (1825 Post St., 415-346-5083, Thai House Express (901 Larkin St., 415-441-2248; 599 Castro St., 415-864-5000), Thai Place II (love the barbecued chicken; 312 Divisadero St., 415-552-6881), Thai Time Restaurant (315 8th Ave., 415-831-3663), Turtle Tower (p. 153), Udupi Palace (1007 Valencia St., 415-970 8000)

Rehearsal Dinner (Private Rooms) (p. 83)

1300 on Fillmore (p. 128), 2223 Restaurant (p. 91), Absinthe (p. 7), Acquerello (p. 89), Ame (p. 88), Americano (8 Mission St., 415-278-3777), Ana Mandara (891 Beach St., 415-771-6800), Aziza (p. 79), Betelnut (p. 82), Big 4 (p. 89), Boulevard (p. 80), butterfly (p. 138), Delfina (the patio is available from April 1–October 31; p. 137), Dining Room at the Ritz-Carlton (p. 38), E&O Trading Company (314 Sutter St., 415-693-0303), EPIC Roasthouse (p. 91), Farina (p. 127), Garibaldi's (347 Presidio Ave., 415-563-8841), Harris' (p. 18), House of Prime Rib (Mon.–Thurs.; p. 158), Incanto (p. 92), Kokkari (p. 103), La Mar (p. 134), Le Charm French Bistro (315 5th St., 415-546-6128), LuLu (816 Folsom St., 415-495-5775), Moss Room (p. 68), North Beach Restaurant (1512 Stockton St., 415-392-1700), One Market (p. 99), Pauline's Pizza (p. 72), Quince (p. 137), Saha (1075 Sutter St., 415-345-9547), Shanghai 1930 (133 Steuart St., 415-896-5600), Spruce (p. 100), Terzo (p. 5), Waterbar (p. 105), Zaré at Fly Trap (p. 112)

(1075 Sutter St., 415-345-9547), Shanghai 1930 (133 Steuart St., 415-896-5600), Spruce (p. 100), Terzo (p. 5), Waterbar (p. 105), Zaré at Fly Trap (p. 112)

Kid-Friendly (Other Kids Will Be Throwing Food) (p. 93)

Arlequin (p. 122), Barney's Gourmet Hamburgers (various locations; barneyshamburgers.com), Bill's Place (p. 144), Bistro Boudin (160 Jefferson St., 415-928-1849), Blue (2337 Market St., 415-863-2583), Burgermeister (various locations; burgermeistersf.com), Capp's Corner (1600 Powell St., 415-989-2589), Chenery Park (Tues. night; p. 81), Chow (215 Church St., 415-552-2469), Ella's Restaurant (brunch; 500 Presidio Ave., 415-441-5669), Flipper's (p. 130), Gaspare's Pizza House and Italian Restaurant (p. 154), Gialina (p. 62), Giorgio's Plzzeria (p. 81), Goat Hill Pizza (300 Connecticut St., 415-641-1440), Goood Frikin' Chicken (p. 142), Hard Knox Café (2526 3rd St., 415-648-3770), Home (2100 Market St., 415-503-0333), Il Pollaio (555 Columbus Ave., 415-362-7727), Jitlada Thai Cuisine (1826 Buchanan St., 415-292-9027), Just for You Cafe (732 22nd St., 415-647-3033), Kingdom of Dumpling (1713 Taraval St., 415-566-6143), Little Star Pizza (p. 115), Lotus Garden (3216 Mission St., 415-282-9088), Mario's Bohemian Cigar Store Café (566 Columbus Ave., 415-362-0536), Max's Opera Café (p. 81), Memphis Minnie's (576 Haight St., 415-864-7675), Mijita (great people and bird watching; 1 Ferry Bldg., 415-399-0814), Miller's East Coast Deli (1725 Polk St., 415-563-3542), Moki's Sushi and Pacific Grill (615 Cortland Ave., 415-970-9336), Mo's Grill (1322 Grant Ave., 415-788-3779), Old Clam House (299 Bayshore Blvd., 415-826-4880), Outerlands (p. 110), Pacific Catch (2027 Chestnut St., 415-440-1950; 1200 9th Ave., 415-504-6905), Papalote (p. 145), Park Chalet (p. 133), Park Chow (1240 9th Ave., 415-665-9912), Patxi's (511 Hayes St., 415-558-9991; 3318 Fillmore St., 415-345-3995), Pauline's Pizza (crayons included; p. 72), The Pizza Place on Noriega (3901 Noriega St., 415-759-5752), Pizzeria Delfina (p. 66), The Plant Café Organic (p. 144), Q (225 Clement St., 415-752-2298), Quixote's Mexican Grill (406 Dewey Blvd., 415-661-1313), Rigolo (stroller central; 3465 California St., 415-876-7777), Savor (3913 24th St., 415-282-0344), Schmidt's Deli (p. 12), St. Francis Fountain (p. 34), Taylor's Automatic Refresher (p. 144), Ti Couz (3108 16th St., 415-252-7373), Tommaso's (p. 154), Tony's Pizza Napoletana (p. 96), Woodhouse Fish Company (1914 Fillmore St., 415-437-2722; 2073 Market St., 415-437-2722)

Inexpensive Vegetarian (p. 111)

Ananda Fuara (1298 Market St., 415-621-1994), Angkor Borei (3471 Mission St., 415-550-8417), Atlas Café (p. 129), Bang San Thai (505 Jones St., 415-440-2610), Barney's Gourmet Hamburgers (20 kinds of veggie burgers; various locations; barneyshamburgers.com), Burma Superstar (p. 66), Chez Maman (p. 50), Chow (215 Church St., 415-552-2469), Chutney (511 Jones St., 415-931-5541), Citrus Club (1790 Haight St., 415-387-6366), Delica rf-1 (1 Ferry Bldg., 415-834-0344), Enjoy

3253 Mission St., 415-826-6288), Kasa Indian Eatery (4001 18th St., 415-621-6940; 3115 Fillmore St., 415-896-4008), La Méditerranée (2210 Fillmore St., 415-921-2956; 288 Noe St., 415-431-7210), Layaly (2435 Clement St., 415-668-1676), Lers Ros (p. 75), The Little Chihuahua (p. 63), Little Star Pizza (p. 115), Lotus Garden (3216 Mission St., 415-282-9088), Lucky Creation (wheat gluten puffs!; 854 Washington St., 415-989-0818), Mariachi's (all kinds of vegetarian burritos and nachos; 508 Valencia St., 415-621-4358), Old Jerusalem (p. 148), Osha Thai (various locations; oshathai.com), Outerlands (p. 110), Out the Door (various locations; outthedoors.com), Pakwan (various locations; pakwanrestaurant.com), Papalote (p. 145), Park Chow (1240 9th Ave., 415-665-9912), Pizzeria Delfina (p. 66), The Plant Café Organic (p. 144), Saha (1075 Sutter St., 415-345-9547), Samovar Tea Lounge (p. 8), Shalimar (532 Jones St., 415-928-0333), Shangri-La (2026 Irving St., 415-731-2548), Sultan (340 O'Farrell St., 415-775-1709), Thai House Express (901 Larkin St., 415-441-2248; 599 Castro St., 415-864-5000), Ti Couz (3108 16th St., 415-252-7373), Truly Mediterranean (p. 149), Udupi Palace (1007 Valencia St., 415-970-8000), Yamo Thai (3406 18th St., 415-553-8911)

Music, Maestro, Please! (p. 128)

Ana Mandara (live jazz Thurs.–Sat.; 891 Beach St., 415-771-6800), Beach Chalet (various Tues.–Sat.; 1000 Great Hwy., 415-386-8439), Big 4 (piano nightly; p. 89), BIX (live jazz nightly; p. 20), butterfly (DJs Thurs.–Sat.; p. 138), Café Claude (live jazz and vocals Thurs.–Sat.; p. 31), Chez Spencer (piano and vocals Fri.–Sat.; p. 9), CODA (nightly; 1710 Mission St., 415-551-CODA), Eastside West (live jazz Tue.–Wed.; 3154 Fillmore St., 415-885-4000), El Mansour (belly dancing nightly; 3119 Clement St., 415-751-2312), Enrico's (nightly, variety of styles; p. 212), farmerbrown (live jazz Sun.; p. 64), Fiddler's Green (acoustic music, better atmo during the week; 1333 Columbus Ave., 415-441-9758), Harris' (live jazz trio Thurs.–Sat.; p. 18), Kan Zaman (belly dancing and DJs Thurs.–Sat.; 1793 Haight St., 415-751-9656), Katia's Russian Tea Room (accordion on Sat.; p. 12), Le Charm French Bistro (live jazz Thurs.; 315 5th St., 415-546-6128), Peña Pachamama (world music Wed.–Sun.; 1630 Powell St., 415-646-0018), Poleng Lounge (live acts/DJs in the back room; p. 72), Puerto Alegre (mariachi; 546 Valencia St., 415-255-8201), Rasselas (live jazz nightly; 1534 Fillmore St., 415-567-5010), Rose Pistola (live jazz Fri.–Sun.; 532 Columbus Ave., 415-399-0499), Shanghai 1930 (live jazz Mon.–Sat.; 133 Steuart St., 415-896-5600), Thee Parkside (live bands Tues.–Sun.; 1600 17th St., 415-252-1330), Tonga Room (live music Wed.–Sun.; 950 Mason St., 415-772-5278), Yoshi's (can order food during a performance; 1330 Fillmore St., 415-655-5600), Zuni Café (piano Wed.–Thurs.; p. 52)

Outdoor Dining (p. 131)

BREAKFAST

Americano (8 Mission St., 415-278-3777), Angelina's (6000 California Ave., 415-387-2222), Arlequin (p. 122), Atlas Café (p. 129), Boogaloos (3296 22nd St., 415-824-4088), Boulettes Larder (p. 123), Café de la Presse (352 Grant Ave., 415-249-0900), Café Reverie (848 Cole St., 415-242-0200), Chez Maman (p. 50), Chloe's Café (p. 132), Crown & Crumpet (p. 12), Flipper's (p. 130), The Grove Fillmore (2016 Fillmore St., 415-474-1419), Pork Store Café (16th St. location; p. 34), Rose's Café (p. 10), Savor (3913 24th St., 415-282-0344), Squat and Gobble (various locations; squatandgobble.com), Thorough Bread and Pastry (p. 133), Toast (1748 Church St., 415-282-4328), Zazie (p. 35)

WEEKEND BRUNCH

Absinthe (p. 7), Americano (8 Mission St., 415-278-3777), Aperto (1434 18th St., 415-252-1625), Arlequin (p. 122), Atlas Café (p. 129), Axis Cafe (p. 84), B Star Bar (p. 19), Bazaar Café (5927 California St., 415-831-5620), Beretta (p. 4), Boogaloos (3296 22nd St., 415-824-4088), Boulange (various locations; baybread.com), Boulettes Larder (p. 123), The Butler & The Chef (p. 131), Cane Rosso (1 Ferry Bldg., 415-391-7599), Chez Maman (p. 50), Chouquet's (p. 124), Dolores Park Café (501 Dolores St., 415-621-2936), Duboce Park Café (2 Sanchez St., 415-621-1108), EPIC Roasthouse (p. 91), Ferry Building Marketplace Farmers' Market vendors (Sat.), Flipper's (p. 130), Foreign Cinema (p. 32), The Grind (783 Haight St., 415-864-0955), The Grove Chestnut (2250 Chestnut St., 415-474-4843), The Grove Fillmore (2016 Fillmore St., 415-474-1419), Il Fornaio (1265 Battery St., 415-986-0100), Le Zinc French Bistro (4063 24th St., 415-647-9400), Mijita (1 Ferry Bldg., 415-399-0814), Park Chow (1240 9th Ave., 415-665-9912), Pork Store Café (16th St. location; p. 34), The Ramp (855 Terry Francois St., 415-621-2378), Rex Café (2323 Polk St., 415-441-2244), Rose's Café (p. 10), Savor (3913 24th St., 415-282-0344), Slow Club (p. 30), Spork (p. 20), Squat and Gobble (various locations; squatandgobble.com), Tartine Bakery (p. 131), Thorough Bread and Pastry (p. 133), Ti Couz (3108 16th St., 415-252-7373), The Tipsy Pig (p. 94), Toast (1748 Church St., 415-282-4328), Waterbar (p. 105), Zazie (p. 35), Zuni Café (p. 52)

LUNCH

54 Mint (p. 61), Americano (8 Mission St., 415-278-3777), Angelina's (6000 California Ave., 415-387-2222), Aperto (1434 18th St., 415-252-1625), Arlequin (p. 122), Atlas Café (p. 129), Axis Cafe (p. 84), Bar Bambino (p. 6), Barney's Gourmet Hamburgers (various locations; barneyshamburgers.com), Betelnut (p. 82), B Star Bar (p. 19), Boulettes Larder (p. 123), Café Bastille (22 Belden Pl., 415-986-5673), Café Claude (p. 31), Café de la Presse (352 Grant Ave., 415-249-0900), Café du Soleil (p. 27), Café Flore (2298 Market St., 415-621-8579), Café Reverie (848 Cole St., 415-242-0200), Café Tiramisu

(28 Belden Pl., 415-421-7044), Cane Rosso (1 Ferry Bldg., 415-391-7599), Chez Papa Resto(4 Mint Plaza, 415-546-4134), Chouquet's (p. 124), Coffee Bar (p. 109), Crossroads Café (p. 27), EPIC Roasthouse (p. 91), The Grove Fillmore (2016 Fillmore St., 415-474-1419), Hog Island Oyster Co. (p. 151), Houston's (p. 23), Il Fornaio (1265 Battery St., 415-986-0100), La Mar (p. 134), Le Charm French Bistro (315 5th St., 415-546-6128), Le Zinc French Bistro (4063 24th St., 415-647-9400), Mijita (1 Ferry Bldg., 415-399-0814), MoMo's (760 2nd St., 415-227-8660), Monk's Kettle (sidewalk seating coming in 2010, p. 23), Park Chalet (p. 133), Piccino (p. 52), Piperade (p. 87), Pizza Nostra (p. 134), Pizzeria Delfina (Mission location p. 66), Pizzetta 211 (p. 49), The Plant Café Organic (p. 144), Plouf (40 Belden Pl., 415-986-6491), The Ramp (855 Terry Francois St., 415-621-2378), Red's Java House (p. 212), Rose's Café (p. 10), Samovar Tea Lounge (Castro and Yerba Buena; p. 8), Sam's Grill (p. 100), Slanted Door (p. 98), Slow Club (p. 30), Sociale (p. 37), Stable Café (2128 Folsom St., 415-552-1199), Tartine Bakery (p. 131), Taylor's Automatic Refresher (p. 144), Ti Couz (3108 16th St., 415-252-7373), Tony's Pizza Napoletana (p. 96), Town Hall (p. 103), Umi (1328 18th St., 415-355-1328), Waterbar (p. 105), Zazie (p. 35), Zuni Café (p. 52)

AFTERNOON BEER/WINE/HAPPY HOUR

Absinthe (p. 7), Americano (8 Mission St., 415-278-3777), Atlas Café (p. 129), Balboa Cafe (p. 21), Bar Bambino (p. 6), Betelnut (p. 82), BIN 38 (3232 Scott St., 415-567-3838), B Restaurant & Bar (720 Howard St., 415-495-9800), Café Bastille (22 Belden Pl., 415-986-5673), Café Claude (p. 31), Café Divine (1600 Stockton St., 415-986-3414), Café du Soleil (p. 27), Café Flore (2298 Market St., 415-621-8579), Connecticut Yankee (p. 22), The Cosmopolitan (121 Spear St., 415-543-4001), Ducca (50 3rd St., 415-977-0271), Eastside West (3154 Fillmore St., 415-885-4000), El Rio (Fridays free oysters, Sundays salsa; 3158 Mission St., 415-282-3325), EPIC Roasthouse (p. 91), Hog Island Oyster Co. (p. 151), Jay'n Bee Club (pub grub and margies; 2736 20th St., 415-824-4190), Le Zinc French Bistro (tapas; 4063 24th St., 415-647-9400), Liverpool Lil's (2942 Lyon St., 415-921-6664), Lucky 13 (2140 Market St., 415-487-1313), MarketBar (1 Ferry Bldg., 415-434-1100), Mars Bar (798 Brannan St., 415-621-6277), Mojo Bicycle Café (639-A Divisadero St., 415-440-2338), MoMo's (760 2nd St., 415-227-8660), Ottimista Enoteca-Café (1838 Union St., 415-674-8400), Paragon (701 2nd St., 415-537-9020), Piccino (p. 52), Pier 23 (Pier 23, The Embarcadero at Broadway, 415-362-5125), The Plant Café Organic (p. 144), The Ramp (855 Terry Francois St., 415-621-2378), Revolution Café (3248 22nd St., 415-642-0474), Rose's Café (p. 10), Taylor's Automatic Refresher (p. 144), Thee Parkside (1600 17th St., 415-252-1330), The Tipsy Pig (weekends; p. 94), Trademark (56 Belden Pl., 415-397-8800), Wild Side West (p. 208), Zazie (p. 35), Zeitgeist (p. 116), Ziryab Mediterranean Grill (528 Divisadero St., 415-522-0800), Zuni Café (p. 52)

Absinthe (p. 7), Americano (8 Mission St., 415-278-3777), Aperto (1434 18th St., 415-252-1625), Bar Bambino (p. 6), Barney's Gourmet Hamburgers (various locations; barneyshamburgers.com), Beretta (p. 4), Betelnut (p. 82), BIN 38 (3232 Scott St., 415-567-3838), Bistro Aix (reopening in 2010; 3340 Steiner St., 415-202-0100), Blue Plate (p. 19), B Star Bar (p. 19), Café Bastille (22 Belden Pl., 415-986-5673), Café Claude (p. 31), Café Tiramisu (28 Belden Pl., 415-421-7044), Chez Papa Resto (4 Mint Plaza, 415-546-4134), Chez Spencer (p. 9), Chouquet's (p. 124), Contigo (p. 49), Ducca (50 3rd St., 415-977-0271), Enrico's (p. 212), EPIC Roasthouse (p. 91), Farina (p. 127), Fattoush Restaurant (1361 Church St., 415-641-0678), Ferry Plaza Seafood (1 Ferry Bldg., 415-274-2561), Foreign Cinema (p. 32), Gitane (p. 24), Houston's (p. 23), Le Charm French Bistro (315 5th St., 415-546-6128), Le Colonial (p. 84), Le Zinc French Bistro (4063 24th St., 415-647-9400), MoMo's (760 2nd St., 415-227-8660), Nettie's Crab Shack (2032 Union St., 415-409-0300), Park Chow (1240 9th Ave., 415-665-9912), Piccino (p. 52), Piperade (p. 87), Pizzeria Delfina (Mission location; p. 66), Pizzetta 211 (p. 49), Plouf (40 Belden Pl., 415-986-6491), Rose Pistola (532 Columbus Ave., 415-399-0499), Rose's Café (p. 10), Slanted Door (p. 98), Slow Club (p. 30), Sociale (p. 37), Spork (p. 20), Terzo (can reserve a table out front; p. 5), Ti Couz (3108 16th St., 415-252-7373), The Tipsy Pig (p. 94), Tony's Pizza Napoletana (p. 96), Town Hall (p. 103), Umi (1328 18th St., 415-355-1328), Universal Cafe (p. 26), Waterbar (p. 105), Zazie (heated during dinner!; p. 35), Ziryab Mediterranean Grill (528 Divisadero St., 415-522-0800), Zuni Café (p. 52)

NOTE: In listings with multiple entries, the page number for the main entry appears in bold below.

notes